# My Website is Better Than Yours

## Learn HTML & Web Design from the Inside Out

Dr. Nicholas Longo

*Founder and CEO*

CoffeeCup Software

# My Website is Better than Yours

Learn HTML & Web Design from the Inside Out.

International Standard Book Number: 0-9767569-0-0

Printed in the United States of America

First Printing: April 2005

## Trademarks

## Warning and Disclaimer

## Published By

CoffeeCup Software, Inc.
226 South Tancahua Street
Corpus Christi, TX 78401 USA
Tel: +1 (361) 887-7778
Fax: +1 (361) 887-8788 Fax
Web: http://www.coffeecup.com/

# Dedication

This Book is dedicated to my wife Serena and our two
lovely daughters, Elizabeth and Victoria. When all three of
you go to sleep I work alone and think of you.
I love you with every breath, whispered word, and
quiet smile. Sweet Dreams.

I also want to thank all of our users for giving us so much
to write about. In the last 10 years you have asked a lot of
questions and most are answered here.

A very special thank you to the people who made this book real:

Dr. Peter Aitken — My partner on the content of the book.
J Cornelius — VP of Operations
Scott Swedorski — VP of Software Development
The Team — John Doerfler, Mike Dixon, Jennifer Freeman,
Clint Armstrong, Zeke Tamez

"Veni, Vedi, Vici."

# TABLE OF CONTENTS

Being the CEO of CoffeeCup Software, I probably could have gotten someone famous to write the foreword for this book. Instead I chose someone that uses our Web design software and who understands what we are about. This was taken directly from his Website without his knowledge until this book went to print. I did this because it would not be fake or contrived. For me, it's always been about the users.

I first discovered CoffeeCup Software in 1997 when the company was only about a year old and they only had only one program, an HTML Editor. About six months later I contacted the company while doing some research about the Internet. My telephone conversation was brief. I had no idea what would follow.

Three days later, without solicitation, one of their programmers called to make sure that I had gotten an appropriate and complete answer to my question. The programmer knew that further detailing the information meant no revenue for their company. I was simply doing some research in an attempt to learn more about the Internet. Later that same week the programmer called again with another programmer on a long distance conference call and further detailed their answer.

During that last call I asked the programmer why he had taken so much time to research my question, and to call me twice, and what about my question sparked his concern. He explained to me that the team at CoffeeCup Software was passionately committed to being an organization about helping people communicate and express themselves. He told me that he believes that if they pay attention to each and every question or concern that comes from their potential customers like the answer would either make or break their company, thus their dreams, that some day the sincere effort to help will be rewarded. Then he told me that he gets his reward each evening when he goes home to be greeted by his young son while knowing that he has done his very best to truly help someone.

The passionate professionalism that I found at CoffeeCup Software is second to none and I am honored to do all that I can to spread the word about this wonderful organization and its wonderful people.

— Keith T. Dove

# An Introduction and History of CoffeeCup

My name is Nicholas Longo and I am the CEO of CoffeeCup Software. I started CoffeeCup in 1996 from a real coffeehouse I owned called The Raven and The Sparrow Gourmet Cafe. In 1995 I added free Internet access, which was very new at the time. Looking back, I created one of the first Internet cafes, but I had motives besides just being tech savvy. I thought if I could get the business travelers that come to Corpus Christi, Texas (our hometown), to check their e-mail and surf this new thing called the World Wide Web, they would buy cappuccino and espresso and sit around all day spending money and drinking coffee. Little did I know that things would move quickly from there. I created the first Website for the coffeehouse using Notepad because there was no real software at the time to create Websites. Once people started coming in to use the Internet, we received some attention through news stories on local TV news and in newspapers. Now it was about the Internet, not the coffee, and the most-asked question was, How do I create a Website?

That's when I started becoming a Webmaster for money. I charged $500 to $1000 to create local business Websites and had plenty of business because we were known for having the first commercial Website in Corpus Christi. You probably have heard that necessity is the mother of invention, and it is absolutely true. It was a real pain to create Websites without good software, and in one sentence CoffeeCup Software was born. The sentence was simple and the idea would grow well beyond my expectations. After being overwhelmed by doing everything by hand, I said out loud, "I should make software so people can make their own Websites." It just didn't feel right charging people $1000 to make a Website if they could not only do it themselves, but it would be cheaper and easier. It's funny how your whole life can change by saying one thing. I then took this idea to a regular coffeehouse customer who I knew programmed software. We played with the first version of the CoffeeCup HTML Editor for three months before releasing it. Once it was available for download, I never thought about selling it until a user e-mailed and told me that I could charge money for it. He explained how trial software works. You let people use the software for 30 days for free and then after the 30 days they pay for it if they want to continue to use it. Very cool idea.

I charged $20 for the first HTML Editor and took orders by phone written on sales receipts because e-commerce didn't really exist at the time. Since we didn't have a credit card machine in the coffeehouse, we just jotted down credit card info and sent users the software. Once I got a merchant account and could take credit cards, I looked at all the sales I had collected. They were on a little board with a big nail stuck through them. There were so many that the stack was as thick as a phone book. After processing almost $20,000 in orders by hand, I knew what I would be doing from here on out. I would make more software and services to help others create Websites. Four months after releasing the CoffeeCup HTML Editor, I closed the coffeehouse for good.

I finally decided to get this book written simply out of necessity—to help CoffeeCup Software users. Since 1996 we have had over 11 million people use our Web design software. We make a very easy-to-use HTML editor and 20 other programs, but most of our daily work at CoffeeCup is about supporting some misguided people who are enthusiastic but do not understand the fundamentals. They buy a computer and want a Website the same day. It just doesn't work that way. Anyone can create a great Website, but you have to learn how first.

You need to know the basics of creating a Website, and you should know a lot more if you want a really nice Website. It's not just going to happen. There are a lot tools out there that will make it easier though (like ours), but it is important to remember that the best Websites are made with a very good knowledge of HTML. A real Webmaster can write HTML code blindfolded and with something as simple as Notepad (and even better with our software).

This book is not a sales pitch for our software either. We make a lot of software programs, and I only mention five in this book. What I want to do here is to help beginners and intermediate Webmasters get better so they can create a Website better than ours. It's a very good test, and if you can create a Website like ours, then our job at CoffeeCup is truly complete. If you would like to use some of our software to make your Website, that's great, but there's plenty of other software available. You can download our trial software from www.coffeecup.com.

Now I try to cover a lot in this book, but being a Webmaster takes practice too. The biggest secret that I pass on to people is actually very simple, and it's the fastest way to learn HTML and other tips and tricks. Just right-click in a Web page in your browser and choose View Source. You can also save any Web page to your hard drive to open in an HTML editor by clicking File and then Save As in the top toolbar of your browser.

Now you have some power. Visit a very popular Website or one that you personally like a lot. Save the page to your hard drive. Now in Notepad or the CoffeeCup HTML Editor, open that HTML document. You now have the source code that makes that page look so good or navigate so well. All you have to do is fiddle with the code and text on the page and save it. If you open the page in a browser, you will see the changes you have made. You can play with it all you want, and if you mess it up, who cares? Just save the page again and start over. I show you the source code of over 10 popular Websites in this book so you can understand what is good and/or bad about them. This "deconstruction" is just like viewing the source in your browser, only with me as your guide with a critic's commentary.

Now you should not be copying other people's hard work; but it's perfectly okay to use these pages as a guideline for what you would like to accomplish for your own Website. This is exactly how I learned, and now it's odd that I can even write a book about it and, even more so, make software that helps people create Websites. The Web is indeed a very interesting place.

HTML is just a form of the English language. A lot of people think that it's confusing because it looks like crazy computer code. This is not true. It is actually very simple text that is written in English. Here's one example I like to give:

```
<center> Hi There </center>
```

Guess what happens to the words "Hi There" on the page. If you say anything other than "It centers it on the page," I want you to take a five-minute break and come back to read the next paragraph later. It is really that easy; you just have to take your time and you will get it. Even the hard stuff.

There is a moment of enlightenment, I promise you. All of my experience shows that a light will come on in your head about two weeks into the learning process. Then you will be hard to stop, and you just might take this book and put it on a shelf and say to yourself, "I can't believe I ever bought that."

Don't make the Web ugly and have fun!

— Nick

# PART 1

· · · · · · · · · · · · · · · · · · · · · · · · ·

# The Building Blocks
# of Great Websites

It's always best to start with the basics. When it comes to

designing Websites it is best to learn about the basic building

blocks that are the foundation of all Web pages. These first five

chapters provide the foundation you will need to start on your

way to becoming a successful Webmaster.

· · · · · · · · · · · · · · · · · · · · · · · · ·

# CHAPTER 1

# My Website Is Better Than Yours!

Well I finally did it. After nine years of making software and Websites, I have put pen to paper and created my first book. The title of this chapter, and of the whole book, is not intended to be nasty, but to call attention to what I see as a glaring fact. The number one reason most Websites are never as good as they could be is that the people making them jump into the process without a solid understanding of HTML, good Web design principles, and the components of a great Website. This book is intended to highlight this common problem through various examples and to help show you how to avoid falling victim to it.

Lots of people want to have a Website these days, and if you are reading this book you are probably one of them. Maybe you want a simple personal site where you can share information about your family, pets, hobbies, or whatever else you like. Maybe you are putting together a Website for a club or church you belong to, or maybe you want to start an online business. The fact is you will have to create the pages that make up your Website. Despite what you may have heard elsewhere, it is not an overnight process. In particular, it's not quite as easy as you may think to create a Website that is attractive and easy to use and that will keep drawing visitors and customers.

That's where this book comes in. My Websites probably are a lot better than yours, but that's only because I have years of experience and you're just getting started. With some training, this book, and a little experience, you too can create terrific Websites. My goal in this book is to provide the fundamentals that you need to know to do just that. So, read on!

## Web Design and Web Hosting

There are two basic parts to having a Website. The first, and the topic of this book (as you probably already know), is Web design. This is the process of planning, creating, testing and saving Web pages, and putting them all together to make a Website.

The other is Web hosting. This is placing your Website on a server (a fancy computer with specialized software that is connected to the Internet and lets other people access your Website). Very few people host their own Websites; it is much more common to purchase a hosting plan with a commercial hosting provider. This really is the way to go. For a modest fee your hosting provider takes care of all the details of networking, bandwidth, software configuration, backups, and security. For the examples given in this book, I will assume you already have a hosting plan set up for your Website.

Now, back to making your Website. Some sites may have only a single page, others will have hundreds, but in any case these pages need to be created. This is where most potential Webmasters run into problems. They are eager to get their site up and running (understandably enough), so they rush ahead without the proper preparation. The result is often a Website that neither looks good nor works as well as it should.

You have probably heard the saying "An ounce of prevention is better than a pound of cure." There's a similar saying for Webmasters: "An ounce of preparation is better than a pound of fixing it later." Okay, I just made that up, but it's really true, By spending a little time now to learn the fundamentals of Web design, you'll save yourself lots of headaches down the road fixing things that you didn't do right the first time. You are holding that ounce of preparation in your hands right now!

**Figure 1.1.** The CoffeeCup home page displayed in a browser.

## What Exactly Is a Web Page?

I am sure that you've seen lots of Web pages from the perspective of a user, viewing them in your browser. But what about the perspective of your new role as a Web designer? Beneath the surface a Web page is quite different from what you see in a browser, and when you are creating Web pages, it's this "beneath the surface" aspect that you will be working with. This is the source code that makes a Web page work.

Every Web page is basically a text file. You can see this text, the "source," behind any Web page by going to the page in your browser and selecting Source from the browser's View menu (this is the command in Internet Explorer; other browsers, such as Firefox and Netscape, have similar commands). An easier way to do this is to right-click your mouse and select View Source. This way, you can look at the source for any page on the Internet.

This will be an instrumental tool for you to learn the ins and outs of Web design. Figure 1.1 shows the CoffeeCup Software home page in a browser and Figure 1.2, you can see its source (or at least part of it) displayed in Notepad.

Don't worry about the details of the source code yet. You'll be learning about that throughout this book. The point I am trying to make is that as a Web designer, you must know and understand the source code because it is what determines how pages look and behave. Web pages are all written using a language called Hypertext Markup Language (HTML). Fundamentally, all HTML code in a Web page serves two functions:

- Tells the browser what text and images to show the visitor
- Tells the browser how to format and display those text and images

You'll start learning more about HTML in Chapter 2.

**Figure 1.2.** The source code for the CoffeeCup Website displayed in Notepad

## Website Design Software

You may have heard about Website design software that lets you create pages without knowing any HTML. With these programs you create a page in WYSIWYG (which stands for "what you see is what you get") mode, adding and formatting text and images much as you do in a word processor. Behind the scenes the program creates the necessary HTML for you. Sounds like a pretty good idea, but is it?

Yes and no. It's true that these programs save a lot of time, but just as you can't learn really English by using Microsoft Word, you can't learn HTML (or about Web design, for that matter) from a WYSIWYG program. So why is this important? Because without an understanding of HTML, you will never be a decent Webmaster. Even if you eventually decide to use such a program, you will be able to do a lot more with it if you know the fundamentals of HTML and Web design. In addition, as sophisticated as these programs are, they can't do everything. Sometimes you need to go in and tweak the HTML manually, which requires knowledge of HTML on your part. My advice is to start by designing your Web pages manually; writing HTML code by hand with a code editor. There are many good code editors out there (and I wouldn't be a very good businessman if I didn't mention the CoffeeCup HTML Editor here) and you can make the decision of which one is best for you. This book will provide all you need to know to start , and before you know it, you'll find that you are developing the expertise needed to create really great Websites.

## Summary

Website design is actually rather easy when you don't make the mistake of jumping in without learning the basics first. This book is the ideal guide. You'll start by learning the fundamentals of HTML in Chapter 2, and later chapters cover everything else you will need to know, from Cascading Style Sheets (CSS), scripting, and dynamic HTML to images and uploading your pages the the server we talked about earlier. Time to get started!

# Getting Started with HTML

The best way to start learning HTML is by learning the basics. It's not really all that complicated, and once you know the basics it will be easy to learn the more advanced stuff that comes in later chapters.

## The Origins of HTML

Hypertext Markup Language (HTML) had its origin back in the early days of the Internet. The Internet was already being used, primarily by research scientists, to exchange research, manuscripts, and data. Many people realized that this new electronic communication medium had great potential. What was needed was a standard way of creating documents so they would be accessible and viewable over the Internet. Central to this was the idea of a *hyperlink*, a way of linking related documents together so the user could easily move from one document to the other.

At this time, Tim Berners-Lee was a researcher at a lab in Europe. He took on this challenge and soon came up with a simple markup language that met the most important requirements:

- A means to link documents together no matter where on the Internet they were located

- A way to add simple formatting to a document, such as paragraphs, bold and italicized text, and headings

- A method for displaying images in the document

With some help from others, Tim developed the first version of HTML. It was a lot simpler than what we use today, but all the basic pieces were in place. Tim did not try to patent his invention but put it in the public domain where it was and still is freely available for anyone to use (Bravo, Tim!). Its use spread rapidly and hence the World Wide Web was born. It may be hard to believe, but the first version of HTML came out in the early 1990s, barely more than a decade ago. This does not seem like nearly enough time for the Web to have grown to its current size and importance, but that's what happened.

The picture would not be complete without a browser. While today's browsers are quite complex, with all sorts of bells and whistles, their primary function is simple and exactly the same as it has always been: to read an HTML document (note that I use the terms *HTML document* and *Web page* interchangeably) and display it on-screen according to the markup that the document contains. This relates to an important distinction between source code and HTML rendering:

- The rendering of an HTML document is what the user sees in their browser. It is formatted content only—no HTML tags are seen.

- The HTML source code is what's actually in the document, content and HTML alike. It's what you'll be working on as you create and edit Web pages.

Browsers offer a way to view the source code for the current HTML document. In Internet Explorer it is View|Source; in Mozilla Firefox it is View|Page Source. We'll be using these commands a lot in this book because viewing the source is a great way to understand the HTML behind great—and not so great—Web pages.

## Internet vs. World Wide Web

Some people use these two terms interchangeably, but they really mean different things. The Internet is the physical structure that provides the connectivity—the servers, routers, cable and satellite connections, fiber optics, and computers all over the world. The World Wide Web is the entire collection of all linked documents and images that are available on the Internet.

# Fundamental Concepts of HTML

At its core, HTML is very simple. In fact, it is so simple in concept that some people are surprised that it has proven to be so powerful a tool. I think that this simplicity is in fact part of the reason for its success. Let's look at the basic concepts of HTML.

## HTML Is Plain Text

That's right, folks—there's nothing special about an HTML document. It contains nothing but plain text, the characters you can type from your keyboard. There are two big advantages to this:

- Cross-platform compatibility. Text is handled essentially the same way on all computers, whether it be a Windows PC, a mainframe, a Linux box, or a Macintosh. This means that an HTML document created on a PC will work fine on all other computers and *vice versa* providing it was written using valid HTML. This is essential for something that's supposed to be universal, such as the World Wide Web.

- Ease of editing. You can create and edit HTML documents with any text editor, such as Notepad and WordPad on Windows systems.

What about different languages? What constitutes "text" in Russia or Japan will be very different from text in the United States or Canada. This is handled by different *character sets* for different locations. Fortunately, you needn't worry about this yet; if your computer is set up properly for where you live, it will already be using the proper character set. You can also specify what character set you want your pages to use, but we'll talk more about that later.

## HTML File Names

HTML documents are stored on your computer like any other type of document. They are identified by the file name extension—the part after the period. It can be either .htm or .html for an HTML document. Even if a file contains HTML, most programs will not recognize it as an HTML document without the proper file name extension.

## Tags vs. Content

Any HTML document is made up of two things—tags and content. This is central to the way HTML works.

Tags are the HTML itself—in other words, the markup (remember Hypertext *Markup* Language). All HTML tags are enclosed in angle brackets < and >. Here are some actual HTML tags:

```
<title>
<p>
<img>
<table>
```

Most, but not all, HTML tags are used in pairs—there is a starting tag and an ending tag. These tags are called container tags because they can "contain" or wrap around other tags and content. The ending tag is the same as the starting tag with the addition of a leading slash (/). So, **</title>** is the ending tag for **<title>**. The tags that do not have a separate closing tag are known as *self-closing*. All you do is add a space and the slash just before the > to close the tag.

The **<img>** tag is a good example of this. Since it doesn't have a closing tag, we close it as follows, with a closing slash:

Wrong: <img src="logo.gif">

Correct: <img src="logo.gif" />

Content in an HTML document is anything that is not an HTML tag. Another way of looking at it would be that content is the information you want to show the user. Content can be included in an HTML document in two ways:

- Included as part of the document. This is the way text content is handled.
- In a separate file and referenced from the document. This is the way images are handled.

Here's an example of HTML that illustrates how tags and content relate to each other:

```
<p>HTML is <b>easy to learn!</b></p>
```

Let's dissect and analyze this short piece of HTML:

- **<p>** is the paragraph tag. It marks the start of a paragraph.
- **HTML is** is content. It will be displayed to the user.
- **** is the boldface tag. It marks the start of boldfaced text.
- **easy to learn!** is more content. It will be displayed to the user in boldface text.
- **** is the boldface ending tag. It turns boldface off.
- **</p>** is the paragraph ending tag. It marks the end of the paragraph.

The relationships between tags and content will become clearer as you learn more about HTML.

## White Space

The term *white space* refers to characters that take up space in a document but do not actually display. They are the space, the tab, and the new line, which causes subsequent text to move to the next line (the new line is sometimes called the line feed or carriage return). HTML handles white space in content by ignoring it. Well, not quite—any white space is simply converted to a single space. This is sometimes referred to as *white space normalization*. The white space can be a row of 10 spaces, a pair of new line characters, several tabs, or any combination of these, and the resulting display will have just a single space in the content.

Let's see this in action. The following HTML will display as a single line, with one space between words, just as you would expect:

```
<p>one two three four five</p>
```

Because of the way HTML handles white space, the following HTML will display exactly the same way:

```
<p>one
       two three
four
five
</p>
```

White space normalization in HTML has two practical consequences:

- You can use white space to format your HTML source code as you like, using new lines, tabs, and spaces to organize the code in a way that's clear and easy to read. It will have no effect on the final rendering of the document.

- You cannot use white space to format the content because it will have no effect. You must use HTML tags for this purpose.

You can tell HTML not to normalize white space by including text within the preformat **<pre>** tags. This can be useful when you have some text that is already formatted the way you want with white space, such as a poem. I will cover the **<pre>** tag in Chapter 3.

## Comments

A comment is an HTML tag that does not affect how the document is displayed or what is shown to the user. It can be used by Web designers to insert comments such as reminders and explanations. You create a comment like this:

```
<!- this is the comment ->
```

Simple HTML documents usually do not need comments, but they can be useful in other situations. For example, if you are editing an HTML document and want to see how it looks with some material removed, simply enclose the material in comment tags. If you decide to keep the material, all you have to do is remove the tags.

## Special Characters

Certain characters have special meaning in HTML, such as the < and > characters that are used to enclose tags. This means that you can't just go ahead and use these characters in your content but must use a special code to represent them. These are called *character entities* and they are represented by a letter or number code preceded by an ampersand and followed by a semicolon. For example, **&lt**; is the code for the "less than" symbol (<). Here are a few commonly used character entities:

| CODE | CHARACTER | |
|---|---|---|
| &lt; | < | less than |
| &gt; | > | greater than |
| &amp; | & | ampersand |
| &quot; | " | double quote |

Here's an example of some character codes used in some HTML code:

```
<p>The new product name is &quot;Nice &amp; Tasty&quot;</p>
```

And here's how it will be rendered by a browser:

```
The new product name is "Nice & Tasty"
```

Another character entity that is commonly used is the *non-breaking space*. You'll recall from the section on white space earlier in this chapter that HTML's default behavior is to normalize white space in a document, collapsing multiple spaces, tabs, or new lines to a single space. But what if you actually want multiple spaces in the document? Then you must use the non-breaking space character entity ** **. Each one of these is displayed as a space and is never collapsed. For instance, here is a line of code in which the non-breaking space is used:

```
<p>Total cost:       $15.95</p>
```

This line is rendered like this:

```
    Total cost:         $15.95
```

Finally, there are character entities for special characters that do not appear on most keyboards, such as the cent symbol and the accented letters that are used in many European languages. There are many dozens of these; the few that you are most likely to use are listed in Table 2.1 (see the back of the book for a more complete list)

**Table 2.1.** Character entities for non-keyboard characters.

| CHARACTER | NAME | ENTITY |
|---|---|---|
| £ | Pound sterling symbol | &#163; |
| ¥ | Yen symbol | &#165; |
| ¢ | Cent symbol | &#162; |
| © | Copyright symbol | &#169; |
| ® | Registered trademark | &#174; |

# Basic HTML Document Structure

Any and all HTML documents have a certain basic structure that must be adhered to:

- The entire document is enclosed in **<html>** tags.

- The second tag in the document is the **<head>** tag. This tag is used to contain other tags, which hold information about the document, such as its title. Items in the **<head>** tag are not displayed to the user.

- The **<head>** tag is followed by the **<body>** tag. The **<body>** tag contains the document content.

The simplest possible HTML document is made up of these three tags, as shown here:

```
<html>
<head>
</head>
<body>
</body>
</html>
```

This document is empty and if loaded into a browser will simply display a blank page. But this is where every HTML document starts, and if you're creating a new document from scratch, you might as well start by putting these tags into it because they are required.

# The <!DOCTYPE> Tag

Strictly speaking, every HTML document should start with a **<!DOCTYPE>** element. This is a stand-alone tag that is placed before the first **<html>** tag. Its purpose is to provide information about the version of HTML that the document uses. With this information, the browser can precisely interpret the document's HTML tags. Without it, the browser has to guess and may not render things as precisely as you like.

To be honest, most Web pages omit the **<!DOCTYPE>** tag and work just fine. Even so, I recommend using it. It can't hurt, it may help, and it certainly is a good idea for future compatibility. For most of this book I will use the tag for HTML version 4.01 Transitional, which is the *de facto* standard for HTML these days.

With this tag your basic HTML document looks like this:

```
<!DOCTYPE HTML PUBLIC "-//W3C//DTD HTML 4.01 Transitional//EN"
    "http://www.w3.org/TR/html4/loose.dtd">
<html>
<head>
</head>
<body>
</body>
</html>
```

I'll mention other **<!DOCTYPE>** definitions as needed in other chapters.

## What's a URL?

URL stands for *Uniform Resource Locator*. This is just a fancy name for a Web address such as www.coffeecup.com. Sometimes you'll see URLs written with http:// at the beginning. This is not part of the URL but is used to specify the protocol or data transfer method that the browser will use. All Web pages use some variant of HTTP, or Hypertext Transfer Protocol.

A URL identifies the location of a resource (a file) on the Internet. There are at least two parts to this: the name of the Web server where the file is located and the name of the file. Sometimes a third part is added as well, identifying the folder on the server where the file is located. Let's look at some examples.

www.coffeecup.com is a URL that identifies a specific Web server but without a file name. If someone navigates to this URL they will get a file—a Web page—because the server is programmed to return the default page in this situation. Essentially all Websites have a default page and it is often named index.html.

www.coffeecup.com/index.html is a URL that includes a file name. It specifies a certain file, index.html, in the default, or root, folder on the Web server.

www.coffeecup.com/images/logo.jpg is a URL that includes a folder and a file name. It specifies the file logo.jpg in the folder images on the Web server.

## Document Information Tags

Document information tags are placed within the **<head>** tag and, as I mentioned before, provide various kinds of information about the document. There are only two information tags you need to know about at this point: the **<title>** tag and the **<meta>** tag.

### The <title> Tag

As you may have guessed, this tag defines the document's title. This is important because most browsers display the document's title in the title bar. If a document lacks a title, the browser will display its URL or the name of the browser instead.

Another reason to include a title is that Web directories and search engines such as Yahoo! and Google rely on page titles to help locate, index, and categorize pages properly. You should select a fairly short title that accurately describes your page. Simply include the title in the document head and you are all set:

```
<head>
<title>Jane Smith's Personal
Web Page</title>
</head>
```

## The <meta> Tag

The **<meta>** tag is a clever invention. It lets you include essentially any information you want in an HTML document. A **<meta>** tag has two attributes, **name** and **content**. You write a **<meta>** tag like this:

```
<meta name="tag name" content="tag content" />
```

You can use any text you want for the **name** and **content** attributes. The **<meta>** tag stands on its own—there is no closing tag required. You can have as many **<meta>** tags as you like in a document.

What do **<meta>** tags do? Nothing. They are simply a way to include additional information in an HTML document. It does not affect how the document is displayed, but the information is available for programs that are looking for it. For example, many people use **<meta>** tags to include a description and a list of keywords in a document. Many search engines are programmed to look for these meta tags and use the contained information as an aid for indexing and listing the page. For example if you were creating a Web page that explained the basics of HTML, you could use **<meta>** tags to include a description and keywords like this::

```
<meta name="description" content="Introduction to HTML" />
<meta name="keywords" content="HTML, Web page design" />
```

## Other Information Tags

There are four more information tags that can be placed in an HTML document's head section. I will describe them briefly in Table 2.2 but will not go into more detail at this point because you will not need them unless you progress to advanced HTML editing. We'll return to the **<link>** and **<style>** tags in Chapter 7. With this basic information, however, you will understand the tags should you see them in an existing Web page.

**Table 2.2.** Other information tags that can be included in the head section of an HTML document.

| TAG | DESCRIPTION |
| --- | --- |
| <base> | Defines a base URL that will be used for all links on the page. |
| <link> | Links the HTML document to another document such as a style sheet. |
| <script> | Identifies script code, such as JavaScript, in the document. |
| <style> | Defines a style in the document. |

## Tags for Presenting Simple Text

Strictly speaking, text content in the body of an HTML document does not need to be enclosed in tags. Practically speaking, however, it always should be because using tags gives you the maximum control over how your Web page looks. There are two tags you need to know about when working with text.

The **<p>** tag is used to define paragraphs. A paragraph is set apart from other text by a blank line. Its width depends on the size of the browser window, and the text will automatically wrap to fit (You can control the width of text by using tables, which we'll get to in Chapter 4).

To see how the **<p>** tag works, look at this HTML (I will omit the head section in this and other examples because it does not affect the rendering). Then, see how it is rendered in a browser in Figure 2.1.

```
<body>
<p>This is the first paragraph in the document. It is
enclosed in paragraph tags to set it apart from other text.
Note that the text wraps automatically to fill the browser
window. If the user changes the size of the browser
window,the text adjusts too.</p>
<p>This is a second paragraph enclosed in its own set of
paragraph tags. It is separated from the previous paragraph
by a blank line.</p>
</body>
```

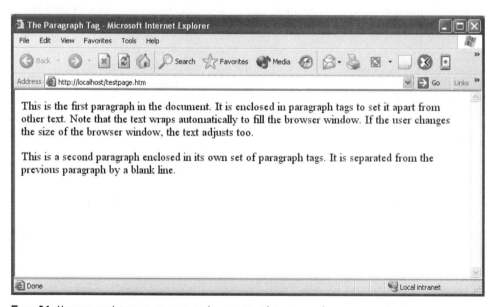

**Figure 2.1.** Use paragraph tags <p> to separate document text into paragraphs.

The **<br />** tag lets you start a new line of text without starting a new paragraph. It is used alone, with no closing tag. It is usually used within a paragraph as shown in this example, with the browser display shown in Figure 2.2.

```
<body>
<p>When you report for your first day of
camp, please be sure that you have all of
the following items with you:</p>
    <p>Sneakers<br />
    Sun hat<br />
    Bathing suit<br />
    Towel</p>
    <p>We'll be going swimming for part of
    the afternoon and then reporting to the
    dining hall for a general meeting.</p>
</body>
```

## Using <p> without </p>

Sometimes you'll see a paragraph marked by an opening **<p>** tag but without a closing **</p>** tag. While this works most of the time because the browser is smart enough to figure out where the paragraph ends even without the closing tag, it's a bad habit to get into. I recommend that you always use the closing **</p>** tag in your documents. It will make your pages more valid and help you down the road; trust me on this one.

## Tags for Creating Lists

HTML supports two kinds of lists: the ordered list, in which items are numbered sequentially, and the unordered list, in which items are displayed with bullets. They

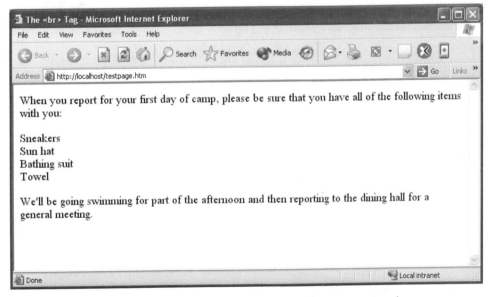

**Figure 2.2.** Use the <br /> tag to start a new line of text without starting a new paragraph.

work essentially the same way. First, you use the ordered list tag **&lt;ol&gt;** or the unordered list tag **&lt;ul&gt;** to enclose the entire list. Then within the list you use the list item tag **&lt;li&gt;** to enclose each list item. Here's an example (Figure 2.3 shows how these lists are displayed):

```
<body>
<ul>
<li>Item 1.</li>
<li>Item 2.</li>
<li>Item 3.</li>
</ul>
<ol>
<li>Item 1.</li>
<li>Item 2.</li>
<li>Item 3.</li>
</ol>
</body>
```

## Tags for Displaying Images

Images can really spice up a Web page, and it's pretty rare to find a page that does not use at least a few images. Images are not actually included in an HTML document. Rather, you use a tag to tell the browser the name and location of the

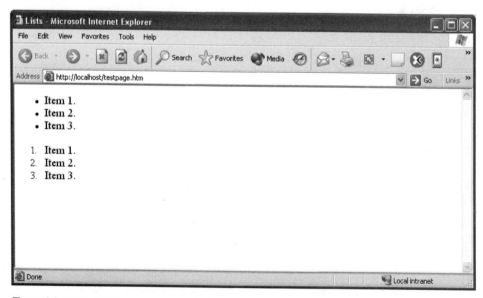

**Figure 2.3.** With HTML, you can include both ordered and unordered lists in your Web pages.

image file. When the browser loads the document, it automatically retrieves the image and displays it at the proper location on the page.

You use the <img> tag to display an image. There is no closing </img> tag—the information about the image is part of the tag itself. The most basic use of the <img> tag is as follows:

```
<img src="url" />
```

The **src** attribute identifies the image file. It is specified as a URL (as defined earlier in the chapter). It's essential that you specify the image URL correctly. If the browser cannot locate the image file it displays a small box with a red X in it, like this:

You definitely do *not* want visitors seeing these "missing image" symbols on your Web pages—it is a real sign that the page was authored by an amateur and is a great way to scare visitors off. We need to look at URLs in some detail to be sure you understand this.

## Specifying the Image URL

In order to avoid the problem of broken image links on your Web pages, you need to understand how to specify the image URL in an <img> tag. There are two types of URLs you can use: *relative* and *absolute*.

A relative URL gives the location of the image file relative to the location of the HTML document that contains the tag. This is the type of image URL you will use when the image file is on the same server as the document, which is almost always the case. If the image file and Web page are in the same folder, then all you need to include is the image file name, as in this example:

```
<img src="logo.gif" />
```

The browser translates this as "the file logo.gif in the same folder on the same server as the current document."

Keeping your HTML documents and images together in the root folder is okay for small Websites, but a separate folder for the images—the folder is usually called images, as you might expect—is generally preferred. This folder will be a subfolder of the root folder where the HTML document is located, as in this diagram:

Then, you would write an <img> tag like this:

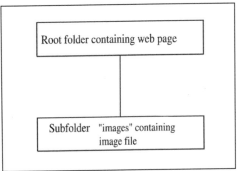

```
<img src="images/logo.gif" />
```

Another situation has the Web page and the image in separate subfolders, as diagrammed here:

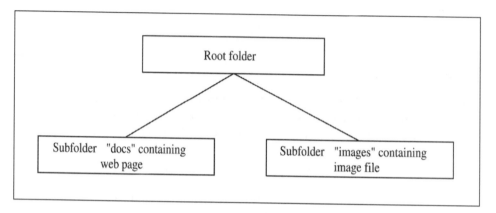

In this case, you would write the **<img>** tag as follows:

```
<img src="../images/logo.gif" />
```

The .. notation means "move up one folder level," so this URL is translated as "move up one folder level and then down to the images subfolder to find the file logo.gif."

Using relative URLs in **<img>** tags is common practice. You just have to be sure the URL is correct! One disadvantage is that if you move either the Web page or the image to another folder, you must change all the URLs to reflect the new location. This is one reason to select a good folder structure for your Website and stick with it—don't move things around without a good reason.

An absolute URL specifies the precise location of the image file—the location of the Web page itself does not matter. An absolute URL identifies the Website, the file name, and the folder (only if the file is not in the site's root folder). Here's an example:

```
<img src="http://www.coffeecup.com/images/logo.gif" />
```

You can use an absolute URL to refer to a file that is on any Website in the world. Of course, you cannot display someone else's images on one of your Web pages without permission. You could use an absolute reference to refer to images on your own Website, but relative URLs are easier to use for this purpose. One advantage of using absolute URLs for **<img>** tags is that you can move the Web page (but not the image file) without having to revise the URLs.

You can also omit the Web address in absolute URLs for images and other files that are on your Website. This tells the browser to start at the root of your Website and go from there. I feel this is the best way because you can move your pages around and they will always point to the images and other files you reference in the same way.

```
<img src="/images/logo.gif" />
```

## Image Size Attributes

When you use a basic **<img>** tag as was described in the previous section, the browser will display the image at its "natural" size. This means that each pixel in the image will get one pixel on the screen. You can see how big this is when you preview the Web page you are working on, but you can get an idea ahead of time if you know the pixel size of the image. These simple formulas give you the approximate "natural" size of an image:

Display width in inches = horizontal image pixels / 96
Display height in inches = vertical image pixels / 96

You can modify the display size of an image by using the width and height attributes in the **<img>** tag. Here's an example:

```
<img src="logo.gif" width="60" height="40" />
```

This will tell the browser to display the image 60 pixels wide and 40 pixels high regardless of its actual size. The picture will be expanded or shrunk as needed. By using the width and height attributes, you can precisely size images to fit in your page layout.

However, there are some important precautions.

The first is maintaining the image's *aspect ratio*, the ratio of its width to height. You can change this using the width and height attributes, but the result may look weird. If you don't believe me, here's proof. The following HTML code displays the same image twice on a Web page, the first time at its natural size of 600 x 200 pixels, so it is three times as wide as tall for an aspect ratio of 3:1. Then the image is displayed with the width attribute changed to 300 so the aspect ratio is now 1.5:1. As you can see in Figure 2.4, that second fish photo definitely looks...well, fishy! The take-home message is that if you want to use the width and height attributes to change an image's size, change them both by the same factor to retain the original aspect ratio.

## Determining an Image's Pixel Size

You can determine the pixel dimensions of an image by opening it in any graphics program and using the Image Size command, or something similar, to display the size. Windows XP users have it even easier—simply locate the image file in Windows Explorer and point at the file name (do not click)—a small pop-up window will appear with information about the image, including its pixel dimensions.

```
<body>
<img src="images/fish.jpg" width="600" height="200" />
<img src="images/fish.jpg" width="300" height="200" />
</body
```

While you can use the **width** and **height** attributes to display an image at a smaller than normal size, I recommend against it. It's better to use a graphics program such as Adobe Photoshop or Paint Shop Pro to make a copy of the image at the size you want it and use that. You'll save download time and your users will see faster-loading pages—always a good thing!

## Should You Ever Omit Width and Height?

If you want an image displayed at its normal size, you can just omit **width** and **height**, right? Well, you can but you shouldn't, and here's why. You must include the height and width of an image for the page to be good HTML. Without the **width** and **height** information, the browser has to download the entire image to know how big it is and how much space to reserve for it on the page. If you include this information in the <**img**> tag, the browser knows how much space to reserve *before* the image is downloaded and can continue rendering other page elements while waiting for the image to download. The result is a faster page download experience for your users. It's not a significant difference in all situations, but particularly with large images it can have a real effect.

**Figure 2.4.** At its normal aspect ratio, the photo looks fine (top), but with a distorted aspect ratio, it definitely looks weird (bottom).

## Other <img> Tag Attributes

This section describes a few other attributes of the <**img**> tag that help control images on your Web page.

You use the **alt** attribute to specify alternate text for the image. This text is displayed in the browser if it is unable to download the image or if the person visiting your site has images turned off. More importantly, it is used by special software designed to let vision-impaired people surf the Web. A Web page's content is converted to audible speech, and images are converted according to their **alt** attributes. There is also the benefit of telling search engines and other screen readers what the image is and therefore giving them a better idea of what your page is about.

The **border** attribute defines a border around the image. The default is no border; set this attribute to a value specifying the border width in pixels. Here's an **<img>** tag that uses both the **alt** and **border** attributes:

```
<img src="fish.jpg" border="2" alt="Lake Trout" />
```

Although it's not used as much anymore , the final **<img>** tag attribute that I will mention is **align**. It is used to control the way text wraps around an image when the **<img>** tag is within a paragraph—that is, between a **<p>** and a **</p>** tag along with text.

The align and border tags are not supported in XHTML. In addition they are deprecated (not recommended) in HTML 4.01.

The default alignment is **bottom**—the image appears inline with the text at the bottom and no wrapping, meaning that there are blank areas to the right and left of the image. You get this result if you do not include the **align** attribute in the <img> tag or if you explicitly specify **align="bottom"**. This is shown in Figure 2.5.

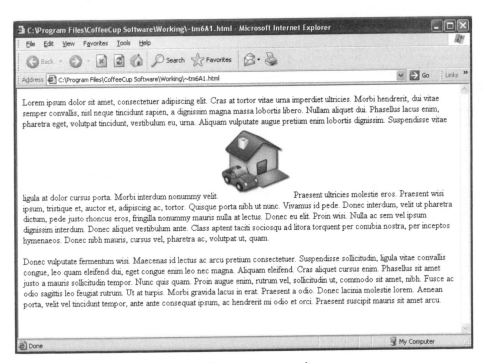

**Figure 2.5** The default image alignment provides for no text wrapping

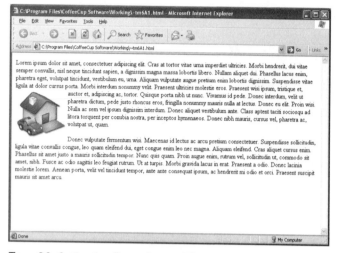

**Figure 2.6.** Setting the **align** attribute to **left** gives this result.

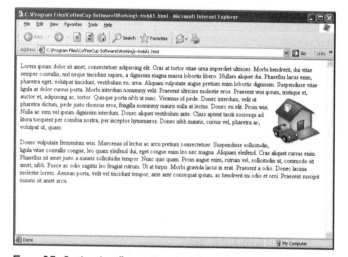

**Figure 2.7.** Setting the **align** attribute to **right** gives this result.

Setting the **align** attribute to **left** places the image against the left edge of the browser window with the text wrapping in the space to the right of the image. This is shown in Figure 2.6.

Conversely, setting **align** to **right** places the image against the right edge of the window with the text wrapping in the space to the left of the image. This is shown in Figure 2.7.

Two other supported values for the **align** attribute are **top** and **middle**. I rarely see these used; you can explore them on your own if you like. We will talk more about the best way to align and add borders to your images using style sheets later in Chapter 7.

## Tags for Creating Hyperlinks and Anchors

Hyperlinks are, of course, central to the Web, and it's difficult to imagine a Web page that does not contain at least a few. An anchor is a way to identify a specific location in a Web page so that a hyperlink can link to that location and not just to the page as a whole.

## Hyperlinks

To create a hyperlink, you use the **<a>** tag. The syntax is as follows:

```
<a href="URL">Link text</a>
```

In the browser, **Link text** will be displayed with the special hyperlink formatting, usually a blue underline. When the user clicks the link, the browser will navigate to the location specified by **URL**. You can also use an image for the link by inserting an **<img>** tag within the **<a>** tags:

```
<a href="URL"><img src="linkimage.gif" /></a>
```

In both cases, the mouse pointer changes to a hand icon when it's over a link in the browser. In either case, it is important to include the http:// part of the URL:

```
<a href="http://www.coffeecup.com">CoffeeCup Software</a>
```

Many links on a Web page are often to other pages on the same Website. If the target page is in the same folder as the current page, then the <a> tag needs to include only the name of the target page:

```
<a href="privacy.htm">Privacy policy</a>
```

If the target page is in a different folder on the same Website, then the link must indicate the file location:

```
<a href="docs/privacy.htm">Privacy policy</a>
```

To link to an anchor in a Web page, put the anchor name at the end of the URL, separated by a pound sign (#):

```
<a href="http://www.coffeecup.com#AnchorName">CoffeeCup
Software</a>
```

You can also link to an anchor that is in the same document as the hyperlink. In this case, use just the anchor name, preceded by #, as the URL:

```
<a href="#AnchorName">Link
text</a>
```

You can use a hyperlink to let the user download a file onto their computer. All you need to do is specify the file name as the **href** attribute. This link, for example, will let the user download the specified ZIP file:

```
<a href="SourceCode.zip">
Download source code</a>
```

Please see the sidebar "Links to Other File Types" for more information on downloading files.

# Links to Other File Types

You can create a hyperlink to any kind of file: images, word processing documents, Excel spreadsheets, ZIP files, executable program files, and so on. What happens when a user clicks a link depends on the file extension, which identifies the type of file.

If the file is a recognized Web file, it is opened in the browser. This includes HTML documents (.htm and .html extensions), Web images (.gif, .jpg, and .png extensions), and script files (.asp, .php, and .jsp extensions).

If the file is another type, the user has the option to download it or to, in most cases, open it. For downloading, the user will be permitted to select the download folder. The opening option is available only if the user has the associated application installed, such as Microsoft Word for files with the .doc extension. If the user chooses the Open option, the file is downloaded to a temporary folder and then opened.

## Anchors

You also use the **<a>** tag to create an anchor, using the **name** attribute instead of the **href** attribute:

```
<a name="AnchorName">Text to be anchored</a>
```

Each anchor name must be unique within the document. Text that is anchored is not displayed in any special way. You can create an "empty" anchor by simply not including any text within in **<a>** tag:

```
<a name="AnchorName"></a>
```

Anchors function the same, however, whether empty or not.

## Linking to the Top of a Page

When you have a long Web page, it's a good idea to include some links that let the user return to the top of the document with a single click. First, place an anchor named **top** at the start of the document:

```
<a name="top"></a>
```

Then, place hyperlinks like this one at the desired locations in the document:

```
<a href="#top">Return to top</a>
```

## Review and Practice

It's time to take what you have learned and see it in action. In this section, I'll present a complete (though basic) Web page that uses only tags presented in this chapter. By examining the HTML code and looking at the rendered page, you will get a better feel for how all the elements of an HTML document come together to create the final product. Then in later chapters, as you learn more HTML tags, we will improve and expand the page.

The project that we will tackle is a Web page for an amateur photographer. It will be a one-page site, at least for now, and because it is a photographer's site, it will include lots of images, providing good practice for this important part of Web design. I'll be using my own images for the examples—if you want to work through it yourself, you will have to locate some images to use.

What are the goals for the page? It's usually a good idea to think about this before you get started. For now, our goals are fairly simple:

- A title or heading at the top of the page that gives the photographer's name

- A list of the types of photographs that he specializes in

- A small selection of photographs to tempt prospective customers

- At the bottom of the page a brief resume of the photographer's education and experience

- Near the top of the page, a link that takes the user to the resume
- <title> and meta tags that describe the page

I'll warn you now that this page will not be finished in any sense—you would not want to put in on the Web! But that's okay; you're just getting started. We will improve the page in later chapters.

Listing 2.1 shows the HTML for this first try at a Web page. This HTML uses only the tags you learned about in this chapter. The result is shown in Figure 2.8.

Listing 2.1. The HTML source code for the photographer's Web page, first try.

```
<html>
<head>
   <title>Dave Davison Photographer</title>
   <meta name="keywords" content="photography, photographer"
/>
</head>
<body>
<p>Dave Davidson, Photographer</p>
<p><a href="#resume">View my resume</a></p>
<img src="image01.jpg" />
<img src="image02.jpg" />
<img src="image03.jpg" />
<img src="image04.jpg" />
<ul>
<li>Fine Art</li>
<li>Landscapes</li>
<li>Architecture</li>
</ul>
<p><a name="resume">Resume</a></p>
<p>Dave Davidson has been an active photographer since 1992.
He specializes in
portraits and fine art prints.</p>
<p>Education</p>
<ul>
<li>BS, Art History, University of Pennsylvania, 1988</li>
<li>MS, Photography, Chicago School of Design, 1991</li>
</ul>
<p>Exhibitions</p>
<ul>
<li>Images From Nature, Smith Gallery, Los Angeles, 1994</li>
<li>Dave Davidson, Photographer in Nature, Oak Creek Center,
Houston, 1996</li>
<li>Architecture of Manhattan, Bowles Museum, New York,
1999</li>
</ul>
</body>
</html>
```

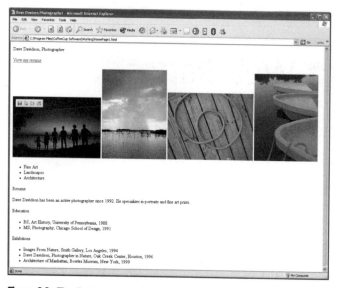

Looking at this Web page, several problems are immediately apparent. Here are the most obvious ones:

- The text is all the same, with no differences between headings, regular text, and so on.

- The images are just lined up with no attention to their placement relative to each other and the text.

- The white background does not look particularly attractive.

While this page is a start, it certainly can use some improving. We'll start with these improvements in the next chapter.

**Figure 2.8.** The first try at the photographer's Web page.

## Summary

Welcome to the world of Web design! You're just getting started, but already you have learned enough HTML to create a basic Web page on your own. It would be a good idea for you to try out what you have learned in this chapter. Go ahead and create a Web page, even if it's just for you to play around with. Or, work with the page created in the Review and Practice section, making changes to the HTML and seeing what effects they have. Try out the tags for paragraphs, lists, images, hyperlinks, and the other page elements that were covered here. There's nothing like some practice to hone your skills.

# Formatting Your Web Pages

The previous chapter showed you how to use the most basic HTML tags to create a Web page to display text and images. I bet this is not enough for you—you want to do more to make your Web pages even better. In this chapter I'll show you some more HTML techniques to change the appearance of your Web pages.

## HTML and Colors

HTML provides you with control over the colors of items on your pages. There are two ways to specify a color.

The first and easiest is to simply use the color name. You can select from the following 16 keywords: **aqua, black, blue, fuchsia, gray, green, lime, maroon, navy, olive, purple, red, silver, teal, white**, and **yellow**. Of course you can use this technique only if you want one of these colors.

The second way, which allows specifying any color you want, is using hex codes. This is the preferred way to specify colors because it is universally understood and you'll never get stuck trying to find the name for that certain shade of blue.

To use this technique, you need to understand how colors on a computer screen are created. Any color is a combination of the three additive primary colors red, green, and blue. This is why you will sometimes see computer colors referred to as RGB colors. In any given color, each of the three primary colors has a value ranging from 0 (none) to 255 (maximum), so any color can be represented by its RGB value of three numbers—and this is how you can specify colors for your Web page elements. There are three formats for doing this:

- Use the **rgb(r, g, b)** function, where r, g, and b are numbers in the range 0 to 255 that specify the level of red, green, and blue, respectively.

- Use the **rgb(r%, g%, b%)** function, where r, g, and b are numbers in the range 0 to 100 that specify the level of red, blue, and green as a percentage of the maximum.

- Use a hexadecimal (base 16) number in the form #RRGGBB, where RR, GG, and BB is each a hexadecimal number in the range 00-FF (0-255 in decimal notation).

Table 3.1 shows some examples of colors using the **rgb()** function and hexadecimal notation. You can experiment with colors using your HTML editor and browser to see what different values look like.

**Table 3.1.** RGB and hexadecimal codes for some colors.

| Color | rgb() | Hexadecimal |
|---|---|---|
| Black | rgb(0,0,0) | #000000 |
| White | rgb(255,255,255) | #FFFFFF |
| Medium gray | rgb(153,153,153) | #999999 |
| Blue | rgb(0,0,255) | #0000FF |
| Red | rgb(255,0,0) | #FF0000 |
| Green | rgb(0,255,0) | #00FF00 |
| Yellow | rgb(255,255,0) | #FFFF00 |
| Purple | rgb(255,0,255) | #FF00FF |
| Light blue | rgb(51,255,255) | #33FFFF |
| Pink | rgb(255,51,153) | #FF3399 |
| Brown | rgb(153,51,0) | #993300 |

A full list of HTML color codes can be found at http://html-color-codes.com/.

# The <body> Tag

You saw in the previous chapter how every HTML document includes the <body> tag to enclose its content. When used by itself, the <body> tag results in a document that displays with certain default characteristics. By including attributes in the <body> tag, you can control certain aspects of document rendering.

The presentation attributes of the <body> tag are not supported in XHTML and are deprecated in HTML 4.01.

## The Background

Unless you specify otherwise, a browser will render an HTML document on a white background. You can specify either a color or an image for the background.

To specify a background color other than white, include the **bgcolor** attribute in the <body> tag. You can specify either a color name or a numerical value for the color. For example, the following <body> tag creates a document with a medium gray background:

```
<body bgcolor="#C0C0C0">
```

To display an image in the page background, use the **background** attribute to specify the URL of the image:

```
<body background="URL">
```

Here's an example:

```
<body background="images/chalk.gif">
```

If the image is smaller than the browser window, it will be tiled (repeated) to fill the area.

## Link Appearance

Text that is a hyperlink is displayed differently from regular text on the Web page. By default, a link is blue underlined text. If the link has been visited recently (the period is determined by the user's browser settings), it displays as purple underlined text. You can control how links display to the user by including the following attributes in the **&lt;body&gt;** tag:

- **link:** the color of normal links
- **alink:** the color of an active link (the user has pressed but not yet released the mouse button on the link)
- **vlink:** the color of links the user has visited

Each of these attributes could be set to a color name, RGB color value, or hex color value as described earlier in this chapter. You can do a lot more with link appearance using styles, as I will show you in Chapter 7.

## Default Text

The default text color is black. To specify a different text color, use the **text** attribute in the **&lt;body&gt;** tag and set it to a different color (color name, RGB value, or hex color value). This **&lt;body&gt;** tag, for example, sets the default text color to blue.

```
<body text="#0000FF">
```

You can still set selected portions of text to different colors using the **&lt;font&gt;** tag, which is covered later in this chapter.

# Changing Text Style

By default, text on a Web page is displayed with the default style. This style is best defined by what it is not—it is not boldface, it is not italicized, and it is not

## Background Cautions

When using a background for your Web page, either a color or an image, it is important to ensure that the text on the page remains easily readable. Black text against a dark blue background, for example, can be pretty tough to read. Likewise, a busy background image can make it hard to decipher the text. One useful technique is to use a graphics program, such as Adobe Photoshop, to reduce the contrast of the background image. This will make it a lot easier to read the text.

underlined. If you want to use any of these text effects, you have to include the proper HTML tags. They are **<b>**, **<i>**, and **<u>**:

```
<b>This text will be boldface.</b>
<i>This text will be italicized.</i>
<u>This text will be underlined.</u>
```

The **<u>** tag is not supported in XHTML and is deprecated in HTML 4.01. You can use styles to underline text, but many people believe it is better to avoid underlining text because the user may confuse it with a hyperlink.

These tags can be nested and overlapped to get the effect you want. Here's an example:

```
<p>You <b>can combine <i>boldface </i></b><i>and
italics.</i></p>
```

The preceding line of code is rendered like this:

```
You can combine boldface and italics.
```

# Changing Font Appearance and Size

Each browser displays text in its own default font. But sometimes you want to specify the precise font that will be used. You can use the **<font>** tag to control the font that text is displayed with. There are three attributes that you use with this tag to control different aspects of the font. The following sections explain the attributes that you can use with the **<font>** tag. Then, I'll present an example of using this tag.

The **<font>** tag is not supported in XHTML and is deprecated in HTML 4.01. You should use styles to control fonts in your Web pages when you are coding to these standards.

## The Face Attribute

The **face** attribute defines the style of the font—the shape of the individual letters. Font faces are identified by names; Arial, Times New Roman, and Courier are some commonly used fonts. When specifying a font in a Web page, you must be aware that users' browsers will be limited to displaying the fonts they have installed on their system. In other words, you cannot be assured that your end users will be able to view the font you specify in the **face** attribute. The good news is that browsers handle this situation well. If the requested font is not available, the browser will choose a similar font that is available. In the worst case scenario, it will fall back on the default font. Your text *will* be displayed even if not in the exact font you wanted.

How can you tell what fonts are available even on your own system? The method I like best is to open a word processing program and open its Fonts list. All the available fonts will be listed, and some programs will even display each font so you can see what it looks like. This is shown for Microsoft Word in Figure 3.1.

Another technique to view the available fonts is to open the Windows Control Panel and double-click the Fonts icon. Windows will display a list of all the available fonts, as shown in Figure 3.2. To see what a font looks like, double-click its name.

The following fonts are widely used on the Web and you can assume that essentially all your site visitors will have them installed. When in doubt, stick to this list—it includes a good selection of styles.

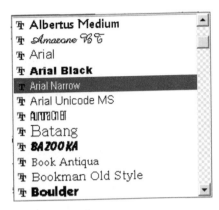

**Figure 3.1.** Using a word processing program to view available fonts.

Arial
**Arial Black**
Courier New
Times New Roman
**Impact**
Comic Sans MS
Georgia
Trebuchet MS
Verdana

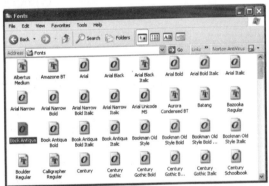

**Figure 3.2.** Using the Fonts entry in Control Panel to view available fonts.

## The Size Attribute

The **size** attribute controls the size of text. Rather than using the more usual points, HTML specifies font size as a value from 1 to 7, with 1 being very small, 3 normal, and 7 large. The point equivalents are as follows (recall that 1 point equals approximately 1/72 inch):

| HTML SIZE | POINTS |
|:---:|:---:|
| 1 | 8 |
| 2 | 10 |
| 3 | 12 |
| 4 | 14 |
| 5 | 18 |
| 6 | 24 |
| 7 | 36 |

## The Color Attribute

The **color** attribute determines the text color. The default is black. There are two ways to specify the **color** attribute. The first is to use one of the predefined HTML color names. The other is to specify a numeric color value using the **rgb()** function or hex notation. You learned how to specify colors earlier in this chapter. Thus, you could make text blue like this:

```
<p><font color="blue">This text is blue</font> and this
text is not.</p>
```

## Using the <font> Tag

Now that you have learned how to use the **<font>** tag to control the font in your document, let's look at an example. Here's some HTML code that uses the **<font>** tag:

```
<p>This is normal black text, <font size="5"
color="red">this is larger red text.</font></p>

<p><font size="7" color="blue">This is blue in the largest
size</font>, now back to normal!</p>

<p><font size="4" color="#008080">Green large, <font
size="7" color="brown">brown larger,</font> back to green
large.</font></p>
```

The rendering of this in a browser is shown in Figure 3.3. The important thing to note about the third example is that **<font>** tags can be nested. Each **<font>** tag controls the text that it encloses; when the ending **</font>** tag is reached, the text reverts to whatever it was before. This might be the default font or it might be a font as defined by a previous **<font>** tag.

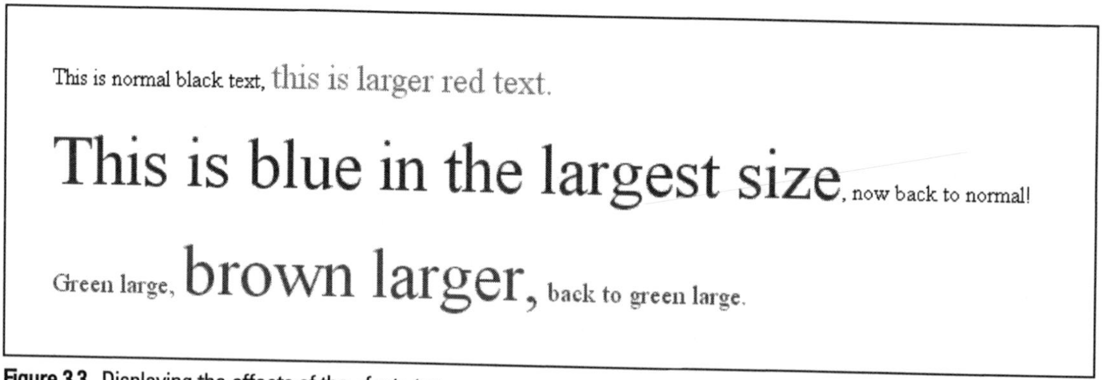

This is normal black text, this is larger red text.

This is blue in the largest size, now back to normal!

Green large, brown larger, back to green large.

**Figure 3.3.** Displaying the effects of the <font> tag.

# Preserving White Space

You learned in Chapter 2 how HTML normalizes white space in your document. Any white space in your content—spaces, tabs, and new lines—is collapsed to a single space. This works well in most situations, but there are times when you have text that you want displayed exactly as is, white space and all. An example might be a poem that has been carefully laid out with spaces and tabs to get the exact indentation that the author wants. In this situation, use the **<pre>** tag, which stands for preformatted. White space is not normalized within **<pre>** tags—it is displayed exactly as entered. The **<pre>** tag also forces the browser to use a monospaced font, in which all characters are the same width.

The following HTML will demonstrate this. It contains two paragraphs that are identical except that the second one uses the **<pre>** tag to preserve white space. Figure 3.4 shows how this HTML is rendered.

```
<body>
<p>one
    two            three

four
five
</p>
<p><pre>one
    two            three

four
five
</pre></p>
</body>
```

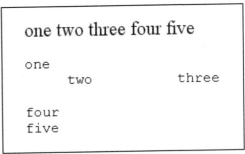

**Figure 3.4.** Use the <pre> tag to display content with white space preserved and in a monospaced font.

# Creating Headings

HTML defines six levels of document headings, numbered from level 1 (the highest) to level 6. The higher the level, the larger the font used to display it. This is shown in Figure 3.5.

Heading levels 5 and 6 are rarely used because they display so small—in any event, it's a rare document that needs so many levels of headings! You create headings in your document with the tags **<h1>** for heading level 1 through **<h6>** for heading level 6. In this example, two heading levels are used:

```
<body>
<h1>Jason's Web Page</h1>
```

**Figure 3.5.** HTML defines six levels of document headings.

```
<p>Welcome to my Web page. I hope you enjoy it!</p>
<h2>My family</h2>
<!-- images and text here-->
<h2>My hobbies</h2>
<!-- more images and text here-->
</body>
```

# Changing Paragraph and Heading Alignment (<center> and the Align Attribute)

By default, paragraphs and headings in a Web page are left-aligned. For some Web page layouts, you may want to position them in the center or even aligned on the right edge of the page. You accomplish this by including the **align** attribute in either the heading or the paragraph tag:

```
<p align="center">Centered paragraph text</p>
<h2 align="right">A right aligned heading</h2>
```

The **align** attribute is not supported in XHTML and is deprecated in HTML 4.01. You should use styles to control paragraph and heading alignment in your documents.

## Horizontal Rules

When you need to divide your Web page into sections, you can use the **<hr>** tag to place a horizontal rule, or line, across the page. When used alone, the **<hr>** tag creates a thin gray line that extends across the page almost, but not quite, to the left and right edges. By using the attributes that are listed in Table 3.2 you can modify the appearance and position of the rule.

None of the attributes of the **<hr>** tag are supported in XHTML, and they all are deprecated in HTML 4.01.

**Table 3.2.** Attributes of the **<hr>** tag.

| ATTRIBUTE | VALUES | DESCRIPTION |
|-----------|--------|-------------|
| align | left, right, center | Controls the horizontal alignment of the rule. The default value is center. |
| noshade | true, false | Determines whether the rule displays as a solid line (true) or as a two-color "groove" (false). Has no visible effect on thin rules. |
| size | A number | Sets the thickness of the rule in pixels. |
| width | A number or percentage | Sets the length of the rule in pixels or as a percentage of the window width. |

The following HTML code displays four different horizontal rules. The results are shown in Figure 3.6.

```
<body>
<p>Example 1</p>
<hr />
<p>Example 2</p>
<hr size="5" width="50%" noshade="false" />
<p>Example 3</p>
<hr size="8" width="65%" align="left" />
<p>Example 4</p>
<hr size="10" width="45%" align="right" noshade="true" />
</body>
```

# Frames and Why Not to Use Them

Using frames is an HTML technique that divides the browser window into two or more rectangular regions. You might see, for example, a table of contents on the left side of the screen and the content on the right. Each frame displays a separate HTML document. Because the individual frames scroll independently, you can in theory create some attractive and easy-to-use Web pages this way.

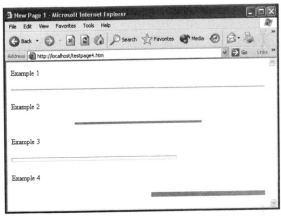

**Figure 3.2.** Examples of using the <hr> tag.

Note that I say *in theory!* In practice, frames usually introduce a variety of problems that may not be apparent to the Web page author. Let's take a brief look at them.

The success of the World Wide Web is based in part on the simplicity of the underlying concepts. One URL refers to one and only one page. With frames, this correspondence is lost. A frames-based page has its own URL, but the page itself rarely contains any content. Rather, it contains links to *other* Web pages that contain the actual content; it is these pages that are displayed in the frames. Suddenly the situation changes—a URL no longer points to a page of content but rather points to a frames page, which then points to the actual content. The fundamental structure of the Web is broken.

This alone is enough reason to avoid frames, but there is more. Browser support for frames varies, both between browser brands and between versions within a brand. The overwhelming use of Microsoft Internet Explorer has lessened this problem but not made it go away.

The final problem with frames that I'll mention is search engines such as Yahoo! and Google. The break in the URL-content link mentioned earlier can be fatal to a search engine trying to index your page. While some search engines have been programmed to "drill down" through a frames page to the underlying content, you cannot count on it. Given the importance of the search engines in locating Web content and drawing visitors to your site, this is a serious shortcoming.

This is not to say that there are no situations in which frames can be used to advantage. With advanced Web authoring techniques, some of the disadvantages can be overcome. Someone just getting started with Web design, however, should not use them. Frames are created using the **<frameset>** and **<frame>** tags. I mention this only so you'll recognize them when you see them in the source code for someone else's Web page. Frames will not be covered further in this book.

## Review and Practice

In Chapter 2 we started creating a Website for a photographer. We were limited to using the HTML tags that were covered to that point, and the resulting site was pretty basic—not really ready to publish, to be honest. With what you have learned in this chapter, you are ready to take that site to the next level. To remind you of what that page looked like, refer to Figure 3.7.

What would this page benefit from? There are quite a few things, but as for the changes we can accomplish with the tags you learned about in this chapter, let's focus on these:

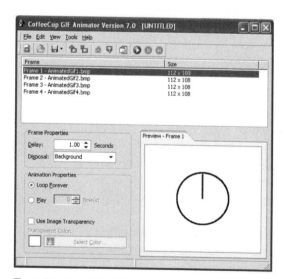

- Displaying a page background
- Changing the appearance and alignment of some of the text
- Using headings in the resume
- Using a horizontal rule to separate parts of the page

Listing 3.1 shows the HTML source code for the page after making the changes, and Figure 3.8 shows the resulting display. You should look specifically for these things:

- Addition of the **background** attribute to the **<body>** tag to use the image paper1.gif as the page background. This image provides the appearance of high-quality stationery, and while it may not be visible in the figure, it really is a professional touch.

**Figure 3.7.** The original Web page as created in Chapter 2.

- Use of the **<font>** tag to display the page's main heading in a different font.
- Use of the **<font>** tag to display the first bulleted list in a different font.
- Use of the **<hr>** tag to create a horizontal rule to separate the resume from the rest of the page.
- Use of **<h2>** and **<h3>** tags for the headings in the resume.

All in all, I think you'll agree that this version of the Web page is a lot better than the original. You might even consider publishing this one—but there are still some improvements we could make, particularly to the layout. Those improvements will have to wait for the next chapter.

Listing 3.1. HTML source for the modified Web page.

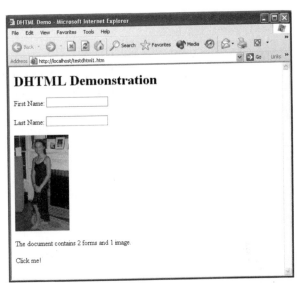

**Figure 3.8.** The modified Web page looks a lot nicer than the original.

```html
<html>
<head>
   <title>Dave Davison Photographer</title>
   <meta name="keywords" content="photography, photographer"
/>
</head>
<body background="paper1.gif">
<p align="center">
<font size="7" face="Calligrapher" color="#0000FF">Dave
Davidson, Photographer</font></p>
<p><a href="#resume">View my resume</a></p>
<img src="image01.jpg" />
<img src="image02.jpg" />
<img src="image03.jpg" />
<img src="image04.jpg" />
<font size="4" face="Cornerstone"><ul>
<li>Fine Art</li>
<li>Landscapes</li>
<li>Architecture</li>
</ul></font>
<hr>
<h2><a name="resume">Resume</a></h2>
<p>Dave Davidson has been an active photographer since 1992.
He specializes in portraits and fine art prints.</p>
```

```
<h3>Education</h3>
<ul>
<li>BS, Art History, University of Pennsylvania, 1988</li>
<li>MS, Photography, Chicago School of Design, 1991</li>
</ul>
<h3>Exhibitions</h3>
<ul>
<li>Images From Nature, Smith Gallery, Los Angeles, 1994</li>
<li>Dave Davidson, Photographer in Nature, Oak Creek Center,
Houston, 1996</li>
<li>Architecture of Manhattan, Bowles Museum, New York,
1999</li>
</ul>
</body>
</html>
```

## Summary

HTML provides the Webmaster with a decent set of tags for formatting the page content. No, you do not have the same formatting flexibility that is provided by a modern word processor or desktop publishing program, but for Web pages, you rarely if ever need that. You can get a lot more Web page formatting power when you learn about styles in Chapter 7.

# Magic with HTML Tables

The HTML tags that you have learned so far will let you create some very nice Web pages. But what if you want a more attractive and complex layout than those tags provide for? Surely there's something more behind those terrific and attractive Web pages that you see so often! Indeed there is—and it usually is tables. More advanced Websites will use style sheets for layout and positioning text and images on the page, but we'll talk more about that later. This chapter shows you all the ins and outs of using tables to create complex Web page layouts.

## Table Fundamentals

At its most basic, a table is a grid of one or more rows and columns. At the intersection of each row and column is a *cell*. Table cells can hold HTML content such as text, hyperlinks, and images. While tables were designed to display tabular information like price lists and charts, they are probably the main layout technique behind many of the Web pages you may have been admiring. Look, for example, at the cnn.com Web page in Figure 4.1. Note how the various page elements—text, images, links, and so on—are arranged in a visually attractive manner that lets visitors find what they are looking for quickly. There's no way you could create a Web page like this one with the HTML tags you learned about in Chapters 2 and 3—tables are the key.

Some HTML tables are used in what might be called the traditional manner: for

**Figure 4.1.** The www.cnn.com Web page makes extensive use of tables to achieve an attractive and efficient layout.

the presentation of rows and columns of data. That's fine, but it just scratches the surface when it comes to the possibilities of tables. What makes tables so special is that you can change the relationships between rows and columns. One row can be tall, the other short. One column will be wide, the other narrow. As you manipulate the table rows and columns, the content of the cells will move along too. As a result, you can use tables to create essentially any arrangement of elements on your page. When you make the table borders invisible, the contents seem to "float" in position on the Web page. Let's see how you can use tables for Web page layout.

## The Basic Table Tags

A table requires at least three HTML tags:

- The **<table>** tag defines the table itself.

- Within the **<table>** tag there will be one <tr> tag for each row.

- Within each **<tr>** tag there will be one <td> tag for each cell, or column.

- Within each **<td>** tag you place the content for that cell.

| row 1, cell 1 | row 1, cell 2 |
| row 2, cell 1 | row 2, cell 2 |

**Figure 4.2.** A simple two-row, two-column table.

The following HTML creates a basic table with two rows and two columns; the resulting table is shown in Figure 4.2. Note that I have included the **border** attribute, which I'll get to later in the chapter. You can omit this but then the table would display without borders, which would not have been appropriate for this example.

```
<body>
<table border="1">
<tr>
<td>row 1, cell 1</td>
<td>row 1, cell 2</td>
</tr>
<tr>
<td>row 2, cell 1</td>
<td>row 2, cell 2</td>
</tr>
</table>
</body>
```

Most of the remainder of this chapter is devoted to showing you how to modify this basic table to get exactly what you want.

## Adjustable vs. Fixed-Width Tables

In the basic table shown in the preceding section, each column is just wide enough to hold its content, and the total table width is simply the sum of all the column widths. Most of the time, however, you'll want to specify the width of the table rather than simply letting it adjust to its contents. You use the **width** attribute for this, and there are two ways to do it:

- As a percentage of the browser window width. The table will grow or shrink to fill the specified percent of the window.

- As a number of pixels. The table will always display at the same fixed width regardless of the window size. Depending on the window size, the table may extend past the edge.

To specify width as a percent, use a number followed by the % sign. To specify a pixel width, use a number alone. Here are examples:

```
<table width="90%">
<table width="365">
```

Go ahead and try it! Put the following HTML, modified from the preceding example, in the body of an HTML document and preview it in the browser when you resize the window. It will look like Figure 4.3. Then change the **width** attribute to "**365**" and see how the table looks.

```
<table width="90%" border="1">
<tr>
<td>row 1, cell 1</td>
<td>row 1, cell 2</td>
</tr>
<tr>
<td>row 2, cell 1</td>
<td>row 2, cell 2</td>
</tr>
</table>
```

> ## Empty Table Cells
>
> If you want to have an empty cell in a table, be sure to put a non-breaking space character in it. You use the character entity ** ** for this purpose.

**Figure 4.3.** Displaying a table with the width set at 90%.

When should you use each kind of width setting? There's no clear answer to this question—it's something you'll develop a feel for as you gain experience. In general, though, people use fixed-width tables for layouts that contains a lot of graphics and other elements that must retain the same spatial relationship to each other. Variable-width tables are more appropriate when the table contains mostly or all text that can reflow and wrap without affecting the page's usability.

## Attributes of the <table> Tag

The **<table>** tag has quite a few other optional attributes that control various aspects of how the table is displayed. These are described in Table 4.1.

The **align** and **bgcolor** attributes of the **<table>** tag are not supported in XHTML and are deprecated in HTML 4.01. You should use styles to control table alignment and background color in your Web pages when you are authoring to these standards.

**Table 4.1.** Additional attributes of the <table> tag.

| ATTRIBUTE | VALUES | DESCRIPTION |
|---|---|---|
| align | **left**, **center**, or **right** | Controls how the entire table is aligned on the page. |
| bgcolor | a color name, an **rgb()** value, or a hex value (#xxxxxx) | Specifies the background color of the table. |
| border | A number 0 or higher | Determines the width of the border in pixels. Set to 0 for no border. |
| cellpadding | A number with or without % | Sets the space between the cell contents and borders, expressed in pixels or as a percentage of the cell width. |
| cellspacing | A number with or without % | Sets the space between cells, expressed in pixels or as a percentage of the cell width. |

Let's take a look at how the **cellpadding** and **cellspacing** attributes work. The following is a modification of the HTML code presented earlier to include these two attributes:

```
<table width="400" border="2" cell
padding="10" cellspacing="10%">
<tr>
<td>row 1, cell 1</td>
<td>row 1, cell 2</td>
</tr>
<tr>
<td>row 2, cell 1</td>
<td>row 2, cell 2</td>
</tr>
</table>
```

## Single Borders

The best way to get a single table border is to include the following attribute in the **<table>** tag:

```
style="border-collapse: collapse"
```

You'll learn more about using styles with tables in Chapter 7.

The resulting table is shown in Figure 4.4 with callouts to the cell spacing and cell padding. This shows how cell padding is *within* cells and cell spacing is *between* cells.

**Figure 4.4.** Displaying a table with the width set at 90%.

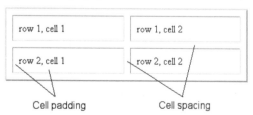

# Working with Table Rows

Each row in an HTML table is defined by a **<tr>** tag. The height of each row is by default determined automatically as the amount of space required to hold the contents of the tallest cell in the row plus the cell padding. The one exception to this rule is if you use the **height** attribute in the **<td>** tag as described in the next section. You can control other aspects of how the row is displayed using the attributes that are described in Table 4.2.

The **align** and **bgcolor** attributes of the **<tr>** tag are not supported in XHTML and are deprecated in HTML 4.01. You should use styles to control alignment and background color in table rows when you are authoring to these standards.

**Table 4.2.** Attributes of the <tr> tag.

| ATTRIBUTE | VALUES | DESCRIPTION |
|---|---|---|
| **align** | **right, left, center, justify** | Determines the horizontal alignment of text or images with the cells of the row. The default is **left**. |
| **bgcolor** | a color name, an **rgb()** value, or a hex value (#xxxxxx) | Specifies the background color of the row. |
| **valign** | **top, middle, bottom** | Determines the vertical alignment of content in cells of the row. The default is **middle**. |

From this table you can conclude that individual table rows can have a different background color than the table as a whole—a useful technique for some more sophisticated page designs.

Now let's see how the **valign** attribute works. First of all, you must realize that this attribute has an effect only if the individual cell is taller than needed to hold its content. This will happen only when the content in another cell in the same row is larger, forcing the row height to increase.

Figure 4.5 shows a two-column, three-row table in which a different **valign** setting is used in each row. Note that the second column contains dummy content in order to make the rows taller so the **valign** setting will have an effect. If you omit the **valign** attribute, the **middle** alignment setting is used.

# Working with Table Cells and Columns

Each row in an HTML table contains one or more cells, with each cell defined by a **<td>** tag. This is important—each row has its own cells defined separately from other rows, which means

| valign = top | Dummy content |
|---|---|
| | Dummy content |
| | Dummy content |
| | Dummy content |
| | Dummy content |
| | Dummy content |

| | Dummy content |
|---|---|
| | Dummy content |
| valign = middle | Dummy content |
| | Dummy content |
| | Dummy content |
| | Dummy content |

| | Dummy content |
|---|---|
| | Dummy content |
| | Dummy content |
| | Dummy content |
| valign = bottom | Dummy content |
| | Dummy content |

**Figure 4.5.** The effects of using different **valign** settings in the **<tr>** tag.

that there is no such thing as a "column" in an HTML table. In most tables the cells do in fact fall into nice neat vertical columns, but they do not have to. There is no "column" tag that you can use to affect the appearance of an entire column in a table. Rather, you must work with the **<td>** tags within each row.

Within a row tag **<tr>**, you will place one or more **<td>** tags to define the row's cells in left-to-right order. The cell's content is placed within the **<td>** tag. For now I will limit discussion to tables in which each row has the same number of cells. The **<td>** tag supports a variety of attributes that control how it and its contents are displayed. These are described in Table 4.3.

The **height**, **width**, and **bgcolor** attributes of the **<td>** tag are not supported in XHTML and are deprecated in HTML 4.01. You should use styles to control cell size and background color in tables when you are authoring to these standards.

**Table 4.1.** Additional attributes of the <table> tag.

| ATTRIBUTE | VALUES | DESCRIPTION |
|---|---|---|
| align | right, left, center, justify | Determines the horizontal alignment of text or images with the cell. The default is **left**. |
| bgcolor | a color name, and **rgb()** value, or a hex value (#xxxxxx) | Specifies the background color of the row. |
| height | A number | Sets the height of the cell in pixels. |
| valign | top, middle, bottom | Determines the vertical alignment of content in cells of the row. The default is **middle**. |
| width | A number | Sets the width of the cell in pixels or as a percent of the table width. |

You'll note that the **<td>** tag shares the **align**, **bgcolor**, and **valign** attributes with the **<tr>** tag. Settings for an individual cell override settings for the row it's in, just as settings for an individual row override settings for the table as a whole.

Can you use the **height** attribute to create a table that has cells with different heights in the same row? No—the row's height will be set to the largest height value that is specified for any of the cells in the row. This means that you can set the **height** attribute for only one cell in the row to change the entire row's height. Thus, the following two **<tr>** tags result in the same row height, 50 pixels (I have omitted the cell content for this example):

```
<tr><td height="50"></td><td height="25"></td><td
height="15"></td></tr>
<tr><td height="50"></td><td></td><td></td></tr>
```

You should note that the **height** setting specifies the minimum height of a cell. If the cell's contents require more space to display, the cell's height (and also the entire row's height) will increase to fit it.

# Merging Cells

The tables I have presented so far have a standard structure in which each row has the same number of cells as any other row and each column has the same number of cells as any other column. When you need more flexibility in your table layout, you can merge cells, combining two or more adjacent cells into a single cell. The resulting merged cell can span two or more original cells horizontally, vertically, or both.

You create merged cells by using either or both of the following two attributes in a **<td>** tag:

- **colspan**: set to the number of cells to be spanned horizontally.
- **rowspan**: set to the number of cells to be spanned vertically.

Here's a simple example. This HTML code creates a table with a basic structure of four rows and two columns. By inserting the attribute **rowspan="4"** into the first **<td>** tag in the first row, the top left cell in the table is merged over four rows — its own row and the three below it. The resulting table is shown in Figure 4.6.

```
<table border="1" cellpadding="5" width="100%">
  <tr>
    <td width="50%" rowspan="4">Merged cell</td>
    <td width="50%">Original cell</td>
  </tr>
  <tr>
    <td width="50%">Original cell</td>
  </tr>
  <tr>
    <td width="50%">Original cell</td>
  </tr>
  <tr>
    <td width="50%">Original cell</td>
  </tr>
</table>
```

When you look at the HTML code for this table, please note the following: The first **<tr>** tag contains two **<td>** tags, as you would expect. The other three **<tr>** tags, however, each contain

| Merged cell | Original cell |
|---|---|
| | Original cell |
| | Original cell |
| | Original cell |

**Figure 4.6.** A table with a cell that is merged vertically over four rows.

only a single `<td>` tag. This is because the top left cell is merged down into these three rows, so they only need one additional cell to make up the overall two column structure of the table.

Next, let's look at an example of merging horizontally. The principle is the same but the details are slightly different. Here's the HTML code to define the table shown in Figure 4.7.

```
<table border="1" cellpadding="5" width="90%" >
  <tr>
    <td width="33%">Original cell</td>
    <td width="33%">Original cell</td>
    <td width="34%">Original cell</td>
  </tr>
  <tr>
    <td width="33%">Original cell</td>
    <td width="67%" colspan="2">Merged cell</td>
  </tr>
  <tr>
    <td width="33%">Original cell</td>
    <td width="33%">Original cell</td>
    <td width="34%">Original cell</td>
  </tr>
</table>
```

| Original cell | Original cell | Original cell |
|---------------|---------------|---------------|
| Original cell | Merged cell   |               |
| Original cell | Original cell | Original cell |

**Figure 4.7.** A table with a cell that is merged horizontally over two columns.

Finally, we'll look at a table that contains a cell that is merged both vertically and horizontally. This requires including both the **colspan** and **rowspan** attributes in the `<td>` tag of the merged cell. Here's the HTML; the table is shown in Figure 4.8.

```
<table border="1" cellpadding="5" width="90%">
  <tr>
    <td width="25%">Original cell</td>
    <td width="25%">Original cell</td>
    <td width="25%">Original cell</td>
    <td width="25%">Original cell</td>
  </tr>
  <tr>
    <td width="25%">Original cell</td>
    <td width="50%" colspan="2" rowspan="2">Merged cell</td>
    <td width="25%">Original cell</td>
  </tr>
  <tr>
    <td width="25%">Original cell</td>
    <td width="25%">Original cell</td>
  </tr>
  <tr>
    <td width="25%">Original cell</td>
    <td width="25%">Original cell</td>
    <td width="25%">Original cell</td>
    <td width="25%">Original cell</td>
  </tr>
</table
```

| Original cell | Original cell | Original cell | Original cell |
|---|---|---|---|
| Original cell | Merged cell | | Original cell |
| Original cell | | | Original cell |
| Original cell | Original cell | Original cell | Original cell |

**Figure 4.8.** Merging a cell both vertically and horizontally.

When creating merged cells, the most important thing to remember is that you must reduce the number of cells — the number of **<td>** tags — in the rows and columns that the merged cell is being merged into. While browsers are usually pretty forgiving in dealing with less-than-perfect code, you may get unpredictable results if you ignore this warning.

## Embedding a Table in Another Table

Some of the most flexible page design techniques involve the use of nested tables. This technique is surprisingly simple — all you need to do is create the main table (the outer table) and then insert another table (the inner table) in one of the cells. Here's a very simple example of HTML that nests one table in another, with the rendering shown in Figure 4.9.

```
<table border="1" cellpadding="5" width="250">
  <tr>
    <td width="50%">
      <table border="1" cellpadding="5" width="100%">
    <tr>
      <td>inner</td>
    <td>inner</td>
      </tr>
    <tr>
      <td>inner</td>
      <td>inner</td>
    </tr>
      </table>
    </td>
    <td width="50%" height="12">outer</td>
  </tr>
  <tr>
    <td>outer</td>
    <td>outer</td>
  </tr>
</table>
```

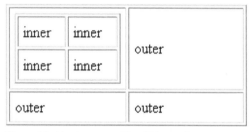

**Figure 4.9.** Nesting one table within another.

The size of the inner table, and the size of the cell it is in, interact as follows:

- If the inner table's width is specified as a percent, it's width will be that percentage of the width of the cell it is in.

- If the inner table's width is specified in terms of pixels, it will display at that width. The cell it is in will expand if needed to accommodate.

- The inner table's height will be determined by its content or by the **height** attribute of the **<td>** elements it contains.

- The containing cell's height will expand, if needed, to accommodate the inner table.

# Merge or Embed — Which Is Better?

You may have already realized that these two distinct techniques, merging cells and embedding tables in tables, are similar in some respects. They are both techniques that let you escape from the strict rectangular grid structure of a basic table. Which should you use for a given design task? There's no real answer to this question. Many layouts could be created either way. As you work with HTML tables and gain additional experience, you'll gain an intuitive feel for which technique would be better for a particular layout. Also, remember that you can combine merged cells and embedded tables, providing you with even more flexibility.

There's no theoretical limit to the number of levels of table nesting. In my experience, two levels, as in the example in this section, is all that you need for most design tasks. Three levels (table A is within table B which is within table C) is rarely called for.

# Review and Practice

It's time to get back to the photographer's Web page that we have been developing. You'll remember that in Chapter 3 we added some formatting to the page and it was starting to look good, but there were still layout problems. That version of the page is shown in Figure 4.10.

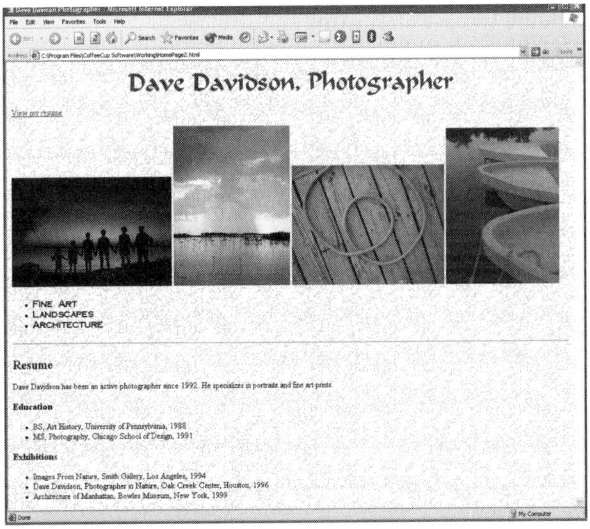

What we need to do with the page now is make some changes to the layout, the way the text and images are arranged. Tables, which you learned about in this chapter, are just the tool for this job! So, let's get to work.

First, the plan: For the top part of the page we will insert a three-row, three-column table. The three cells in the first row will be merged to a single cell that will hold the page's main heading. The second

**Figure 4.10.** The practice Web page before modifications.

row will hold an image in the left cell, the list of photo services in the center cell, and another image in the right cell. The last row will have the resume link in the center and images on the two ends.

At the bottom of the page we'll insert another table, this one with a single row and two columns. The left cell will hold the education part of the resume and the right cell will hold the exhibitions information.

Both tables will be set to have no borders so the images and text elements simply appear to "float" on the page. Padding and alignment will be set as needed for the best appearance.

The final source code is presented in Listing 4.1. Because the photos are now displayed in two rows rather than one, the page is longer, so it cannot be shown in a single image. Figure 4.11 shows the top part of the modified page in a browser and Figure 4.12 shows the bottom part.

**Listing 4.1.** The modified HTML source code after adding tables to the page.

```
<html>
<head>
  <title>Dave Davidson Photographer</title>
  <meta name="keywords" content="photography, photographer"
/>
</head>
<body background="paper1.gif">
<table border="0" cellpadding="5" width="100%">
  <tr>
    <td width="100%" colspan="3">
<p align="center"><font size="7" face="Calligrapher"
color="#0000FF">Dave Davidson, Photographer</font></p>
    </td>
  </tr>
  <tr>
    <td width="33%">
    <p align="center">
<img src="image01.jpg" width="314" height="210" /></td>
    <td width="33%"> 
<font size="4" face="Cornerstone">
    <p align="center">Fine Art</p>
    <p align="center">Landscapes</p>
    <p align="center">Architecture</p>
    </font>
    <td width="34%">
    <p align="center">
  <img src="image02.jpg" width="230" height="307" /></td>
  </tr>
  <tr>
    <td width="33%">
    <p align="center">
  <img src="image04.jpg" width="225" height="300" /></td>
    <td width="33%">
    <p align="center"><a href="#resume">View my resume</a></p>
    </td>
    <td width="34%">
    <p align="center">
  <img src="image03.jpg" width="307" height="230" /></td>
  </tr>
</table>
<hr>
<h2><a name="resume">Resume</a></h2>
<p>Dave Davidson has been an active photographer since 1992.
He specializes in portraits and fine art prints.</p>
<table border="0" width="100%">
  <tr>
    <td width="50%" valign="top">
```

```
<h3>Education</h3>
<ul>
<li>BS, Art History, University of Pennsylvania, 1988</li>
<li>MS, Photography, Chicago School of Design, 1991</li>
</ul>
      </td>
      <td width="50%" valign="top">
<h3>Exhibitions</h3>
<ul>
<li>Images From Nature, Smith Gallery, Los Angeles, 1994</li>
<li>Dave Davidson, Photographer in Nature, Oak Creek Center,
Houston, 1996</li>
<li>Architecture of Manhattan, Bowles Museum, New York,
1999</li>
</ul>
      </td>
   </tr>
</table>
</body>
</html>
```

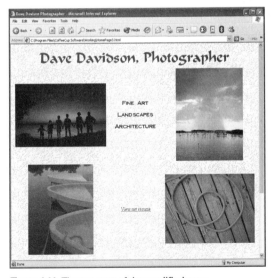

**Figure 4.11.** The top part of the modified page.

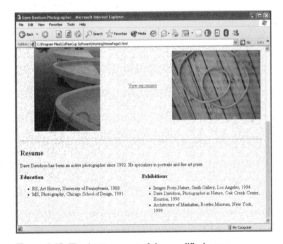

**Figure 4.12.** The bottom part of the modified page.

I hope that you'll agree with me—the page looks really nice now and is ready to be uploaded to the Web. That does not mean it could not be improved further! We'll be revisiting this page in later chapters.

## Summary

HTML tables are an essential part of any Web designer's arsenal of tools. It's difficult to imagine any even slightly sophisticated Web page being authored without the use of tables. While some Web gurus are proclaiming the demise of tables for layout, I think they are a little premature. It's true that you can create the same layouts using CSS, and we will talk about this in Chapter 7, but there are still quite a few issues with getting CSS-based layouts to display the same way in all browsers. Internet Explorer in particular has a few bugs that make CSS-based layouts tricky even for experienced Web designers. Because of this, I'm sure that layouts based on HTML tables will be with us for quite some time.

# CHAPTER 5

# Creating and Uploading Your Web Pages

The previous several chapters taught you some HTML that you can use to create basic, yet attractive Web pages and even to start adding some more sophisticated elements. Now it's time to get to some of the practical nuts and bolts that a Webmaster must be concerned with. These are not concerned directly with page design, but they are essential to know.

## Website Editing Tools

As you have already learned, HTML documents are plain text and as such can be created and edited with any text editor. For example, the program Notepad that is part of every Windows installation is perfectly adequate, as are the many other freeware and shareware text editors that are available from Download.com. Of course, these types of editors provide no tools to simplify the more tedious aspects of authoring a Web page. Can't you find something better, or at least easier?

Yes you can, as I'll discuss soon. But for now I recommend against it. When you use a text editor such as Notepad, you are working directly with the HTML code. You must think about where to put every tag and every attribute and about all the other little details of HTML authoring. This may slow you down at first, but it is the best way to learn HTML. Later, when your HTML skills are improving, you might consider saving time by moving to a specialized HTML editor, but not now.

### The CoffeeCup HTML Editor

If you are determined to get away from a basic text editor, then you should take a look at the CoffeeCup HTML Editor. You can download a free trial version at www.coffeecup.com and then, if you like it, buy the full version for a very reasonable price. The reason I recommend this program is that it provides some time-saving tools but at the same time lets you work directly with the HTML code.

The CoffeeCup HTML Editor is shown in Figure 5.1. I am not going to cover all of its features—that would be almost a book in itself—but I will point out some of the more interesting features:

- The large central area is the editing pane where you enter and edit HTML. You can see that the code lines are numbered. In addition, although not visible in the figure, different elements—tags, content, and comments—are displayed in different color text.

- There is also the Visual Editor where you can drag and drop items in your page and see how the resulting code changes. This is a great learning and design tool.

- The Preview tab enables you to see what the document will look like in a browser.

- The panels on the left are for browsing folders and locating files.

- The buttons on the right are used to insert some commonly used HTML tags, such as hyperlinks, paragraphs, images, and line breaks.

Later in this chapter I'll show you how to use the Editor's FTP capability to upload Web pages to your Website.

## WYSIWYG vs. Code Editors

The main feature of these specialized programs is that they provide WYSIWYG (what you see is what you get) Web page authoring. In other words, you are not editing the HTML for a Web page; you are editing the rendering, or display, of the Web page. The program works behind the scenes to generate the HTML that is required to generate the display you are creating. For example, to insert a table into a Web page, all you need do is click a button and specify the number of rows and columns—all the required <table>, <tr>, and <td> tags are created automatically. Some of these programs also provide a host of other time-saving features, such as link management, automatic publishing, and image editing. They are quite impressive and can be a very useful tool for the professional Web designer.

There's a serious problem, however—these programs isolate the user form the page's

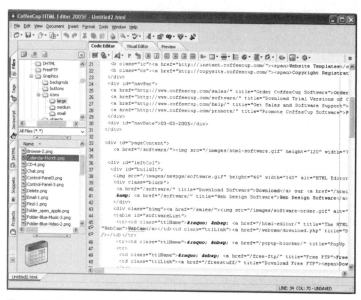

**Figure 5.1.** The CoffeeCup HTML Editor.

HTML. In fact, many people who use such programs regularly do not know one thing about HTML. When a problem arises, or the page does not render exactly as they want, they do not have the skills to edit the HTML directly and fix the problem. This is not a good way to approach Web design, and for this reason alone you should stay away from this kind of program until you have a thorough knowledge of HTML

## Best of Both Worlds

The CoffeeCup HTML Editor incorporates both the power and flexibility of a code editor and the ease of use of a WYSIWYG editor in one program. For this reason, I think it is absolutely one of the best options for any Webmaster.

# Web Servers and Publishing

Once you have your first Web pages done, you want everyone else to be able to see them, right? They cannot see them on your computer, so you need a place to put them that everyone on the Internet can access. This place is called a Web host or Web server. You need an understanding of how Web servers work and how to copy your Web pages to a server. This process is called uploading.

## Servers and Domain Names

A Web server is a computer that meets two requirements. First, it must be connected to the Internet. Second, it must have special server software installed that lets it interact with users on the Internet. Specifically, when a user navigates to a Web page, the server must receive that request and send the page back to the user. How does this work? The following is a somewhat simplified account, but it is enough for now.

When a computer is connected to the Internet, it is assigned a special unique number (like a phone number) called an IP address (IP stands for *Internet Protocol*). The address consists of four numbers separated by periods; each number can range from 0 to 255. For example, the popular search engine Yahoo! has the IP address 216.109.112.135. You can browse to a server using just the IP address. Go ahead and try it—start your browser and enter 216.109.112.135 and you'll go to the Yahoo! Website.

Of course, IP addresses are hard to remember. In the early days of the Internet, someone realized that recognizable names would be a better way to identify and locate Web servers, and the domain name was born. For example, www.coffeecup.com is the domain name for CoffeeCup. This has three parts:

- www, for World Wide Web, is the traditional prefix, but other prefixes can be used also.

- coffeecup is the unique name for this Website.

- com is the extension that identifies the type of site. The most common ones are com for commercial sites, edu for educational sites, org for nonprofit organization sites, and gov for government sites.

Most Web surfers do not surf to IP addresses but to domain names (URLs). How does this work? On the Internet there are computers called DNSs (*domain name servers*). Each of these DNS computers maintains a database that contains all the domain names and the associated IP addresses. For example, there will be an entry that associates www.yahoo.com with the IP address 216.109.112.135. Thus, when you browse to a domain name, it is looked up on a DNS computer to obtain the IP address, and the IP address is used to route your request to the proper Web server. This all happens automatically and most users are not even aware that it is happening.

Okay, so your request is on its way to the correct Web server—then what? Well, since you are connected to the Internet through your service provider, your computer also has an IP address. The request that is sent when you browse to a Website includes your IP address. When the server receives your request, it can retrieve the requested file and use your IP address to send it back to you. When the file is received, your browser reads it and displays it. All this happens in a fraction of a second—okay, it's not always that fast, but most of the time it is so fast you never see it happen!

One of the major advantages of the domain name system is that domain names are portable—they are not tied to a specific location as IP addresses are. Suppose CoffeeCup decided to move its operations to another state. In all likelihood, its servers would be assigned a new IP address. But that doesn't matter because it can change its domain name registration so that www.coffeecup.com points to the new IP address instead of the old one. Within a day or two, the new IP address will be propagated through all the DNS computers on the Internet, and anyone browsing to www.coffeecup.com will be directed to the new location.

## Web Hosting

Very few individuals or companies host their own Website. It almost always makes more sense to pay a Web hosting company to host your site. Not only is it almost always cheaper than doing it yourself, but these companies provide other services, such as email, and have the expertise, personnel, and equipment to maintain backups and keep everything running smoothly. My company is a Web hosting provider as well as a software company. When selecting a hosting provider, choosing one that is free is not always the best. You need to balance the possibly less than stellar reliability of a free service with the improved service and reliability of a hosting provider that charges a monthly fee.

Once you have a host picked out, you will create an account and select a domain name for your Website. Next, the host will send you a user name and password to access your account. Once you have this information, you are ready to upload your Web pages, as described later in this chapter. Uploading is a process that copies your Web pages to the server; once this is done, anyone in the world can see your pages by browsing to your domain name. In most cases they'll also be able to send you email at that domain.

# Understanding and Using FTP

FTP stands for *File Transfer Protocol*, and that name says it all—it is a widely used and accepted standard for transferring files from one computer to another over the Internet. When you transfer a file from one computer to another, you are either uploading or downloading the file. If you move the file from your computer to the other one, that's uploading. If you copy the file from the other computer to yours, that's called downloading. FTP is the most common technique for uploading a Website. FTP capability is built into many Web design tools such as the CoffeeCup HTML Editor. If you're using a basic text editor to create your Web pages, you can use a stand-alone FTP program such as CoffeeCup Direct FTP.

## Publishing Your Website with Direct FTP

When you first install and start Direct FTP, it will not have any servers set up. You must set up your Web server before you can upload your pages, as follows:

1. Start Direct FTP.

2. Click the Servers button on the toolbar. You'll see the My Sites dialog box, which lists any servers that are set up. If you are just getting started, this list will be empty. Click the Add button.

3. The next several dialog boxes ask you for the following information about your server. Fill in each dialog box and click Next to continue.

   • Profile Name: Assign a nickname to this profile, such as My Website.

   • Username and password: Fill in the username and password that were provided to you by your Web hosting company.

   • Hostname: Fill in the name of your Web server as provided by your Web host; for example, www.mysite.com. (Note: Check the information provided by your Web host because you may need to specify ftp.mysite.com or some thing similar instead.)

   • Default folder: Enter the default folder that was provided by your Web host. If there is no default folder, leave this blank.

- Proxy server: Most people do not use one and should click No. If you do use a proxy server, click Yes and fill in the proxy server details.

4. Finally, click Finish to complete the server setup.

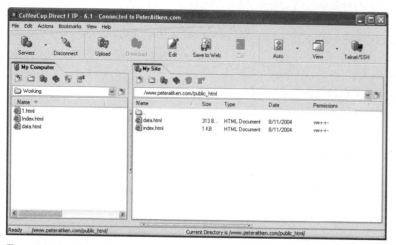

**Figure 5.2.** The Direct FTP screen after connecting to your site.

Once you have set up your Web server with Direct FTP, you are ready to upload. Start by clicking the Servers button on the toolbar to display the My Sites dialog box. Then, in the My Sites list, click the site you want to upload to and then click the Connect button. Your screen will look something like Figure 5.2.

The panel on the left side of the screen displays files on your local computer. Use the drop-down list at the top to change to a different folder. The list below displays the files in the current folder. The panel on the right side of the screen displays the files on the remote server. Use the drop-down list at the top of the panel to change to a different folder on the server. Here are some of the actions you can take:

- To upload a file, drag it from the left panel to the right panel. Or, you can click the file and then click the Upload button on the toolbar.

- To delete a file from the server, right-click its name in the right panel and then select Delete from the popup menu.

- To rename a file on the server, right-click its name in the right panel and then select rename from the pop-up menu. Type in the new name and press Enter.

- To create a new folder on the server, click the Create a New Folder button just above the server folder drop-down list.

- To move up to the parent folder, click the Go Up One Folder button.

- To move down to a subfolder, double-click the folder name in the file list.

Remember that file names are case sensitive on many Web servers and spaces in the file names are bad news. If you have been told that your default page should be named index.html, then a name of Index.html will not work.

## Uploading Your Website with the HTML Editor

Before you can upload your Web pages to your Web server, you have to tell the CoffeeCup HTML Editor about your server. You'll need the URL of the server as well as your user name and password—all this information will have been sent to you by your Web hosting company.

Then, in the editor, select File|Upload File to Server|Add or Edit Servers. You'll see the Server Configuration dialog box, which lists any servers you already have listed; since you are just getting started, this list will be empty. Click the Add button to add a new server. You'll see the dialog box shown in Figure 5.3.

In this dialog box, make entries as follows:

- Nickname of the Server Profile: Enter a name such as My Website that will be used for this profile.

- Username: Enter the username provided by your Web host.

- Password: Enter the password provided by your Web host. Note that passwords are case sensitive on most servers.

- Port: Leave this at the default of 21 unless you have been instructed to change it.

- Web Server Address: Enter the URL of your Website.

- Remote Directories: For each folder or directory on the remote server that you will be publishing to, enter the name here and click Add.

Once all the information has been entered, click the Cool button. You'll be returned to the Server Configuration dialog box (Figure 5.4), which will now have an icon for the Website you just entered. If you need to modify a configuration, click its icon then click the Edit button. Otherwise, click the Close button to return to the editor.

Once you have defined your Web server and folders, you are ready to publish files from the HTML editor. It's really quite simple:

**Figure 5.3.** You use this dialog box to enter information about your Web server.

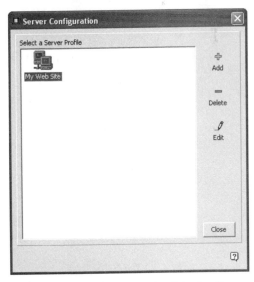

**Figure 5.4.** The Server Configuration dialog box lists your Web server entries.

1. To upload the page you are currently editing, right-click in the editing pane. To upload another file, right-click it in the file list pane.

2. Select Upload File to Server from the pop-up menu.

3. Select the desired server from the next menu.

4. Select the desired destination folder from the next menu.

   The file will be uploaded to the specified folder on the server.

## Summary

Creating and editing your Web pages is one thing, but no one will be able to see them until you put them online by uploading them to your Web server. This chapter has showed you how to do so with two useful tools, the CoffeeCup HTML Editor and Direct FTP.

# PART 2

· · · · · · · · · · · · · · · · · · · · · · ·

# Moving Beyond the Basics

A basic cup of coffee can be great, but a cup of coffee with

whipped cream, chocolate, and cinnamon is even better! Now

that you know the basics of Web Design it's time to move on to

some more advanced topics. These techniques will help your

Web pages stand out from the crowd.

· · · · · · · · · · · · · · · · · · · · · · ·

# Creating and Using HTML Forms

I am sure you have seen HTML forms before. Whenever you enter information on a Web page, such as when registering for an online news service or entering your address and credit card information for a purchase, you are almost always using an HTML form. When you need to gather information from your Website's visitors, you'll need to create a Web page that uses a form. This chapter shows you how.

## Form Fundamentals

A form is a section of an HTML document that is marked by <form> tags (what else?). A form always contains two things and usually a third:

- Input elements where the user enters information, such as a text box for entering text or a check box for selecting an option.

- A Submit button that the user clicks to send the information to its destination.

- An optional Reset button that clears the form.

Figure 6.1 shows what a simple form looks like. This form has two text boxes, one check box, and Submit and Reset buttons. A Web page can contain multiple forms, each one being completely independent of the others.

Much of the power of HTML forms comes from the fact that you can control how the data is submitted. It can be placed in an email message and sent to a specified address, or it can be sent to a specialized program on the server that will process the data (for example, inserting it into a database).

### An Easier Way

CoffeeCup makes a program called CoffeeCup Form Builder that takes all the hassle out of making and uploading Web forms. Using Form Builder, you can make great looking Web forms without knowing any HTML or scripting languages. It is available for a trial download at www.coffeecup.com.

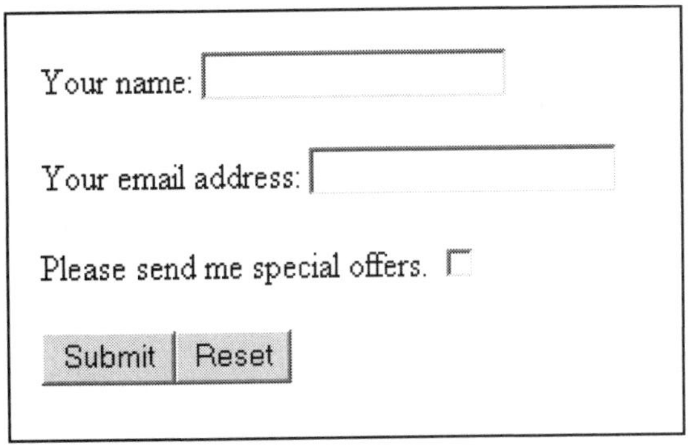

**Figure 6.1.** A simple HTML form.

## Forms and Tables

Not only can you put a form in a table, you can also put a table in a form. This technique can be useful for creating a layout in which the form elements are precisely positioned with respect to each other. You learned about HTML tables in Chapter 4.

# The <form> Tag

The first step in creating an HTML form is to place a **<form>** tag on your page. It can be essentially anywhere in the body section, including inside a table cell. The basic syntax is as follows:

```
<form action="action">
</form>
```

The **action** attribute specifies the URL where the form data will be submitted. Don't worry about this for now—we'll talk about that more later in the chapter.

The **<form>** tag has several optional attributes that you may or may not need to use. These are described in Table 6.1.

**Table 6.1.** Optional attributes of the <form> tag.

| ATTRIBUTE | VALUES | DESCRIPTION |
|---|---|---|
| method | get, post | Use **method="get"** to send the form data in the URL. Use **method="post"** to send the form data in the request body. If this attribute is omitted, then **get** is used. |
| name | Text | Defines a unique name for the form. Used primarily on Web pages that contain more than one form. |
| target | _blank, _top | Specifies where the results of the submission will display. Use **target="_blank"** to open the results in a new window. Use **target="_top"** to open the results in the same window (the default). |

Within the **<form>** tags you place the various HTML elements that are used for data entry and submission. You can also include other HTML elements, such as paragraphs and images, within a form. Let's take a look at the various form elements.

# Form Elements

A form is pretty useless without some elements in it.

Most form elements are defined by the **<input>** tag. There are 10 different types of input elements, specified by the **type** attribute. These types are described in Table 6.2. Following the table I will present details on using each one.

**Table 6.2.** Input element types.

| VALUE OF TYPE ATTRIBUTE | ELEMENT DESCRIPTION |
|---|---|
| button | A button the user can click. |
| checkbox | A check box that lets the user turn an option on or off. |
| file | Lets the user select a file to upload. |
| hidden | Not displayed. Used to submit information that the user does not need to see or change. |
| image | Use an image instead of a standard Submit button. |
| password | A text box that displays dots instead of the actual characters. |
| radio | An on/off button that lets the user choose one from a set of choices. |
| reset | A reset button that resets all form elements to their initial values. |
| submit | A submit button that sends the form data to the URL specified in the **<form>** tag's **action** attribute. |

Note that most form elements also require a **name** attribute. This is a name that uniquely identifies the element on its form. It is used during form submission to identify the data from that element. The **name** attribute is required for button, checkbox, file, hidden, image, password, text, and radio elements.

## The Button Element

Click Me

The **button** element displays a button that the user can click to execute a client-side script. The syntax for a button element is as follows:

```
<input type="button" name="name" value="caption"
onclick="script" />
```

- **name** is a unique name for the button.
- **caption** is the text displayed on the button.
- **script** is the script to execute when the user clicks the button.

You'll learn more about scripts in Chapter 8. Unless you have scripts on your page, you will probably not use the **button** element in your forms.

## The Checkbox Element

☑ I hate spam.

The checkbox element displays a check box that the user can turn on (checked) or off (unchecked) by clicking. The text next to the check box is not part of the element itself—you must add it separately. Here is the syntax for the checkbox element:

```
<input type="checkbox" name="name" value="value"
checked="checked" />
```

- **name** is a unique name for the check box.
- **value** is the data value that is submitted if the check box is checked. If it is not checked, no data is submitted for the element.

Include the **checked="checked"** attribute if you want the check box to be checked when first displayed; omit this attribute if not.

Since the checkbox element does not provide for a label, you must add one yourself. Here's the HTML that was used to create the image of the check box shown at the beginning of this section:

```
<p><input type="checkbox" checked="checked" name="Spam"
value="HateSpam" /> I hate spam.</p>
```
,
## The File Element

You use the **file** element when you want the user to be able to upload a file as part of the submission. The user can either type the name of a file in the box or click the Browse button to browse for the file. Here is the syntax for this element:

```
<input type="file" name="name" size="size" />
```

- **name** is a unique name for the element.
- **size** is the width of the element in characters; the default is about 20 (browser dependent).

It's important to remember that in order to use the **file** element, you must have a script set up on the server that will properly accept and process the uploaded file.

## The Hidden Element

As the name implies, the **hidden** element does not display on-screen. You use it when you want to include information as part of the submission without having the user see or be able to change the data. For example, you could use a hidden input field to identify the page the form is located on. The syntax is as follows:

```
<input type="hidden" name="name" value="value" />
```

- name is a unique name for the hidden element.
- value is the data that will submitted for the element.

You can have as many hidden elements as you need on a form.

## The Image Element

You use the **image** element when you want a form's Submit button to be an image rather than a standard button. You would use this element in place of a **submit** element. The syntax is as follows:

```
<input type="image" name="name" src="imageURL"
value="value" alt="alternate" />
```

- **name** is a unique name for the element.
- **imageURL** is the URL of the image to display.
- **value** is the data passed to the submit target for the element.
- **alternate** is the text to display if the image cannot be found.

## The Password Element

Your password: ●●●●●●●●●●

The **password** element is used for entering passwords. It is identical to the text element except that the characters entered display as dots rather than actual characters. This is to prevent a nosy person looking over your shoulder from seeing your password. The adjacent text is not part of the password element—you must specify it separately. Here is the syntax for this element:

```
<input type="password" name="name" size="size" value="value"
/>
```

- **name** is a unique name for the element.
- **size** is the width of the element in characters; the default is about 20 (browser dependent).
- **value** is the value initially entered in the element. Omit this attribute to have the **password** element initially empty.

The following HTML was used to create the password element shown at the beginning of this section:

```
<p>Your password: <input type="password" name="password"
/></p>
```

## The Reset Element

The **reset** element displays as a button on a form. If the user clicks it, the form is cleared—that is, returned to its initial state. Here is the syntax for this element:

```
<input type="reset" value="value" />
```

• **value** is the text displayed on the button. If this attribute is omitted, the button displays "Reset."

The reset element is optional and, in my opinion, not all that useful. If the user makes a mistake entering data on a form, they will want to edit just the mistake and not clear the entire form. Even so, there may be situations in which you want to use it.

## The Submit Element

Every form needs a submit element—after all, there is no point in a form unless it can be submitted! The element syntax is as follows:

```
<input type="submit" value="value" />
```

• value is the text displayed on the button. If this attribute is omitted, the button displays "Submit."

A form can have more than one submit element. This can be useful when you have a long form and do not want the user to have to scroll to bring a submit button into view. Note that you can use an image as a submit button with the image element, covered earlier in this chapter.

## The Text Element

First name: [                    ]

The **text** element is used for entering text. The adjacent text is not part of the **text** element—you must specify it separately. The syntax for this element is as follows:

```
<input type="text" name="name" size="size" value="value" />
```

• **name** is a unique name for the element.

- **size** is the width of the element in characters; the default is about 20 (browser dependent).

- **value** is the value initially entered in the element. Omit this attribute to have the text element initially empty.

The following HTML was used to create the text element shown at the beginning of this section:

```
<p>First name: <input type="text" name="firstname" /></p>
```

## The Radio Element

C Vanilla

(• Chocolate

You use the **radio** element to create a group of two or more mutually exclusive options. In other words, one and only one of the options in a group can be selected. You will always use **radio** elements in groups of two or more. The adjacent text is not part of the **radio** element—you must specify it separately Here is the syntax:

```
<input type="radio" name="name" value="value"
checked="checked" />
```

- **name** is a unique name for the element group. All radio elements in a group must have the same name.

- **value** is the data that is submitted for the group if the element is selected.

Include the **checked="checked"** attribute in the **radio** element that you want selected initially. You can use this attribute in only one **radio** element in a group.

The following HTML was used to create the radio element group shown at the beginning of this section:

```
<p><input type="radio" name="flavor" value="vanilla" />
Vanilla</p>
<p><input type="radio" name="flavor" checked="checked"
value="chocolate" /> Chocolate</p>
```

You can have as many radio elements in a group as you need. They do not have to be placed adjacent to one another on the form, but it is a good idea to do so.

# Specifying the Form Destination

As I mentioned earlier, forms provide a lot of flexibility in terms of what happens to the data. Basically, in the **action** attribute of the **<form>** tag, you will specify the URL of where the data will be sent. In almost all cases this will be a server side script—a program on the Web server that is designed specifically to accept form submissions and process the data in some way.

## Emailing Form Data

Some Web designers create forms that email data using the **action="mailto:address"** attribute in the **<form>** tag. This works—but only sometimes. Depending on a user's software configuration, it may fail altogether. For reliable emailing of form data, you must direct the form to a script that is on the server and written specifically for emailing data.

As you may have guessed, there's no point in having a form on your Website unless you also have the script to process it as you need. I am not going to teach you how to write scripts—that would take an entire book in itself—but I can provide some background information on scripts, where to find them, and where to install them.

## Script Languages

Server-side scripts can be written in a wide variety of languages. The language does not really matter from the Web designer's point of view as long as the script does its job. Even so, a little background information will be worthwhile.

- Common Gateway Interface, or CGI, is one of the original scripting technologies that is used on the Web. Despite being relatively old, it is still perfectly useful. Because it has been around so long, you will find lots of useful CGI scripts on the Web that you can download and use. CGI is not really a language, but rather a technology, and most CGI scripts are written in Perl.

- Perl, which is an acronym for Practical Extraction and Report Language, is another powerful scripting language. Perl is widely supported and there are lots of useful scripts available on the Web. Perl scripts are stored in files with the .pl extension.

- Active Server Pages, or ASP, is a Microsoft technology that has gained wide popularity. ASP scripts are written using the VBScript language, which can also be used to write client-side scripts. It is very powerful but does not enjoy as wide support as some other scripting technologies. ASP script pages have the .asp extension.

- PHP (which, as far as I know, does not stand for anything) is rapidly gaining popularity as the server-side scripting language of choice for many Webmasters. Why? It's easy to use and learn, it's very powerful, and it's open source and therefore free. A Web hosting provider does not have to pay in order to support PHP on their servers. PHP script pages have the .php extension.

When you locate a script that you want to use on your Website, be sure to check with your Web host. You need to know if they support the kind of script you will be using. You also need details on where on your Website to place the script file. There may be some other configuration steps to take, but only your Web host can tell you exactly what these are.

## Installing and Linking a Script

Once you have found a script you want to use, you will use FTP to upload it to the proper folder of your Website. (For example, CGI scripts are traditionally kept in a folder named cgi-bin off of your site's root folder.) Once the file has been uploaded, you will need to set the form's **action** attribute to point to the script file, as in this example:

```
<form action="cgi-bin/myscript.pl">
```

Once the page containing the form is published, your users will be able to use the form and its attached script. Be sure to test forms and scripts that you publish to make sure they are working correctly.

## Server-Side Script Resources

You are probably wondering what sorts of things can scripts do and, equally important, where can you get the scripts. As to what scripts can do, it might be better to ask what they cannot do! Here are just a few examples, both complex and simple:

- Send a submitted form's data to one or more email recipients.
- Present a user survey and compile the results.
- Create a discussion forum that allows users to read and post messages on your site.
- Display a countdown to a specific date.
- Determine where your visitors come from and which browser they are using.
- Rotate ad banners on your page.
- Conduct online auctions.
- Let users sign a guestbook.

The best way to learn about scripts is to explore some of the online resources that are available. I've listed a few of my favorites in Table 6.3; you can find more by searching Google for "scripts."

### Client-Side vs. Server-Side Scripts

What's the difference? The names say it all. A server-side script is executed on the Web server and the results are returned to the user. A client-side script is embedded in an HTML page and is executed on the user's computer.

**Table 6.3.** Some resources for server-side scripts.

| NAME | URL |
|------|-----|
| Matt's Script Archive | http://www.scriptarchive.com |
| CGI Resource Index | http://cgi.resourceindex.com |
| Hot Scripts | http://www.hotscripts.com |
| Stadtaus.com | http://www.stadtaus.com/en |

## Summary

The form is one of the most powerful features of HTML. When combined with a server-side script, forms bring a great deal of flexibility to your Website. Whether it's just a simple guest book for visitors to sign or a complete online shopping system, you can do it with forms.

# Formatting Web Pages with Style Sheets

I've mentioned style sheets numerous times in the previous chapters. In particular, I have told you that certain HTML elements and attributes are deprecated or not supported in XHTML and that you should use styles instead. This chapter explains what I have been talking about.

Ideally, from a programming perspective you should have several separate "layers" that make up your Website. The content, which is the text and images you display to the visitor, the markup, which is the HTML used to break that content into chunks of information that relate to each other, and the presentation, which is the style and formatting used to display the content. Using style sheets to control how your Website looks helps to separate content from presentation, which is a good thing. This way, when you want to change the look and feel of your Website, all you need to change is the style sheets.

## Style Sheet Fundamentals

Style sheets, or more properly *Cascading Style Sheets (CSS)*, provide a method for specifying formatting in an HTML document. When you use CSS, you can avoid using most or all of the HTML tags and attributes that control formatting. Why would you want to do this? What's wrong with the formatting tags?

The main advantage of CSS is that it allows you to define the formatting of a Web page separately from the content of the Web page, as I mentioned earlier. Let's look at an example. Suppose you want to define a special appearance for certain text in your Web pages: larger than normal text in the Bazooka font, blue. Using regular HTML tags, you would do it like this:

```
<font size="4" face="Bazooka" color="blue">This the
text</font>
```

In fact you would have to use this **<font>** tag for each and every instance of text that you want formatted this way. So far, so good. But then suppose your boss decides that she really wants this text in Arial font, red. Guess what—you have to go through the entire page, not to mention every page in the Website, and change each and every **<font>** tag. This is not cool!

But what if you had used a style to define this special text? Then you are in cool city! Here's what the style definition would look like:

```
.special          { font-family: Bazooka; font-size: 14pt; color:
                    #0000FF; }
```

And here's how you would apply it to text:

```
<p class="special">This is the text</p>
```

Here's what's important: To change the text, all you need do is edit the style and the change will automatically be applied to every instance in the Website. Interested? Then read on.

## CSS Versions

CSS comes in two versions. CSS Level 1 has been around since 1996 and presently enjoys wide browser support. CSS Level 1 includes styles for font formatting, text alignment, line spacing, and similar formatting tasks. CSS Level 2 has been available since 1998, but there is only limited support at present. Level 2 provides a lot more power, particularly when it comes to positioning elements on the page. In fact, some people predict that CSS Level 2 will eventually replace HTML tables for page layout. It's possible, but I'm not holding my breath! Because CSS Level 1 support is so widespread and Level 2 support is patchy at best, I will limit this chapter to the most commonly needed formatting that is available in CSS Level 1.

## Style Sheet Structure

A style sheet contains one or more styles, usually called rules. Each rule has the following structure:

```
selector        {formatting}
```

- **selector** specifies which parts of the HTML document the rule is to be applied to.
- **formatting** defines the formatting for the rule.

Most of the remainder of this chapter is devoted to showing you how to create selectors and formatting rules.

A style sheet can be located either within the HTML document (in the <head> section) or as a separate file that is linked to the HTML document. In fact, a given HTML document can have both internal and external style sheets, one of the CSS features that makes it so flexible.

## What Does Cascading Mean?

The word *cascading* in *Cascading Style Sheets* reflects two aspects of how style sheets work. The first is the way style sheets interact. An HTML document can have more than one style sheet associated with it—for example, one internal and one external. Style rules cascade so that the end result is a combination of the document's various style sheets.

The second aspect of cascading is the operation of *inheritance*. If a certain aspect of formatting is not specified for a child element, it will (in most cases) inherit the formatting of its parent (enclosing) element. For example, a <p>

element that has no font style rule will display in the font specified for its parent, the **<body>** element. The formatting "cascades" down the chain from parent to child.

To create an internal style sheet, place the following in the head section of the HTML document:

```
<style>
<!--
....style rules go here....
//-->
</style>
```

To use an external style sheet, use a text editor to create a text file containing the style rules and save it with the .css extension. Then place a reference to the file in the head section of the HTML document as follows:

```
<link rel="stylesheet" type="text/css"
href="MyStyleSheet.css" />
```

This assumes that the style sheet file is in the same folder on the Web server as the Web page. If not, you must specify the full path in the **href** attribute.

A style sheet can also contain comments. They are ignored in processing and can be useful for documenting your styles. A comment starts with the characters /* and ends with */, as in this example:

```
/* This is a CSS comment. */
/* Comments can be spread over
   two or more lines
   line this one. */
```

## Working with Selectors

A style is not very useful if you cannot associate it with various elements in the HTML document. This is done with a selector, which is the first part of each formatting rule. There are two ways to connect elements with rules: including the name of the element and including the value of a **class** or **id** attribute that an element has. Let's look at these.

To associate a rule with all HTML elements of a specific name, simply use the tag name. For example, the following rule would apply to all **<p>** elements in a document:

   *p     { rule details }*

To associate a rule with all elements that have a specific **class** attribute, place a period before the attribute value:

   *.value     { rule details }*

For example, the rule

*.emphasize    { rule details }*

would apply only to elements where the **class="emphasize"** attribute is present, such as either of these:

```
<p class="emphasize">This text will have the rule
applied.</p>
<td class="emphasize">This table cell will have the rule
applied.</td>
```

You can combine these two techniques to create a selector that will apply only to HTML elements with a certain name and a certain value for the **class** attribute. Here's how:

*ElementName.ClassValue    { rule details }*

Here's an example:

*p.emphasize    { rule details }*

This would apply to the following element:

```
<p class="emphasize">This text will have the rule applied.</p>
```

It would not apply to either of these elements:

```
<p>This text will not have the rule applied.</p>
<td class="emphasize">This table cell will not have the rule
applied.</td>
```

What happens if two style sheet rules conflict? For example, this rule assigns 14-point font to all **<p>** elements:

*p    {font-size: 14pt; }*

Here's a rule that assigns 20-point font to all elements where the class attribute is equal to **large**:

*.large    {font-size: 20pt; }*

What happens, then, to an HTML element such as this one?

```
<p class="large">This is the text.</p>
```

The answer lies in the order of the rules and inheritance—a rule later in the style sheet takes precedence over rules that come before it. You can override this by including the **!important** clause to the rule. Here's an example:

*.large    {font-size: 20pt !important;}*

This ensures that the rule takes precedence over any competing rules even if they come after in the style sheet. This is not a recommended practice; it's much better to lay out the rules in the correct order the first time.

You can assign a single style rule to multiple selectors by separating the selectors with commas. For example, the following selector would assign the rule to <p> elements that had either **emphasize** or **strong** as the value of the **class** attribute:

*p.emphasize, p.strong   { rule details }*

The final selector is for the **id** attribute of HTML tags. You do this with the # symbol. For example, the selector

*#mainTable   { rule details }*

would be applied to the content of any HTML tag that has its id attribute set to "**mainTable**", as in this example:

```
<table width="100%" id="mainTable">
...
</table>
```

The **id** attribute differs from the class attribute in that **id** must be unique in the document. In other words, there can be only one tag with a given **id** value. In practice, browsers do not enforce this rule, but having multiple tags with the same **id** value in one page is invalid HTML and not a good idea.

## Defining CSS Styles

CSS formatting uses a simple box-oriented formatting model. Every formatted element—text or image—will result in one or more rectangular boxes. Each box has a central content area that is surrounded by optional padding, border, and margin areas. These boxes are usually not visible, but you need to understand their uses and relationships in order to work effectively with style sheets. This box model is illustrated in Figure 7.1. The various boxes are related as follows:

- The innermost box, the content area, is where the data is displayed. This can be text or an image. For text, the display is controlled by **font** and **text** properties in the style rule. For an image, the size is controlled by the **height** and **width** properties in the style rule. The **height** and **width** properties can be used with text elements also.

- The padding area provides a space between the content and its border. The size of this area is controlled by the padding properties in the style rule. The background of the padding area is the same as the background of the content area, as controlled by the **background** property.

- The border is an optional box drawn around the element. Its appearance is controlled by the **border** properties.

- The margin provides space around the element, outside the border. In effect, the margin provides the spacing between the element and other elements that are being displayed. The margin size is controlled by the **margin** properties. The margin is always transparent.

**Figure 7.1.** The box-oriented formatting model.

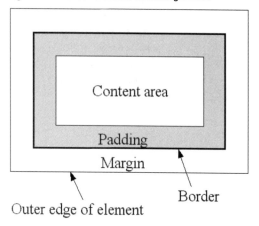

Note that it is this box model that Internet Explorer gets wrong. Because IE doesn't follow the specification correctly, it makes using pure CSS for layouts a little tricky. Other browsers, such as Mozilla Firefox and Opera, display the box model properly.

Now let's look at the various properties that you can use in a style rule. They are described briefly in Table 7.1 and then described in more detail in the following sections.

**Table 7.1.** Overview of CSS formatting properties.

| PROPERTY | DESCRIPTION |
|---|---|
| display | Controls how an element is displayed with relation to the page and adjacent elements. |
| height, width | Controls the size of an element. |
| border | Defines the element's border. |
| margin | Defines the element's margin. |
| padding | Defines the element's padding. |
| font | Defines the text element's font appearance. |
| text | Defines alignment, indentation, and other aspects of text display. |
| color and background-color | Define the element's colors. |

## The display Property

An element on a Web page can be displayed several ways:
- Block: The element is displayed on a separate line from other elements (for example, a paragraph).

- Inline: The element is displayed inline with other elements (for example, an italicized word in a line of text).

- List-item: The element is displayed preceded by a list item mark (for example, an item in a bulleted list).

- None: The element is hidden from view

You specify the way an element is displayed by setting the display property in the style rule to **block**, **inline**, **list-item**, or **none**.

Why would you want to set **display** to **none**? It can be a useful technique for hiding certain elements in the document without actually removing them.

## The height and width Properties

You use the **height** and **width** properties to specify the size of an element's display box. Each property is specified as a numerical value followed by an abbreviation that specifies the unit of measure. These include inches (**in**), centimeters (**cm**), millimeters (**mm**), and pixels (**px**) as well as the following less well known units:

- Ems (**em**): The width of the letter *M* in the current font.

- Ens (**en**): The width of the letter *N* in the current font.

- Picas (**pi**): One sixth (1/6) of an inch.

- Points (**pt**): One seventy-second (1/72) of an inch.

The **em** and **en** units are useful when you want the size of an element to be related to the font that the element uses. This permits the elements to automatically grow or shrink if the font is changed. In my experience, pixels are commonly used for images and points for text.

## The border Properties

The appearance of an element's border is controlled by a set of properties referred to collectively as the **border** properties. The default for most elements is no border, with the primary exception being tables. Every border has three aspects: its width, its style (dotted, dashed, etc.), and its color. With all of these aspects, you can set the appearance of the entire border or you can set the appearance of each of the four individual sides.

To set the width, or thickness, of the entire border, use the **border-width** property. To set the width of individual borders, use the **border-top-width**, **border-bottom-width**, **border-left-width**, and **border-right-width** properties. You can set these properties as follows:

---

## About Semicolons

If a style sheet rule contains more than one rule, you separate them with a semicolon. You will also see rules with a semicolon at the end, just before the closing brace. This final semicolon is optional — you can include or omit it as desired.

- To one of the keywords **thin**, **thick**, or **medium**.
- To a numerical value followed by a unit abbreviation as described earlier in this chapter for the **height** and **width** properties.

To set the border style, use the **border-style** property. There are actually five such related properties:

- If you want all four borders to be the same, set the **border-style** property.
- If you want the four borders to be different, set the **border-top-style**, **border—bottom-style**, **border-left-style**, and **border-right-style** properties individually.

**Figure 7.2.** The appearance of the eight border style settings.

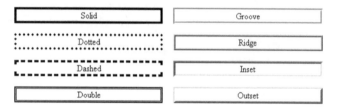

The values that you can set these properties to are **dotted**, **dashed**, **solid**, **double**, **groove**, **ridge**, **inset**, **outset**, and **none** for no border. Figure 7.2 shows how these look when rendered in the browser. This figure was created using a width of 4 pixels for the border because the full effect of the **double**, **groove**, **ridge**, **inset**, and **outset** settings are not apparent with thinner borders.

To set the border color, use the border-color property or the **border-top-color**, **border—bottom-color**, **border-left-color**, and **border-right-color** properties individually. You can set these properties to a color name or a numerical color value (you learned about specifying colors in Chapter 3).

## The margin and padding Properties

These two properties control the size of an element's margin and padding. They work in exactly the same way, with the same syntax, and so are treated together here—simply replace **margin** with **padding**.

To set all four element margins to the same width, use this syntax in the style rule:

*margin:    value*

value can be expressed in the following two ways:

- As a numerical value followed by a measurement unit. The available measurement units were explained earlier in this chapter in the section on the **width** and **height** properties.
- As a numerical value followed by the percent sign. The margin width will be the specified percentage of the width set for the element's closest block-level ancestor.

To set the size of individual margins, use the **margin-top**, **margin-right**, **margin-bottom**, and **margin-left** properties. Be aware that the top and bottom margin settings do not have an effect for inline elements (where **display="inline"** is specified). For inline elements, the line spacing of the content that the element is inline with determines the space above and below the element.

Note that an element's background color extends into its padding but not into its margins.

## The font Properties

The task of designing a reliable way for Web page designers to specify fonts is greatly complicated by the way fonts are handled on PCs. There are hundreds if not thousands of fonts, and each one is a separate install on a user's computer. Of course, any user with the Windows operating system will almost surely have a core set of standard fonts installed, but the bottom line is that the page designer can never be 100-percent sure that a font specified in the page or a style sheet will be available when the page is actually viewed.

The imperfect solution to this dilemma was to define font families—groups of fonts that are similar if not identical in appearance. The four font families are described here, with examples shown in Figure 7.3.

- Serif fonts are so named because they have serifs—small caps and other decorations on the ends of strokes within each character. Serif fonts are proportional. Times New Roman, Georgia, and New Century Schoolbook are popular serif fonts.

- Sans-serif fonts are lacking serifs but are still proportional. Arial, Verdana, and Helvetica are commonly used sans-serif fonts.

- Monospace fonts are those that are not proportional—each character is given the same amount of space. A monospace font may be serif or sans serif. Common examples are Courier New and Andale Mono.

- Cursive fonts are designed to look like human handwriting. The characters are usually composed almost entirely of curves. Amazone BT and Zapf Chancery are two examples of this font family.

> ## So What's a Block-Level Ancestor?
>
> Every HTML element is nested within another HTML element. The sole exception to this rule is the \<html\> element that encloses the entire document. Thus, an element's ancestor is simply the element it is nested within.

**Figure 7.2.** The appearance of the eight border style settings.

Times New Roman is a serif font.

Arial is a sans-serif font.

Courier New is a monospace font.

*Amazone BT is a cursive font.*

89

# Proportional and Monospace Fonts

In a proportional (or variable-width) font, the amount of horizontal space allotted to a character is proportional to the character width. Thus an m gets more horizontal space than an i. Most fonts used in printing and on the Web are proportional, including the one you are reading now. A monospace (or fixed-width) font allocates the same amount of horizontal space to every character. See Figure 7.3 for an example.

The importance of font families is this: Since you cannot be sure that the end user will have a specific font installed, you can always specify a font family in addition to a specific font. If the font is not available, the browser will use a similar font from the specified family.

Now we can get to the specific font-related properties that you use in style sheet rules. They are summarized in Table 7.2 and covered in detail in the following text.

**Table 7.2.** Font-related properties for style sheet rules.

| PROPERTY | DESCRIPTION |
|---|---|
| font-family | Defines the specific font or font family. |
| font-size | Specifies the font size. |
| font-style | Specifies the font style (for example, italics). |
| font-weight | Defines the font weight (for example, bold). |

## Font Family

The **font-family** property can be set to the name of one or more specific fonts and/or to the name of a font family (**serif**, **sans-serif**, **cursive**, or **monospace**). This style rule specifies that a sans-serif font be used for all **<H1>** elements:

h1    {font-family: sans-serif;}

You cannot be sure of which sans-serif font will be used—the browser will select it.

This style rule specifies that the Georgia font be used for all <H1> elements:

h1    {font-family: Georgia;}

If the user does not have this font installed, the browser will fall back to its default font. You can also specify a font family as a second choice:

h1    {font-family: Georgia, serif;}

With this rule, if the Georgia font is not available, the browser will select some other serif font.

You can also specify multiple font names in a rule:

h1    {font-family: Georgia, 'New Century Schoolbook', serif;}

This will cause the browser to look for Georgia first, then for New Century Schoolbook, and if neither is available, to fall back on a serif font. Note the single quotes around New Century Schoolbook. Such quotes are required for any font name that includes a space or a symbol such as $ or #.

## Font Size

Font size is specified using the **font-size** property. You can set the value of this property in the following ways:

- To one of the keywords **xx-small**, **x-small**, **small**, **medium**, **large**, **x-large**, **xx-large**.
- To a specific size consisting of a number followed by a unit abbreviation as described earlier in this chapter. Point (**pt**) is the unit usually used for fonts.
- To a relative size using the keywords **smaller** and **larger** or a numerical value followed by a percent sign.

The size names such as **xx-small** are not guaranteed to give you precise sizes. In theory it is supposed to work like this:

- The medium size is 16 pixels high.
- Each step larger is by a factor of 1.5. Thus **large** should be 16 x 1.5 = 24 pixels.
- Each step smaller is by a factor of 0.66. Thus **x-small** should be 16 x 0.66 = 10 pixels (approximately).

However, different browsers use different factors, so you cannot be sure of exactly what you'll get. These size names are fine for most Web design work but should be avoided for precision design.

The relative font size specifically operates in terms of whatever font size is current. In other words, the font size that would be used without the rule in place. The relative font size specifies operate relative to the current size as follows:

- The keywords **smaller** and **larger** make the font smaller or larger by one step (in theory this is a factor of 0.66 or 1.5).
- A percentage value makes the font the specified percent of the current size.

## Font Style

The font-style property lets you select between **normal**, **italic**, and **oblique** style. **Normal** is the default and displays the letters upright. The styles **italic** and **oblique** both give slanted text and the difference between them is rather subtle:

- Italic is essentially a separate version of a font, with the shapes of the letters altered slightly to look better when slanted.
- Oblique is simply a slanted version of the normal, upright font.

In my experience, most browsers display oblique and italic the same.

## Font Weight

The **font-weight** property controls the weight of text. You can set this property as follows:

- To the keyword **normal** or **bold**.
- To a numerical value 100, 200, 300, 400, 500, 600, 700, 800, or 900.
- To a relative keyword **lighter** or **bolder**.

Most people used to have two font weights available in their word processor: normal and bold. In style sheet rules, these correspond to the numerical values 400 and 700 respectively. In theory, you have a lot of control over font weight, but in reality the degree of control is less than you would expect, depending on the font and font size in use. When using the numerical values, all you can be sure of is that a higher number will produce a font weight that is greater or equal to the next lower number. The reverse is true for smaller font weight numbers. You can experiment with the number settings, but I have never found any use for anything other than **normal** and **bold**.

## Shortcuts Using the font Property

You can use the **font** property as a kind of shorthand when you have several font-related properties to set in a style rule. Rather than specifying all the individual properties, you can just combine them in one **font** property. Here's an example:

*{ font: italic bold 24pt Arial, san-serif;}*

Note however that you *must* include a font size and a font family in a **font** property—you cannot expect the default values to be used if they are omitted.

Another handy way to use the **font** property is to specify one of the system fonts. This is particularly useful when you want a Web page to "blend in" with the appearance of the user's operating system. You can use the following values for this purpose:

**caption.** The font used in captioned controls such as OK buttons.
**icon.** The font used for icon captions.
**menu.** The font used in program menus.
**message-box.** The font used in dialog boxes.
**small-caption.** The font used to label small controls.
**status-bar.** The font used in the status bar of windows.

For example, this style rule specifies the font that the operating system uses for menus:

*{ font: menu;}*

## The text Properties

The text properties control aspects of text display such as indentation, capitalization, and alignment. They are all pretty self-explanatory. I have listed them in Table 7.3 with a description of each.

**Table 7.3.** Text properties that you can use in a style rule.

| PROPERTY | VALUES | DESCRIPTION |
|---|---|---|
| text-decoration | underline, overline, line-through, blink | Specifies the text decoration. |
| text-transform | capitalize, uppercase, lowercase | Specifies the capitalization of text. The **capitalize** value means the first letter of words is uppercase. |
| text-align | left, right, center, justify | Specifies the alignment of text within its content box. The **justify** setting causes the spacing between letters and/or words to be adjusted to align both the left and right end of lines with the margins. |
| text-indent | A number followed by a unit abbreviation or a percent sign | Specifies the indentation of the first line of text as a specific amount or as a percentage of the width of the text element. |
| text-lineheight | A number by itself or followed by a unit abbreviation or percent sign. | Specifies the spacing between lines of text . A number by itself specifies lines (1 = single spaced, 2 = double spaced, etc.). A number with a percent sign specifies a percent of the element's font size. |

## The color and background-color Properties

These properties specify the color of an element and its background. An element's color is used for text as well as for the borders. These properties can be specified as other colors are specified: a color name, a hex color value, or an **rgb**() color value.

# Some Style Sheet Examples

In the following sections, I will present some examples of using style sheets to format Web pages. But first, there are two HTML tags you need to know about.

## The <div> and <span> Tags

The **<div>** and **<span>** tags are essential if you want to use CSS for formatting your Web pages. These tags have no function except to mark off sections of a document, permitting you to assign styles to them by including a class attribute in the tag. The difference between then is that **<div>** is a block element and its content will start on a new line, whereas **<span>** is an inline element and its content will be on the same line as adjacent content. Thus, you could use **<div>** to assign a style to a group of several paragraphs while you would use **<span>** to assign a style to one or more words in a sentence. You'll see examples in the following sections.

## Creating Custom Styles for Headings

The HTML tags **<h1>** through **<h6>** are useful for creating headings in your Web pages. If you do not like the default appearance of these headings, you can use CSS to format them to your liking. This example shows you how to define custom formatting for the first three heading levels. It also shows you how to use an external style sheet with an HTML document.

The first step is to define your formatting goals. For this example, we will write styles that define the following text properties:

- Heading level 1 in red text
- Heading level 2 in Bazooka font, underlined
- Heading level 3 indented by 20 pixels

Now you can create the style sheet as an external file. Here's how:

1. Start your text editor and create a new, blank file.
2. Enter the style sheet rules shown in Listing 7.1.
3. Save the file with the name test1.css. Be sure to save it in the same folder where you will place the Web page.

Listing 7.1. The code in the example style sheet.

```
h1            { color: #FF0000 }
h2            { font-family: Bazooka; font-size: 14pt;
                text-decoration: underline }
h3            { margin-left: 20px }
```

The next step is to create a Web page that uses this style sheet. The HTML code for the one I used is shown in Listing 7.2. Note the use of the **<link>** tag to link the page to the style sheet.

**Listing 7.2.** An HTML page that uses the style sheet from Listing 7.1.

```
<html>
<head>
<title>Heading styles</title>
<link rel="stylesheet" type="text/css" href="Test1.css" />
</head>
<body>
<h1>Heading 1</h1>
<h2>Heading 2</h2>
<h3>Heading 3</h3>
</body>
</html>
```

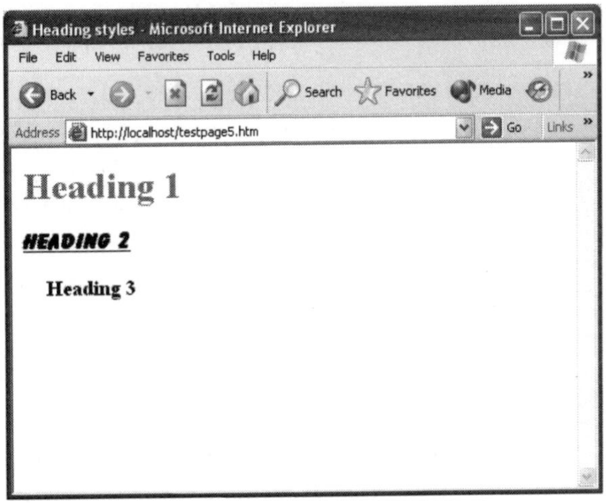

The result is shown in Figure 7.4. It may not be obvious in the figure, but Heading 1 is displayed in red.

**Figure 7.4.** The appearance of the custom heading styles.

## Using Styles for Table Formatting

This next example shows how you can use a style sheet to control the formatting of an HTML table. The objective is to define two styles that can be applied to individual rows. One will be used to display the first row of the table as a header using a large white font on a dark gray background. The other style will be used to format every other row with a light gray background to assist users is reading the table. Each style will be defined with a **class** selector; then the appropriate **class** attribute will be added to the **<tr>** elements as needed.

Listing 7.3 shows the final HTML document, including the internal style sheet and a table of dummy data. Please note how the **class** attribute is used to assign the appropriate style to the table rows. The resulting table is shown in Figure 7.5.

Listing 7.3. Using an internal style sheet to format a table.

```
<html>
<head>
<title>Formattng tables with styles</title>
<style>
<!-
table.info {
    width:100%;
    border:1px solid #111111;
    border-collapse:collapse;
}
.tableheader {
    color:#FFFFFF;
    font:bold 14pt arial,sans-serif;
    background-color:#787878;
}
.alternaterows{
    background-color:#C0C0C0
}
-->
</style>
</head>
<body>
<table class="info">
  <tr class="tableheader">
    <td width="33%">United States</td>
    <td width="33%">Canada</td>
    <td width="34%">Mexico</td>
  </tr>
  <tr>
    <td width="33%">1212323</td>
    <td width="33%">3233434</td>
    <td width="34%">3423432</td>
  </tr>
  <tr class="alternaterows">
    <td width="33%">546778</td>
    <td width="33%">899900</td>
    <td width="34%">432343</td>
  </tr>
  <tr>
    <td width="33%">432343</td>
    <td width="33%">123456</td>
    <td width="34%">899900</td>
  </tr>
  <tr class="alternaterows">
    <td width="33%">546778</td>
```

```
      <td width="33%">546778</td>
      <td width="34%">432343</td>
   </tr>
   <tr>
      <td width="33%">123456</td>
      <td width="33%">432343</td>
      <td width="34%">899900</td>
   </tr>
   <tr class="alternaterows">
      <td width="33%">432343</td>
      <td width="33%">899900</td>
      <td width="34%">546778</td>
   </tr>
  </table>
 </body>
</html>
```

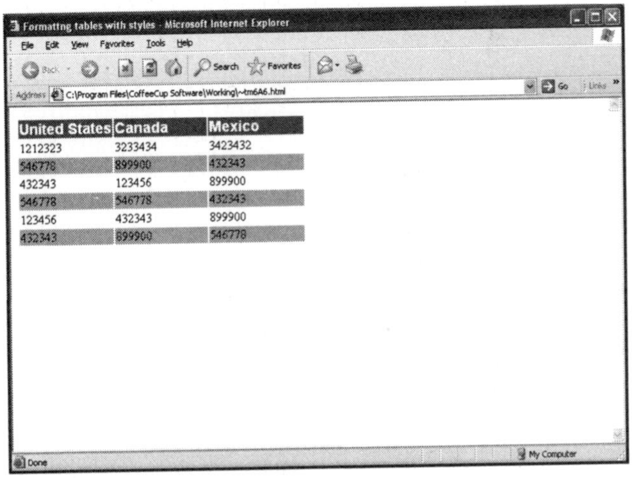

## Using Styles to Format Hyperlinks

**Figure 7.5.** The display of the HTML document from Listing 7.3.

Every browser has default styles for links. For Internet Explorer, this is blue underlined text for unvisited links and purple underlined text for visited links. You can use styles to change the way links are displayed, but first you need to know about *pseudoclasses.*

Every link in a document uses the <a> tag and they all look pretty much the same. In other words, there's no way that you can look at the HTML source code and tell which links have been visited and which have not. What happens is that each browser keeps a history list of links visited within the past so many days (20 days by default in Internet Explorer, but this value can be changed by the user). If a link's URL is found in the history list, it is considered "visited"; otherwise it is not. The browser automatically assigns the **visited** pseudoclass to links that have been visited and the **link** pseudoclass to links that have not been visited. Two other pseudoclasses are available as well: **active** for an active link (one that is being clicked) and **hover** for one the mouse cursor is hovering over. You can use these pseudoclasses as selectors in a style sheet by following the element name with a colon and the pseudoclass name. Thus,

```
   a:link
```

is a selector for unvisited links and

```
a:visited
a:active
a:hover
```

are selectors for visited, active, and hover links respectively. Using these selectors, you can define styles for your page's hyperlinks. Let's look at an example. Suppose you wanted unvisited hyperlinks on a page to be highly visible—for instance, larger white text on a red background, not underlined, with wider left and right margins. Visited links should be the same except for having black text on a gray background. Here are the styles to do this:

```
<style>
<!--
a:link {
    font-size:larger;
    color: #FFFFFF;
    padding-left: 10px;
    padding-right: 10px;
    text-decoration: none;
    background-color: #CC0000;
}
a:visited {
    font-size: larger;
    color: #000000;
    padding-left: 10px;
    padding-right: 10px;
    text-decoration: none;
    background-color: #CCCCCC;
}
//-->
</style>
```

Note that you must include **text-decoration: none** in the style to cancel the default underlining of links. Figure 7.6 shows how the resulting link styles will appear.

**Figure 7.6.** Using styles to define hyperlink appearance.

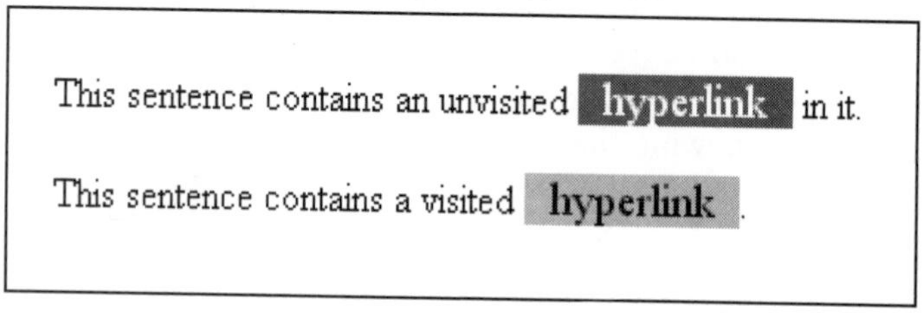

## Style Shortcuts

When you have two or more complex styles that differ only in one or two respects, you can save some time and effort by using the fact that later styles override earlier ones. First, define the base style and assign it to all the relevant HTML elements and classes. Then, below that rule, add new rules that make the necessary changes for each individual element or class. We could have done this with the previous example as follows:

```
a:link, a:visited {
    font-size: larger;
    color: #FFFFFF;
    padding-left: 10px;
    padding-right: 10px;
    text-decoration: none;
    background-color: #CC0000;
}
a:visited {
    color: #000000;
    background-color: #CCCCCC;
}
```

The first rule assigns all the relevant formatting to both visited and unvisited links; then the second rule changes the colors for visited links, leaving the other aspects of the formatting unchanged from the first rule.

# Summary

Style sheets provide a great deal of formatting power and flexibility to the Web page designer. Good design practice dictates that you use style sheets instead of <font> and other HTML tags. For simple personal Websites, the advantage is minimal, but as you get into developing more complex multipage sites, the benefits of style sheets will become more evident.

# CHAPTER 8

# Introduction to Scripting and the Document Object Model

Many terrific Websites have been created using nothing more than HTML and CSS. But what if you want more? What if the capabilities of plain HTML are simply not enough to create the Web pages you want? Then you will probably turn to scripting and the Document Object Model (DOM) to give your Web pages more interactivity and pizzazz. When used together, scripting and the DOM are sometimes referred to as *dynamic HTML*, or DHTML. I can't provide complete coverage of scripting and the DOM in a single chapter, but I can give you a good introduction and let you explore more on your own if you want to.

## What Is Scripting?

A script is a program that is embedded in a Web page. It is kept separate from the page's HTML by special tags, as you'll see soon. The script code is executed when certain events occur, such as the page loading into a browser or the user clicking an element on the page. A script can perform a wide variety of actions, such as figuring mathematical calculations, processing text data, displaying messages to the user, controlling the browser, and changing the appearance of the page. There are also some things scripts cannot do, such as read files on your hard drive or access your system's memory. These limitations are intentional and were put in place for security reasons. Without access to files and memory, it is essentially impossible for a script to cause any mischief on the user's computer. People would be very hesitant to visit Web pages with scripts if they faced the possibility of malicious or unintentional damage to their system and files.

The scripts that are the subject of this chapter are called *client-side scripts* because they are downloaded as part of a Web page and executed on the client's computer. You'll also hear about *server-side scripts*, which are executed remotely on the Web server, but that's a different topic.

Essentially every Web browser in use today includes support for scripts. By far the most popular scripting language is JavaScript, and that's what I'll be using in this chapter. Another commonly used scripting language is VBScript, a Microsoft creation that is intended to have certain syntax similarities with the Visual Basic programming language. If you already know Visual Basic, you might find VBScript a bit easier to learn. For most people, however, I recommend JavaScript.

A scripting language would not be able to do much on its own. It must work in conjunction with the Document Object Model, our next topic.

## The Document Object Model

When a browser loads a Web page, it reads the HTML and holds the document information in memory (as well as displaying it on-screen). The Document Object Model, or DOM, is a specification of how the document is represented in memory and how the document information can be accessed and modified. Much of the power of client-side scripts comes from their ability to use the DOM to manipulate an HTML document in the browser.

The structure of the DOM is based upon the structure of the HTML document. You learned about the structure of an HTML document in earlier chapters, and if you think about it you will realize that it is organized hierarchically—in other words, it is organized in terms of parent elements and child elements. In slightly simplified form, this is as follows:

- At the top of the hierarchy is the **Document** object, which corresponds to the **<html>** tags in the document.
- The **Document** object has two children, the **<head>** and the **<body>** tags.
- The **<head>** element can have a variety of children, including a <title> tag and a <style> tag.
- The **<body>** tag can have a variety of children, including paragraph, image, and table elements.
- The text within a **<p>** tag is considered a child of the paragraph element.

To illustrate, take a look at the simple HTML document in Listing 8.1. The DOM would represent it by the hierarchy shown in Figure 8.1. Each box represents an element or node in the document. The Mozilla Firefox browser also has a DOM Inspector that you can use to have a look at the DOM yourself to see how pages are broken down.

**Listing 8.1.** A simple HTML document.

```
<html>
<head>
<title>Sample</title>
</head>
<body>
<p>Paragraph 1</p>
<p>Paragraph 2</p>
</body>
</html>
```

Before getting to the details of the DOM, there is some terminology you should know:

- **Parent:** The node directly above a node. Every node in an HTML document has one and only one parent except the top-level **Document** node, which has no parent.

- **Child:** A node directly below a node. A node can have zero, one, or more children.

- **Siblings:** Two or more nodes with the same parent.

- **Ancestor:** A node that is one or more levels above another node.

- **Descendant:** A node one or more levels below a node.

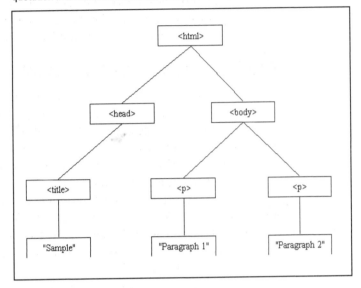

**Figure 8.1.** The DOM hierarchy of the HTML document in Listing 8.1. The quotation marks indicate content elements.

With this background under your belt, you are ready to get to the details.

## Accessing Document Elements

When you are working with the DOM, you need to access specific elements in the document. There are several ways to do this: by unique ID, by name, and by type.

### Getting Elements by Unique ID

One method of accessing individual document elements is to make use of an element's unique **id** attribute. You can add an **id** attribute to any kind of element in the document—paragraphs, tables, table cells, headings, links, and so on. Remember using the **id** attribute for CSS? Here's a few examples:

```
<p id="intro">...</p>
<table id="table1">...</table>
<h1 id="firstheading">...</h1>
```

Each **id** value must be unique within the document. This permits the value of an element's **id** attribute to uniquely identify the element. You can then access the element by using the **document** object's **getElementById()** method. For example, the code

```
document.getElementById("intro")
```

would let you access the **<p>** element from the earlier example. You could then change the text in the paragraph, change its font size and color, and so on. I'll talk more about what you can do with DHTML later in the chapter.

## Warning: Watch Your Case!

DHTML method, property, and function names are case sensitive. This can lead to hard-to-find errors. If you write **getElementByID** instead of **getElementById**, your script won't work. There are some general rules for name case:

- If the name consists of a single word (for example, length), it is all lowercase.

- If the name is made up of multiple words (for example, **getElementByName**), the first letter of each word except the first one is uppercase.

### Getting Elements by Name

The second way to access document elements is with the **name** attribute. This is similar to **id** except that multiple elements in a document can have the same **name** attribute.

```
<p name="section1">First para text</p>
<p name="section1">Second para text </p>
<p name="section1">Third para text </p>
```

Then you use the **getElementsByName()** method to access the elements. Because the **name** attribute does not have to be unique, this method can return one or more elements (or none, of course, if the specified **name** value does not exist in the document). The return is in the form of a collection. You then need to access the individual items in the collection, which I'll cover soon.

### Getting Elements by Type

The final method you can use to access document elements is by virtue of the type of element and its position in the document hierarchy. This works for the following types of elements: anchors (all **<a>** tags), forms, images, and links (those **<a>** tags that are hyperlinks). You do this by using the following properties:

```
document.anchors
document.forms
document.images
document.links
```

Each of these properties returns a collection that contains all of the elements of the specified type. You use the collection as described in the next section.

## Working With Collections

You have seen that several methods of accessing document elements return a collection that contains references to zero, one, or more elements. Once you have a collection, you can go through it and access all the elements in turn or you can access a single element. Let's take a look at how collections work.

A collection has the **length** property that tells you how many items it contains. For example, the expression

```
document.images.length
```

will return the number of image elements in the document. If the value of **length** is 0, then there are no elements of the specified type in the document.

You can access individual elements in a collection by using brackets after the collection name:

```
document.forms[n]
```

The argument n is a number giving the position of the element in the document. It can range from 0 (the first element of the specified type) to length—1 (the last element). The order of elements is the same as their order in the HTML code.

You can also access an element by its **name** attribute as shown here:

```
document.images(name)
```

> ## Alternate Collection Syntax
>
> An alternate method for accessing collection members by position is to use the **item** method:
>
> ```
> document.forms.item(n)
> ```
>
> This is functionally exactly the same as the following:
>
> ```
> document.forms[n]
> ```
>
> You rarely see the first syntax for the simple reason that it takes a bit longer to type.

Note the use of parentheses instead of square brackets. This method is best avoided, however, for two reasons. First, since the **name** attribute is not guaranteed to be unique, it can give unreliable results. Second, it is not supported in Netscape Navigator.

# A Demonstration

Now it's time to look at a simple demonstration of DHTML that will illustrate some of the things you have been learning. The HTML document in Listing 8.2 combines JavaScript and the DOM to create a simple demonstration. When you view the document in your browser, it looks like Figure 8.2. If you click the Click me! text, the main heading in the document changes from black to red. Let's analyze how this document works.

**Listing 8.2.** A simple DHTML demo.

```html
<html>

<head>

<title>DHTML Demo</title>
<script language="javascript">
function changeColor()
{
    document.getElementById('main').style.color="red"
}
</script>

</head>

<body>

<h1 id="main">DHTML Demonstration</h1>
<form name="Form1">
First Name: <input type="text" size="20">
</form>
<form name="Form2">
Last Name: <input type="text" size="20">
</form>
<p><img border="0" src="Claire.jpg" width="125" height="218"
/></p>
<script language="javascript">
document.write("<p>The document contains " +
document.forms.length + " forms and " +
document.images.length + " image.</p>")
</script>
<p onclick="changeColor()"> Click me!</p>

</body>

</html>
```

The first thing you'll notice is this block of script in the document's head section:

```html
<script language="javascript">
function changeColor()
{
    document.getElementById('main').style.color="red"
}
</script>
```

This defines a JavaScript function named changeColor. Because it is a function and located in the head section, is it not executed unless JavaScript code elsewhere in the document specifically calls it. The one line of code in the function changes the color of the element with the id attribute 'main' to red.

At the start of the body section you'll find a heading, two forms, and an image—there's nothing new here. Next, however, there is the following script block:

**Figure 8.2.** Viewing the DHTML demonstration document.

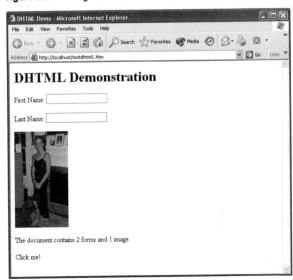

```
<script language="javascript">
document.write("<p>The
document contains " +
document.forms.length + "
forms and " +
document.images.length + "
image.</p>")
</script>
```

The **<script>** tag's **language** attribute is deprecated in HTML 4.0 and is not supported in XHTML. Use the **type** attribute instead: **type="text/javascript"**.

Between the two **<script>** tags is what will be executed as script. Because this code is in the body section of the document and is not a function, it is executed immediately when the page loads. This code writes the text "The document contains 2 forms and 1 image" (with a period at the end) to the document. The following list describes its components:

- **document.write:** A method that writes text to the document.

- Text in quotes, such as "**<p>The document contains**": Literal text that is written as is to the document. Note that the HTML **<p>** tag is included because we are writing HTML to the document and must include the tags.

- The + symbol: Use to combine two sections of text into one. It's also used for adding numbers, but JavaScript can figure out what you want to do by looking at the data.

- **document.forms.length:** Retrieves the number of **<form>** elements in the document.

- **document.images.length:** Retrieves the number of **<img>** elements in the document.

107

The final element in the document is the following:

```
<p onclick="changeColor()"> Click me!</p>
```

This is a normal paragraph element except for the **onclick** attribute. This is an event attribute that specifies what happens when the user clicks the element. The value of the event attribute is the JavaScript code that is to be executed. In this example, it is the name of the function **changeColor()** that is to be called. In other words, when the user clicks the paragraph, the **changeColor()** function is executed to change the color of the document's first heading.

I'll talk more about the DOM later in the chapter, but first let's look at the basics of JavaScript.

# JavaScript Is Not Java

You may have heard of the popular programming language called Java. Is JavaScript related to Java? Only remotely. Java is a full-featured object-oriented language for writing desktop and server applications, whereas JavaScript is a scripting language designed for Web use. There are some syntactical similarities between the two languages, but that's about all.

# JavaScript

You have seen some examples of JavaScript earlier in this chapter, but now you need to learn a bit more so you can use JavaScript effectively in your Web pages. I cannot cover JavaScript in its entirety—that would require its own book—but I can show you enough to get started.

## Syntax

The following sections cover some of the basic syntax rules of JavaScript.

### Case Sensitivity

The first thing you should know about JavaScript is that it is a case-sensitive language. Thus, the terms **COUNT**, **Count**, and **count** will be considered three distinct and totally independent terms in JavaScript. I know this can be really annoying, but there's no getting around it, so you'll just have to get used to it. In my experience, the best approach is to develop a consistent approach to capitalization and stick with it.

JavaScript's case sensitivity can be even more confusing because HTML is not case sensitive. <IMG> and <img> are the same tag, and the same is true of attribute names.

### White Space

JavaScript is similar to HTML in that it ignores most white space (spaces, tabs, and new lines). If, for example, you have a long line of JavaScript code, you can break it up over two or more lines. The only place that white space is not ignored is within literal strings—text that is enclosed in double or single quotation marks.

### Semicolons

In some of the programming languages that JavaScript is related to, a semicolon is used to mark the end of each program statement. JavaScript relaxes this rule—you can end a statement with a semicolon but do not have to as long as each statement is placed on a separate line. If you want to put more than one statement on a line, semicolons are required. For example, this is legal:

```
a = 1;
b = 2;
```

So is this:

```
a = 1
b = 2
```

And this is legal too:

```
a = 1; b = 2;
```

But this is not legal:

```
a = 1 b = 2;
```

### Comments

Just as with HTML, you can enter comments in your JavaScript code. The syntax is different, however. You can enter single-line comments using a pair of slashes. Anything following // on a line is a comment, as in this example:

```
// This is a comment.
a = 1; //This is another comment.
```

You can also create comments using the /* and */ character pairs. Anything following /* up to the next */ is a comment; it can span as many lines as you like (this is the preferred method of commenting code in JavaScript):

```
/* This is
all one large
          multi-line
comment. */
```

The only time that //, /*, and */ do not mark comments is when they are within a quoted string.

### Literals

A literal is nothing more than a data value typed directly into the program code. They fall into three general categories:

- Numbers are typed in normally, such as **123** or **0.045**. You do not use thousands separators, such as the comma in **23,000**.

- Strings, or text, are entered enclosed in single or double quotes. Some examples are "**John's Salary**" and '**Mississippi**'. If a string contains a double quote, it must be enclosed in single quotes and *vice versa*. Otherwise it does not matter which you use.

- The special keywords **true** and **false** representing the corresponding Boolean values, and **null** representing "no data or object."

### Identifiers

An identifier is a name used in a JavaScript program to identify something, typically either a variable or a function. The rules for creating identifiers are simple:

- The first character must be a letter, an underscore (_), or a dollar sign ($).

- Subsequent characters can be any letter, any digit, an underscore, or a dollar sign.

The following are all legal JavaScript identifiers:

```
count
$name
index_12
x
fred_flintstone
```

These are not legal:

```
percent%
12days
john-adams
```

Also, you cannot use a JavaScript reserved keyword as an identifier. These reserved words are listed in Table 8.1.

**Table 8.1.** JavaScript reserved keywords.

| | | |
|---|---|---|
| break | finally | this |
| case | for | throw |
| catch | function | true |
| continue | if | try |
| default | in | typeof |
| delete | instanceof | var |
| do | new | void |
| else | null | while |
| false | return | with |
| | switch | |

## Be Descriptive

When creating variable and function names, it is a good idea to use names that are descriptive of the data the variable holds or the task that the function performs.

## Variables

A *variable* is a location to store data in a script. As the name suggests, the data in a variable can change—unlike a literal, it is not set at one fixed value. When you create a variable, you give it a name; you then use that name to refer to it in your code. To create a variable—called *declaring* a variable—use the **var** keyword:

```
var variablename
```

*Variablename* is any legal JavaScript identifier as described earlier in this chapter. It must be unique within the program or, if it is declared in a function, within that function. You can declare variables one at a time like this:

```
var count;
var total;
```

Or, you can declare more than one in a single **var** statement:

```
var count, total;
```

You can initialize (assign a value to) a variable at the same time you declare it:

```
var name = "Arthur";
```

If you declare a variable without initializing it, the variable's value will be undefined until the program stores a value in the variable. You cannot count on an uninitialized variable having a specific value such as 0.

What happens if you try to use a variable that has not been declared? It depends:

- If your code tries to read the value of the variable, an error occurs.

- If your code sets the value of the variable, JavaScript automatically declares it.

You should not rely on the second point—it is advisable to explicitly declare all variables. One reason for this is that automatically declared variables always have global scope, which can cause problems. You'll learn more about this in the section on variable scope later in the chapter.

## Arrays

An array is a type of variable that can store multiple data items under the same name, distinguishing them by a numerical index. For example, you could create an array named **months** that has 12 elements, one for each month. Then array element 1 could be used for January, element 2 for February, and so on. To create an array, you use the **Array()** function. One option is to specify the number of elements the array has. This declaration creates an array with 10 elements:

```
var myArray = new Array(10);
```

You can also specify the data in the array when you declare it:

```
var myArray = new Array(2, 4, 6, 8, 10);
```

JavaScript assigns the data to the array starting with the first element and automatically sizes the array as needed (five elements in this example).

Finally, you can use an array literal to create an array without using the **Array()** function. Here's an example that has the same result as the previous example:

```
var myArray = [2, 4, 6, 8, 10];
```

To access an array element, you use the array name followed by the element number in square brackets:

```
myArray[4] = "Happy Programming!";
document.write(myArray[4]);
```

You can also specify the index with a variable:

```
myArray[idx] = "Happy Programming!";
document.write(myArray[idx]);
```

If the variable idx has the value 4, these two sections of code are equivalent.

JavaScript has the handy feature that you can change the size of an array at any time. You can both increase and decrease an array's size. To add elements to an array, all you need do is assign a value to one or more new elements as shown here. Look at this variable declaration:

```
var myArray = new Array("red", "yellow", "blue");
```

## JavaScript Arrays Are Zero Based

As with most programming languages, arrays in JavaScript are zero based. This means that the first element in the array has index 0, not 1. It also means that the last element in the array has an index equal to one less than the number of elements in the array. For example, a 10-element array has elements with indexes 0 through 9. A common newbie error is to try to access that nonexistent 10th element at index 10.

This creates an array with three elements with indexes 0, 1, and 2. Then suppose your program executes the following code:

```
myArray[3] = "green";
myArray[4] = "orange";
```

JavaScript will automatically increase the array to five elements, adding the two new elements with indexes 3 and 4.

You can also change an array's size, increasing or decreasing it, by setting its **length** property.:

```
myArray.length = value
```

If *value* is greater than the current array size, new elements are added as needed. If *value* is smaller than the current array size, elements are removed from the end of the array.

## Functions

A *function* is a section of JavaScript code that is set apart from other code and assigned a name. You can execute the code in a function at any time by referring to it by name. Functions are an important part of JavaScript programming, particularly for code that performs actions that are needed frequently. Rather than repeating the code at various locations in your page, you can put it in a function and call it as needed. A function definition consists of the following:

## Determining Array Length

You can use the length property to determine the length of an array. This can be very useful when you need to read out all the elements in an array but do not know how many there are. I'll show you an example of this later in the section on **for** loops.

- The **function** keyword
- The function name, following the rules for JavaScript identifiers that were described earlier in this chapter
- A pair of parentheses that can optionally contain a list of one or more function parameters
- An opening curly brace ({)
- One or more lines of JavaScript code that constitute the function body
- A closing curly brace (})

JavaScript functions are usually placed the head section of an HTML document. A function can contain essentially any JavaScript code, the one exception being that a function definition cannot contain another function definition. Code within a function can, however, call another function.

How much code can you put in a function? There's no real limit, but good programming practice dictates that functions be kept fairly short. How much code is that? I can't give you an exact answer, but in my experience once a function gets beyond 25 lines or so, it is almost always possible to break it into to separate functions. More important, each function should carry out a single discrete task.

Now let's look at some of the details of using JavaScript functions in your Web pages.

### Function Arguments

A JavaScript function can take *arguments* that let you pass information to the function when you call it. Arguments—sometimes also called *parameters—are* optional but are essential for many functions. To include arguments in a function definition, you simply include the argument names, separated by commas if there are more than one, in the parentheses following the function name Here's an example for a function with two arguments:

```
function myFunction(argument1, argument2)
{
...
}
```

When you call the function, you must include the argument values in the call:

```
myFunction(argument1Value, argument2Value)
```

## The Importance of Functions

A lot of JavaScript programming tasks could be accomplished either with or without functions. My advice is to use functions as much as possible even when you do not have to. By dividing your code into discrete named sections, you gain several advantages. First, your code is logically organized, which makes it easier to modify and to debug. Second, you can copy and paste functions from one Web page to another, saving programming time. Finally, there are advantages having to do with variable scope, to be discussed soon.

Let's look at an example. Here's a very simple function that displays a message to the user (you would probably not use a function for something this simple, but it serves as a good example). Note that **alert** is a built-in function that displays a message to the user.

```
function alertUser(msg)
{
alert(msg);
}
```

JavaScript code elsewhere on the page would call the function like this:

```
alertUser("Please enter your name");
```

### Function Return Values

Functions become even more useful when you consider their ability to return a value to the calling code. What exactly does this mean? Some functions, such as the **alertUser()** function presented in the previous section, simply perform an action—there is no data returned to the calling code. However, you can also write a function that performs some sort of calculation or other data manipulation and returns the result to the code that called it. This is a very powerful technique. There are two differences when you are defining and using a function that returns a value.

First, you must use the **return** statement in the function to specify what value is returned. The syntax is

```
return value
```

where *value* is the data to be returned. Here's a simple example—a function that calculates the square of a number:

```
function squareOf(x)
{
return x*x;
}
```

The function multiplies its one argument by itself—that's the definition of a square—and uses the **return** statement to return the value.

Second, the calling code must retrieve the returned value in some way. This is often done by placing the function call on the right side of an equal sign, thereby assigning the return value to a variable:

```
var squareOfFour;
squareOfFour = squareOf(4);
```

You can also use a value-returning function anywhere a value can be used. Here's an example:

```
alert("The square of 4 is " + squareOf(4));
```

## Variable Scope

JavaScript functions bring up the important topic of *variable scope*. This term refers to where in a script a variable is visible—in other words, where it is accessible. This applies to arrays as well. There are two kinds of scope:

- Local scope: A variable declared in a function has *local* scope and is visible within that function only.

- Global scope: A variable declared outside a function has *global* scope and is visible throughout the entire file, both within and outside of functions.

You might think that global scope is the way to go, but that's not the case. Local scope is a valuable tool, particularly when your scripts get long and complex. Let's look at why this is.

When you declare a variable within a function, it is completely hidden from the JavaScript code elsewhere on the page. This means that other code cannot alter the variable—only code in the function can do so. By isolating each function's variables in this manner, you will prevent a lot of pesky and hard-to-find script bugs. Also, it means that you can use the same variable name more than once in different functions—a variable named **count** in one function, for example, is completely independent from a variable of the same name in another function.

Let's look at some examples that will help to bring home the concept of scope. In this first example, a global variable **name** is declared. When the function executes, the value "Peter" is displayed because there is no local variable **name** so the code accesses the global variable:

```
var name = "Peter";
function myFunction()
{
alert(name);
}
```

In the second example, the function declares a local variable **name**. The result is that "**Alice**" is displayed because the code in the function accesses the local variable and not the global one of the same name:

```
var name = "Peter";
function myFunction()
{
var name = "Alice";
alert(name);
}
```

In the final example, **func1** displays "**Alice**" because it uses the local variable name while **func2** displays "**Peter**" because it accesses the global variable **name**:

```
var name = "Peter";
function func1()
{
var name = "Alice";
alert(name);
}
function func2()
{
alert(name);
}
```

## Expressions and Operators

You'll hear the term expression used a lot in programming. It means anything that can be evaluated to a value (a number or text). For example, **2** is an expression—

it evaluates to the value 2, of course. So are **12+5**, which evaluates to 17, and "**Peanut**" + "**Butter**", which evaluates to "Peanut Butter." Functions that return values are expressions, too — they evaluate to whatever value they return.

Many expressions use operators. The JavaScript language provides a rich set of operators to perform a wide variety of operations. Operators are divided into several categories.

### Mathematical Operators

The mathematical operators perform the common operations of addition (+), subtraction (-), division (/), and multiplication (*). The + operator is also used to concatenate, or join together, strings. JavaScript knows whether to add or concatenate based on the data. Note that if an expression contains multiple operators, the * and / will be performed first followed by the + and -. Thus

```
10 + 2 / 4
```

evaluates to 10.5 because the division is done before the addition. You can modify the order of operations by using parentheses. Anything within parentheses is done first. For example,

```
(10 + 2) / 4
```

evaluates to 3 because the parentheses force the addition to be performed first.

Two other mathematical operators are the *increment* and *decrement* operators. They are used when you need to increase or decrease the value of a numerical variable by one—a common operation in programming. The operators are ++ and — and can be placed either before or after a variable name:

```
++count
count++
--count
count--
```

The placement of the operator determines when the increment or decrement is performed, which can affect the evaluation of an expression that the variable is in:

- If the operator is before the name, the operation in performed before the value of the variable is used in the expression.

- If the operator is after the name, the operation in performed after the value of the variable is used in the expression.

Look at this example:

```
var count = 5;
var num1, num2;
num1 = count-- + 10;
num2 = --count + 10;
```

The variable **num1** will have the value 15 because the original value of **count**, 5, is used in the expression and then **count** is decremented to 4. In contrast, the variable **num2** will have the value 14 because the value of **count** is decremented to 4 before it is used in the expression.

The final mathematical operators that you need to know about are a sort of combination—they let you perform an operation and assign the result in a single operation. In programming, it is frequently required to change a variable's value by adding something to it. For example, this code increases the value of **total** by 10:

```
total = total + 10;
```

You can use the assignment with addition operator (+=) to do this as follows:

```
total += 10;
```

Similar shorthand operators exist for subtraction (-=), multiplication (*=), and division (/=).

### Relational Operators

Programs often need to compare one value with another. Is this number larger than a certain value? Are two variables equal in value? You use the relational operators for this purpose. These operators, which can be used for strings as well as numbers, return the logical values **true** or **false** depending on the result of the comparison. They are described in Table 8.2.

**Table 8.2.** JavaScript's relational operators.

| OPERATOR | SYMBOL | DESCRIPTION |
|---|---|---|
| Equal to | == (two = signs) | Returns **true** if the values being compared are equal. Returns **false** otherwise. |
| Not equal to | != | Returns **true** if the values being compared are not equal. Returns **false** otherwise. |
| Greater than | > | Returns **true** if the first value is larger than the second value. Returns **false** otherwise. |
| Less than | < | Returns **true** if the first value is less than the second value. Returns **false** otherwise. |
| Greater than or equal | >= | Returns **true** if the first value is larger than or equal to the second value. Returns **false** otherwise. |
| Less than or equal | <= | Returns **true** if the first value is less than or equal to the second value. Returns **false** otherwise. |

The use of the relational operators with numerical values is straightforward. With strings it is a bit more complex. Characters—letters, digits, punctuation marks, and so on—are represented by numerical codes in the computer. When you compare strings, it is these codes that are actually compared, on a character-by-character basis. This has some strange consequences.

For example, would you consider "apple" to be less than or greater than "cherry"? Most people will say less than because *a* comes before *c* in the alphabet—and that is in fact how it works. The numerical code for *a* is 97, for *b* 98, all the way to 122 for *z*, so the comparisons work as you would expect.

But what about comparing "apple" with "CHERRY"? You may be surprised to find that JavaScript (and most other programming languages as well) considers "apple" to be greater than "CHERRY". This is because the uppercase letters have codes in the range 65-90, so any uppercase letter is "less than" any lowercase letter.

Likewise, is a semicolon less than a period? The question doesn't seem to make sense, but the answer is no because the codes for those characters are 59 and 46 respectively.

While it may not make intuitive sense, this is just the way string comparisons work and you'll have to get used to it. When comparing strings, you should always convert the strings to all uppercase or all lowercase so the comparison will be based on alphabetic order. You use the **toUpperCase()** and **toLowerCase()** methods for this. These methods do not change the original strings but just make temporary converted copies. Here's an example:

```
var s1 = "apple";
var s2 = "CHERRY";
alert(s1 < s2);                        //Displays "false"
alert(s1.toUpperCase() < s2. toUpperCase() // Displays
"true");
```

### Logical Operators

The logical operators perform operations on the logical values **true** and **false**. The simplest logical operator is the NOT operator, represented by the symbol !. It simply reverses the value of its operand, from **true** to **false** or vice versa. Here's an example:

```
var x = true;
var y = !x;     //y has the value false.
```

The other logical operators combine two individual logical expressions to form a single logical value:

- AND (&&) returns **true** if both of its operands are **true** and returns **false** otherwise (if one or both operands are **false**).

- OR (||) returns **true** if either one or both of its operands are **true** and returns **false** otherwise (if both operands are **false**).

Here are some examples:

```
var x = true;
var y = false;
var z = true;
var a;
a = x || y;          // a is true.
a = x && y;          // a is false.
a = y || !z;         // a is false (note the NOT operator).
```

You'll find yourself using the logical operators frequently in loops and if statements, covered soon.

## For Loops

You use a **for** loop to execute a block of statements a specified number of times. Here's the syntax:

```
for (initialize; test; increment)
{
//Statements to execute go here.
}
```

The contents of this statement are as follows:

- *Initialize* is a JavaScript statement that sets up the initial value of a variable that will be used to track the loop.

- *Test* is a logical expression. As long as *test* is **true**, the statement executes repeatedly. As soon as *test* is **false**, the statement terminates.

- *Increment* is a JavaScript statement that specifies how the loop variable is changed with each repetition.

## Single Statement for Loops

When a **for** loop contains only a single statement, you do not have to use the curly braces but can simply place the single statement after the **for** statement. Thus

```
for (var x = 0; x < 20; x++)
document.write(x);
```

is equivalent to

```
for (var x = 0; x < 20; x++)
{
document.write(x);
}
```

Let's start with a simple example. Suppose you want to execute a set of statements 20 times. Here's how you would do it using a **for** statement:

```
for (var x = 0; x < 20;  x++)
{
...
}
```

Here's what happens when execution reaches this **for** loop:

1. The variable **x** is declared and initialized to 0. If the variable has already been declared, you can simply set its value.

2. The expression **x < 20** is evaluated. Since it is **true** at this point, all the statements in the curly braces are executed.

3. The statement **x++** is executed, increasing the value of x by 1.

4. The expression **x < 20** is evaluated. It is still **true** at this point, so all the statements in the curly braces are executed once again.

5. The process repeats 20 times, after which **x** will be equal to 19. When it is incremented to 20, the expression **x < 20** evaluates as **false**, so the statements in the braces are not executed and execution passes to the code following the **for** loop.

Within the body of the loop, the loop variable is available for use in your calculations. In fact, this is a common way to use loops. Here's an example; place the code in Listing 8.3 as the **<body>** section in an HTML document and preview it in a browser. You'll see the results shown in Figure 8.3.

**Listing 8.3.** Demonstrating the **for** loop.

```
<body>
<script language="javascript">
var msg;
var data = new Array(10);
for (var x = 0; x < data.length; x++)
{
// Calculate the square and
store in the array.
data[x] = x * x;
// Write the results to the
document.
document.write("<p>The square
of " + x + " is " + data[x] +
"</p>")
}
</script>
</body>
```

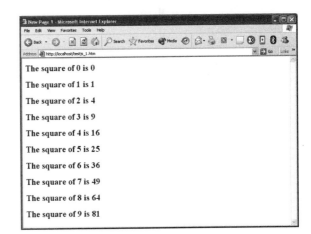

In this example, note how the **length** property of the array was used in the for loop's test condition. This permits the loop to be used for arrays of different lengths.

**Figure 8.3.** The output of the JavaScript code from Listing 8.3.

## Exiting or Repeating a for Loop Early

You can exit a **for** loop early—that is, before the test condition becomes **false**—with the **break** statement. As soon as a **break** statement is encountered within a loop, execution immediately exits the loop and continues with the code that follows.

You can also repeat the loop before it reaches the end using the **continue** statement. When this statement is encountered, a new repetition of the loop is started immediately without executing the statements between the **continue** statement and the end of the loop.

## While and do...while Statements

The **while** statement executes a block of code repeatedly as long as a specified condition is **true**. Here is the syntax:

```
while (condition)
{
//Statements.
}
```

The statements in the block are executed repeatedly as long as *condition* remains **true**. Note that if *condition* is **false** to begin with, the statements will not be executed even once.

The **do...while** statement is a variant of **while** in which the condition is tested at the end of the loop rather than at the start:

```
do
{
//Statements.
}
while (condition)
```

The major difference between **while** and **do...while** is that with **do...while** you are guaranteed that the statements will be executed at least once.

As with the **for** statement, you can use **break** and **continue** to end the loop early or start a new iteration early, respectively.

## If Statements

An **if** statement executes a block of code, one time, only if a condition is **true**. You can optionally include a block of statements to be executed if the condition is **false**. The following code shows the syntax:

```
if (condition)
{
//Statement block 1.
}
else
{
//Statement block 2.
}
```

The **else** statement and its following block of code are optional. If you have only single statements to execute, you can omit the curly braces and use this syntax:

```
if (condition)
   Statement1;
else
   Statement2;
```

When script execution reaches the **if** statement, *condition* is evaluated. If it is **true**, the first block of statements is executed. If it is **false**, the second block of statements is executed or, if there is no **else**, execution continues with the code that follows.

A variant of the **if** statement lets you test more than one condition and execute statements accordingly. You use the **else if** statement for this purpose as shown here:

```
if (condition1)
{
//Statement block 1.
}
else if (condition2)
{
//Statement block 2.
}
else if (condition3)
{
//Statement block 3.
}
else
{
//More statements.
}
```

As before, the **else** and its associated block of statement are optional. You can have as many **else if** statements as you need. The statements associated with the first **true** condition are executed. This is the case even if more than one condition is true—only the statements associated with the first matching condition are executed.

## Event Handlers

An event handler is a section of script code that responds to an event such as a mouse click. In order to create dynamic, responsive Web pages, you must use event handlers so the document can respond to user input. Events are detected by specific elements in an HTML document, such as hyperlinks and images. The event handlers you will use are as follows:

- **onclick**: Occurs when the user clicks an element with the mouse.

- **onmousedown, onmouseup**: Occur when the user depresses or releases the mouse button on an element.

- **onmouseover, onmouseout**: Occur when the mouse cursor moves over or away from an element.

- **onchange**: Occurs when the value of an <input> element changes.

- **onsubmit, onreset**: Occur when an HTML form is submitted or reset.

Because events are associated with specific HTML elements, they are included as part of the element tag in an attribute that has the same name as the event handler. Here's an example for a button element:

```
<input type="button" onclick="javascript code goes here;" ...>
```

If the code to be executed is short, you can place it directly in the attribute. Otherwise you will place the code in a separate function and then place a call to the function in the attribute.

## Summary

Both JavaScript and the Document Object Model are used in Dynamic HTML to provide the script programmer with a great deal of power and flexibility in creating attractive, dynamic, and interesting Web pages. There's a lot to cover in this area, and this chapter has provided you with only an introduction to the details of DHTML. If you decide to move beyond these basics, you will find plenty of information available on the Web and in books. In the next chapter, I will get away from theory and show you how to use DHTML for some real-world Web page tasks.

# CHAPTER 9

# Real-World DHTML

The previous chapter has given you an introduction to the fundamentals of the Document Object Model (DOM) and JavaScript. You should now have enough background information to use these technologies, collectively known as dynamic HTML (DHTML), in your Web pages. In this chapter I will present some examples of useful things you can do with DHTML.

## Restricting Text Box Input

When your Web page includes a form in which users enter data, it is often a good idea to ensure that the data entered into each field is correct. For example, a field that asks for someone's year of birth should not have letters or punctuation marks entered into it—]]just numbers. Likewise a first name field should be restricted to letters. You can validate user input after the fact, as explained later in this chapter in the section "Validating User Form Input." Sometimes, however, it is better to prevent improper input in the first place by restricting the characters that a user can enter into a text box field. For example, a "numbers only" field would accept numbers. but if the user pressed a non-number key. it would be ignored.

The technique that I will show you relies on a field's **onkeypress** event. As you might expect, this event occurs whenever the user presses a key when the field has the focus. The event procedure calls a function that looks at the key that was pressed. If the key is acceptable, the function will return **true**, which lets the text box accept the keystroke. If the key is not acceptable, the function will return **false**, which causes the text box to reject the keystroke, effectively blocking the character.

The input element must be coded with the **onkeypress** event as follows:

```
<input type="text" onkeypress="return numbersOnly(event)">
```

The **event** argument that is passed to the **numbersOnly()** function is a reference to the action—the key press—that triggered the event. The function can extract the character that was entered from this object.

The **numbersOnly()** function is shown in Listing 9.1. The first two lines of this function will look strange to you. I am not going to explain them beyond saying that they are required to extract the value of the character that was entered from the **event** object that is passed to the function. The remainder of the function is straightforward. It accepts only characters with values in the range 48-57, which are the characters 0-9. By also accepting characters with values less than 31, the function passes through backspace and other editing keys.

**Listing 9.1.** A function to accept numbers only.

```
function numbersOnly(evt)
{
  evt = (evt) ? evt : event;
  var c = (evt.charCode) ? evt.charCode : ((evt.keyCode) ?
    evt.keyCode : ((evt.which) ? evt.which : 0));
  if (c > 31 && (c < 48 || c > 57))
  {
    alert("Numerals only are allowed in this field.");
    return false;
  }
  return true;
}
```

This function accepts only the digits 0-9. If you want to accept negative numbers or numbers with a decimal point, you'll need to modify the function to pass through the decimal point and minus sign characters. By modifying the range of character values accepted, you can also create functions that accept letters only, lowercase letters only, or whatever your page needs.

## Writing Text and HTML to the Document

One of the most powerful things you can do with JavaScript is to write text to the document. This means that the document does not have to be static but can change depending on various factors such as user input.

To write content to the document, use the **write()** method of the **document** object. This method writes the text passed as an argument to the document. If the method is executed within the body of the document, the text appears at that location relative to other document content—in other words, where the script is located. Here's an example that displays the current date in the document:

```
<body>
<p>Greetings! Today's date is
<script type="text/javascript">
<!--
var today = new Date();
document.write("<b>" + today.toDateString() + "</b>");
-->
</script>
</p>
</body>
```

The result in the document is text like this:

Greetings! Today's date is **Thu Aug 12 2004**

From this example, it should be clear that **document.write()** is used to write HTML to the document—in other words, it writes tags and/or content. Here's what happens with the previous example:

1. The first part of the content, **<p>Greetings! Today's date is**, is part of the document's static HTML.

2. The script writes out **Thu Aug 12 2004**.

3. The closing **</p>** tag is part of the static HTML.

The exact same result can be obtained with the following, in which the **** and **** tags are part of the static HTML and the **document.write()** method writes out only the date itself:

```
<body>
<p>Greetings! Today's date is <b>
<script type="text/javascript">
<!--
var today = new Date();
document.write(today.toDateString());
-->
</script>
</b></p>
</body>
```

Another way to use the **document.write()** method is to replace the entire content of the document with new HTML. And I do mean entire content—from the opening **<html>** tag to the closing **</html>** tag. The **document.write()** method replaces the entire document when it is executed in a function in the **<head>** section of the document. You can use this in two ways:

• Execute the function when the document loads. This means that the first thing the user sees will be the dynamically generated document. I'll show you how to call a JavaScript function when the page loads later in this chapter in the section "Creating Rollovers."

• Display a static HTML document initially; then execute the function in response to some user action. The user will first see one document, which is then replaced by the dynamically generated document.

Let's look at example of the second method. This is a simple example—it initially displays a Web page with a text box for the user to enter their name and a button. When the user clicks the button, a function is called that replaces the page with a dynamically generated page that greets the user by name. The HTML for the page is shown in Listing 9.2 and the initial page display is shown in Figure 9.1.

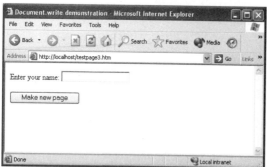
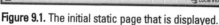

**Figure 9.1.** The initial static page that is displayed.

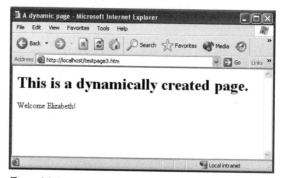

**Figure 9.2.** The dynamic page that is displayed when the user clicks the button.

When the user enters their name in the text box and clicks the button, the document.write() method creates an entirely new page, shown in Figure 9.2.

**Listing 9.2.** Demonstrating the **document.write()** method.

```html
<html>
<head>
<title>Document.write demonstration</title>
<script type="text/javascript">
function writePage(form)
{
  var page;
  page = "<html><head><title>A dynamic page</title></head>";
  page += "<body><h1>This is a dynamically created page.</h1>";
  page += "<p>Welcome " + form.name.value + "!";
  page += "</body></html>"
  document.write(page);
}
</script>
</head>
<body>
<form onsubmit="return false">
<p>Enter your name: <input type="text" name="name"
id="name"></p>
<input type="button" value="Make new page"
onclick="writePage(this.form);" />
</form>
</body>
</html>
```

This example showcases another useful technique. I needed a form on the page because I wanted to display a button, but I did not need to submit the form anywhere. To do this, I included a **<form>** tag that has no **action** attribute and that specifies that the **onsubmit** action returns **false**, which cancels the submit action. The result is a "submissionless" form, useful in many situations such as this one.

## Creating Rollovers

I am sure you have seen rollover effects in many of the Web pages you have visited. A rollover changes some aspect of the page when the mouse cursor moves over it and then changes it back when the mouse cursor moves away. Rollovers are perhaps most commonly use for navigation buttons—when the mouse is over the button it changes appearance so it is perfectly clear which button you are selecting. Rollovers can be used for text effects as well, but I will limit discussion to images.

The first step in creating a rollover is to create or find the images. You'll need two, a "normal" image and a "rollover" image. In most cases, the two images will be the same size and will contains the same text, differing only in color or some other design feature. Figure 9.3 shows an example of two such buttons that I created in a graphics program. I saved then as GIF files with the names HomePageUp.gif (for the "normal" button) and HomePageDown.gif (for the "rolled-over" button).

**Figure 9.3.** Examples of buttons to be used in a rollover.

The next step is to create the hyperlink. If you wanted to use a single image without rollover effects, you would create the link like this (linking to the page index.htm):

```
<a href="index.htm"><img src="imagename"
width="width" height="height" /></a>
```

To create a rollover, you must make use of the **onMouseOver** and **onMouseOut** events to swap your images. The strategy is as follows:

1. The link will initially display the "up" image.

2. The **onMouseOver** event will swap the "down" image to the same location.

3. The **onMouseOut** event will swap the "up" image back.

We will write a JavaScript function called **changeImages()** to perform the swap. For now, let's look at the link tag with the event handlers in place. I have split the tag over several lines to make it easier to read and numbered the lines for easy reference.

### Where Do You Get Buttons?

Many Web designers like to create their own buttons using a graphics program. Some programs even have special features designed to simplify the task of creating rollover effects. You can also find buttons on the Web, and there are a few Websites that let you create custom buttons for download.

```
1. <a href="index.htm"
2.    ONMOUSEOVER="changeImages("HomePageLink",
3.     "HomePageDown.gif"); return true;"
4.    ONMOUSEOUT="changeImages("HomePageLink",
5.     "HomePageUp.gif"); return true;">
6. <img name="HomePageLink" src="HomePageDown.gif" width="140"
7.     height="25" />
8. </a>
```

Now let's see how this works:

- Line 1 is the start of the **<a>** tag including the **href** attribute that specifies the linked-to page.

- Lines 2 and 3 are the **onMouseOver** event handler. This handler calls the **changeImages()** function, passing it two parameters: (1) the name of the image to change, and (2) the name of the new image to display (the "down" image). Be sure to include the **return true**; statement at the end of the handler.

- Lines 4 and 5 are the **onMouseOut** event handler. This works the same way as **onMouseOver**, replacing the "down" image with the "up" image.

- Lines 6 and 7 are the **<img>** tag. Note that the **name** attribute identifies the tag, information that is needed by the **changeImages()** function. The **src** attribute specifies that the "up" image be displayed initially.

- Line 8 closes the link tag.

Now let's look at the **changeImages()** function. It is shown in the following listing:

```
function changeImage(imageName, newImage)
{
    if (document.images)
       document.images[imageName].src = newImage;
}
```

The code in this function is quite simple. The first line—the **if** statement—checks to see that the document does contain at least one image (**<img>** tag). If not, there's nothing to swap so the next line is not executed.

The second line performs the swap. The code **document.images[imageName]** gets a reference to the **<img>** tag with the specified **name** property. Then this image's **src** property is set to the new image. The result is that the new image replaces the original one in the document.

The code presented so far works fine but with one caveat. By default, a browser downloads only those images it is actually displaying. This means that for each rollover, the "down" image will not be downloaded until the first time it is needed. If the network is slow or there is some other problem, this can result in an annoying lag in the rollover effect. You can avoid this problem by precaching the rollover "down" images, downloading them before they are actually needed so they will be instantly available. There are several ways to do this and here's one that I use.

First, create a function called **newImage()** as follows:

```
function newImageX(arg)
  {
     var rslt = new Image();
     rslt.src = arg;
     return rslt;
}
```

This function is passed the URL of an image to preload as its one argument. It then creates a new generic Image object, sets the source to the image to be preloaded, and returns the image to the calling code. This function will be called once for each image that you want to preload.

Next, create another function called **preloadImages()** as shown here:

```
function preloadImages() {
  if (document.images)
  {
     var image1 = newImage("Image1URL");
     var image2 = newImage("Image2URL");
     // additional images as needed.
  }
}
```

For each image that you want to preload, this function calls **newImage()**, passing the URL of the image to preload. To execute this function when the page loads, use the **onLoad** event handler in the document's **<body>** tag:

```
<body ONLOAD="preLoadImages();">
```

The result is that when the page is first loaded, the function is called and the "down" images are preloaded so they are available for instant display. You do not have to preload any images that are displayed in the document when it first loads because they will be downloaded anyway.

## Validating User Form Input

An HTML form provides text and other input fields that let the user enter data in a Web page. When the form is submitted, it is processed on the server and the data is used in whatever way is required, such as placing an online order or entering information in a guest book. In many situations, entry of incorrect data will cause problems on the server, so you would like to check the data that the user enters and verify that it is okay before submitting it. This process is called *validation*.

There are two parts to validation:

1. Checking the data and displaying a message to the user if there is an error.

2. Preventing form submission if the validation fails.

We'll look at both of these tasks here.

There are many different kinds of validation that may be required, most of which apply to text fields where the user will be typing in data. Here are some common examples of things that you might want to verify for a form field:

- The field is not empty.

- The field contains a number.

- The field contains an email address.

- The field data is a certain length, such as 16 characters.

- The field data is a member of a certain list, such as a list of the state abbreviations.

- The field data is a valid telephone number.

I'll present example of the first two types of validation here.

To verify that the field is not empty, we can look at the length of the text in the field. As long as this length is greater than 0, you know the field is not empty. You also need to check that the field data is not **null**, a special JavaScript keyword that means "invalid data." Here's a function for the job:

```
function isNotEmpty(field)
{
    var data = field.value;
    if (data == null || str.length == 0)
    {
        alert("The field may not be left empty.");
        return false;
    }
    else
    {
        return true;
    {
}
```

Verifying that a field contains a number is a bit more complicated. The strategy is to look at each character of the data and make sure the following requirements are met:

- The character - (minus sign) is permitted but only if it's the first character.

- The character . (decimal point) is permitted but only once.

- The digits 0 through 9 are permitted without restriction.

The function shown here does the job:

```
function isNumber(field)
{
    var data = field.value;
    var isNumber = true;
    var alreadyHasDecimal = false;
    var c;

    for (var i = 0; i < data.length; i++)
    {
      c = data.charAt(i).charCode(0);
      if (c == 45) // code for a minus sign.
      {
        if (i == 0)   //OK at first position.
          continue;
        else
        {
          isNumber = false;
          break;
        }
      }
      if (c == 46) //code for decimal point.
      {
        if (!alreadyHasDecimal)
        {
          alreadyHasDecimal = true;
          continue;
        }
        else
        {
          isNumber = false;
          break;
        }
      }
      if (c < 48 || c > 57)   //Codes for the digits.
          isNumber = false;
    }
```

```
if (isNumber)
  return true;
else
{
alert("The field does not contain a valid number.");
return false;
}
}
```

These two validation functions give you the general idea for other kinds of validation—write a function that checks the data in a field and returns **true** if the data is okay, **false** if not. But how then do you combine all these validation functions in a page so that all the form data is validated and the form is submitted only if all validation tests are passed?

First, write a master validation function that calls all the individual validation functions that are needed. For example, you might need to call **isNotEmpty()** on several text fields and **isNumber()** on several others. The master function must return **false** if any of the individual validations failed and true only if none of them failed.

The answer lies in the **<form>** tag. Normally a form is submitted when the Submit button is clicked. But if you put code in the button's **onsubmit** event procedure that returns the value **false**, the submission is aborted. If the return value is **true**, the submission goes ahead normally. Thus, the **<form>** tag will look like this (scriptname is the name of the server script to which the form is being submitted):

```
<form method="GET" action="scriptname" onsubmit=
   "return validateAll(this);">
```

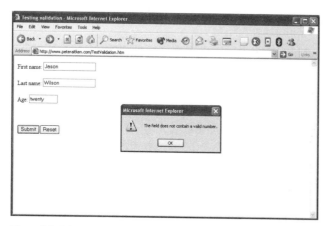

**Figure 9.4.** A forms page with data validation.

Here's how it works. When the user clicks the Submit button, the **onsubmit** event is triggered and the **validateAll()** function is called. The argument **this** is a JavaScript keyword that provides a reference to the current form. Code in the **validateAll()** function calls the individual validation functions as needed and returns **true** or **false** to the event handler. If **true** is returned—if all validation was okay—the submission continues. If **false** is returned, the submission is halted so the user can fix the data.

Listing 9.3 presents the HTML code for a Web forms page that uses this validation technique. Figure 9.4 shows the page after data has been entered and Submit clicked. Because the user entered a word for his age rather than a number, the indicated message is displayed and the form is not submitted.

**Listing 9.3.** An HTML document that uses the validation techniques presented n the text.

```
<html>
<head>
<title>Testing validation</title>
<script type="text/javascript">
<!--
function validateAll(form)
{
    if (isNotEmpty(form.firstname) && isNotEmpty(form.last-
name)
        && isNumber(form.age))
          return true;
    else
          return false;
}

function isNotEmpty(field)
{
    var data = field.value;
    if (data == null || str.length == 0)
    {
        alert("The field may not be left empty.");
        return false;
    }
    else
    {
        return true;
    {
}

function isNumber(field)
{
    var data = field.value;
    var notNumber = false;
    var alreadyHasDecimal = false;
    var c;

    for (var i = 0; i < data.length; i++)
    {
      c = data.charAt(i).charCode(0);
      if (c == 45) // code for a minus sign.
```

```
      {
        if (i == 0)   //OK at first position.
          continue;
        else
        {
          notNumber = true;
          break;
        }
      }
      if (c == 46) //code for decimal point.
      {
        if (!alreadyHasDecimal)
        {
          alreadyHasDecimal = true;
          continue;
        }
        else
        {
          notNumber = true;
          break;
        }
      }
      if (c < 48 || c > 57)   //Codes for the digits.
          notNumber = true;
    }
    if (notNumber)
    {
      alert("The field does not contain a valid number.");
      return false;
    }
    else
      return true;
}
//--></script>
</head>

<body>

<form method="GET" action="cgi-bin/savedata.pl"
   onsubmit="return validateAll(this);">
<p>
  First name: <input type="text" name="firstname"
size="20"></p>
  <p>Last name: <input type="text" name="lastname"
size="20"></p>
  <p>Age: <input type="text" name="age" size="9"></p>
  <p> </p>
```

```
<p><input type="submit" value="Submit" name="B1" />
    <input type="reset" value="Reset" name="B2" /></p>
</form>
</body>
</html>
```

# Formatting Numbers for Display

When you use JavaScript for numerical calculations, you usually want to display the results in the
Web page. Rather than letting JavaScript decide how
to format the number, you can do it yourself, specifying the number of decimal places to use and
whether to use comma separators and/or a currency
symbol.

To control the number of decimal places, you can
use the **toFixed()** method. This method takes one
number as its argument, the desired number of decimal places in the range 0-20. The return is a string
containing the number with the specified formatting.
Here's an example:

```
var num = 123.4567;
var s = num.toFixed(2);
```

At this point, the variable s contains the value
123.46. Note that the **toFixed()** method uses round-
ing. If **num** were equal to 123.4549, the result would
be rounded down to 123.45.

What about currency amounts? Adding a lead-
ing dollar sign seems easy; in this example the value is displayed with two decimals
using the **toFixed()** method:

```
document.write("$" + num.toFixed(2));
```

But what about negative values? You certainly wouldn't want to display a negative currency value as $-123.45, so the technique just presented won't work. By con-
vention, negative money values are displayed in parentheses: ($123.45). The func-
tion **formatCurrency()** showed in Listing 9.4 does the trick. Passed a value and a
symbol, it returns a string consisting of the number formatted with two decimal
places, the leading symbol, and negative values in parentheses. You'd call it like this:

```
var num = -599.95;
document.write(formatCurrency("$", num);
```

## toString() or Not toString()

To be displayed on a page, a number
must be converted into a string. In most
cases JavaScript will do this for you automatically, as in this example:

```
var num = 456.789;
document.write(num);
```

When you need to explicitly convert a
number to a string, as is required for some
of the techniques presented here, you can
use the **toString()** method:

```
var num = 456.789;
var s;
s = num.toString();
```

Now the variable s contains a string
representation of **num**.

**Listing 9.4.** A function to format currency values.

```
function formatCurrency(symbol, value)
{
// Returns value as a string with 2 decimal places, the
specified
// leading symbol, and negative values in parentheses.

  var negative = false;
  //Convert negative values to positive.
  if (value < 0)
  {
    value = -value;
    negative = true;
  }

  var s = symbol + value.toFixed(2);
  if (negative)
    return "(" + s + ")";
  else
    return s;
}
```

# Including JavaScript from External Files

One advantage of using JavaScript functions in your script programming is that you end up with a collection of independent script modules for performing a variety of tasks. You can reuse these functions in multiple pages by simply copying them from the original HTML document and pasting them into a new one. But this can be a lot of work, and it also means that if you modify the code in a function, you will have to copy the changes in all the pages that use the function. A much better idea is to keep your JavaScript functions in a separate file and include it in every HTML document that needs the functions.

An external JavaScript file is simply a plain-text file that contains the JavaScript functions. You do not need to include the **<script>** and **</script>** tags—just the pure JavaScript code. By tradition such files are given the .js extension, although this is not required.

Then, in each HTML document that needs the JavaScript, include a tag like this:

```
<script type="text/javascript" src="URL"></script>
```

*URL* is the URL of the script file. Use just the name if the file is in the same folder as the HTML document. The script file can be located anywhere, even on another server, in which case you must include a full URL. This can be an advantage because a single script file on a single server can be used by multiple pages on multiple servers.

# Displaying Random Images

Many Web authors display images on their pages to make them more attractive and interesting to visitors. But what if the user sees the same old image every time they visit your page—might they get bored? You can avoid this problem by displaying a different, random image each time the page is loaded.

The first step is to gather the images and determine their heights and widths. Then you can write the script that will create an array containing all the information about each image—name or URL, width, and height:

```
var images = new Array();
images[0] = {src:"images/cat.jpg", width:"350", height:"225"};
images[1] = {src:"images/dog.jpg", width:"375", height:"240"};
images[2] = {src:"images/parrot.jpg", width:"225",
height:"290"};
images[3] = {src:"images/gerbil.jpg", width:"260",
height:"200"};
```

This array has only four images, but you can include as many as you like. This code takes advantage of a feature of JavaScript arrays in which each element can contain more than one named data item. In this case, each array item contains a **src** item, a **width** item, and a **height** item. This code should be put in the body section of the page right after the opening **<body>** tag.

The next step is to write a function that randomly selects one of the images and returns the HTML for an **<img>** tag to display the image. Here's the code, which you'll place in the document head section:

```
function selectImage()
{
  var idx = Math.floor(Math.random() * images.length);
  var tag = "<img src='"  + images[idx].src + "' width='"
  tag += images[idx].width + "' height='"
  tag += images[idx].height + "'>";
  return tag;
}
```

The first line of this tag generates an index into the array that we declared earlier. Here's how it works:

- **Math.random()** returns a random number between 0 and 1. Note that the between is important—you will never get exactly 0 or 1, but you may get any value between them, such as 0.00001 or 0.99999.

- Multiplying this value by the length of the **images** array results in a number between 0 and 4 (again the *between* is important).

- Using the **Math.floor()** method returns the next smaller integer—in other words, the value 0, 1, 2, or 3—to serve as the index into the array.

Finally, the function puts together an **<img>** tag containing the source, width, and height of the randomly selected image.

The final step is to write the **<img>** tag to the document at the location where you want the image displayed:

```
<script type="text/javascript">
<!--
document.write(selectImage())
-->
</script>
```

The result is that each time the page is loaded, an image is randomly selected for display.

## Summary

In this chapter I have shown you a few of the things you can do with DHTML. While some Web pages do not need DHTML, many will benefit from it. It's a terrific technique to create interesting Web pages that present information in an eye-catching manner.

# CHAPTER 10

# Selling Online and Site Security

Websites are becoming an ever more important part of business operations. An increasing number of companies are not only making information available on the Web, but are also letting customers shop and place orders on the Web. This kind of Website places whole new demands on the Website developer, including stricter requirements for security. This chapter takes a look at what's necessary if you want to sell online.

## Selling Online

Many people's experience with online shopping is with large retailers such as L.L.Bean, Crate and Barrel, and Amazon.com. These firms have tens of thousands of products, automated ordering, inventory and shipping software, and a team of professional Web experts making sure everything runs smoothly. This type of operation is clearly beyond the scope of this book and almost surely beyond the scope of what you, the reader, needs to do.

But you don't have to be huge to sell online. Many successful merchants have only a few products, filling orders themselves doing the packing and shipping in the garage or a spare bedroom. Website requirements are a lot simpler in such situations, well within the capabilities of most "amateur" Web designers. But there's one unavoidable sticking point—you must be able to accept credit card payments, Visa and MasterCard at a minimum. There are two parts to this:

- Merchant account. You cannot simply deposit credit card payments in a standard bank account; you need a special type of account called a merchant account.

- Security. Customers are understandably leery about giving out their credit card number. You must implement security measures to ensure that their account information is safe, and you must also make potential customers feel safe.

Let's look at these two aspects of online selling.

# Accepting Credit Card Payments

There are several options for the online merchant who needs to accept credit card payments. Which one suits you will depend on the nature of your business. What about fees? Credit card processing cannot be free. The details vary from plan to plan, but in general here's what you can expect:

- There may or may not be a one-time charge for initial account setup.

- There will be a fixed monthly account fee, perhaps from $10 to $20.

- There will be a fixed per-transaction fee, probably in the 20 to 50 cents range.

- There will be a percent fee per transaction, typically from 2 to 5 percent.

When shopping for a merchant account, you need to pay attention to the fees, of course, but there are other questions to ask. For example, how quickly do the proceeds from a charge appear in your account, and how does the provider handle chargebacks (when a customer disputes a charge)?

## Your Own Merchant Account

For many operations, the simplest approach may be to get your own merchant account. Customers will send you their credit card information along with the order, and then you process the payment yourself. If you already have a merchant account, perhaps for a phone order business, this would be an obvious choice. The downside is that each charge must be processed manually, and if your order volume increases, this may take too much time.

In a typical scenario, you would design an HTML form for the customer to enter the order and credit card information. You would program the form to send you the information by email or one of the other available methods (see Chapter 6 for details on using HTML forms). You would need to implement the appropriate security on your site to protect the customers' sensitive information. This is discussed later in the chapter.

You can inquire at your bank about setting up a merchant account. There are also online services for setting up a merchant account.

## Automated Credit Card Processing

Some merchant accounts offer a service by which Web orders are processed automatically. The customer enters their card information on a special Web page, which might be part of your site or might be part of the merchant account provider's site. When they submit the order, the credit card is processed right away. If the charge is accepted, the money is credited to your account and you receive an email with the order details so you can fill it. This removes the need for manual processing of charges and is better suited for online businesses that process more than a few orders a day. One place offering this service is www.charge.com.

## PayPal

PayPal (www.paypal.com) started as a secure and convenient way for making secure electronic payments and has become very popular with users of the online auction services such as eBay (which now owns PayPal). The basic premise was simple. If you wanted to be able to receive payments via PayPal, you had to set up an account. Anyone wanting to pay you would go to the PayPal Website and send a payment to you, either from their credit card or from their own PayPal account. You would receive notification of the payment and could safely ship the goods that had been bought. PayPal would take a small commission from each transaction.

As online commerce became more widespread, the PayPal folks realized that a lot of people would like to be able to accept credit cards on their own Website without the hassles of setting up a shopping cart or their own merchant account.

If you are selling only one or a few items, you may want to consider PayPal's Buy Now buttons. Each button, an example of which is shown in Figure 10.1, is linked to a single specific product. When the user clicks the button, they go to a custom PayPal payment page to enter their ordering information. What's nice about this approach is that you can customize the payment page to have the same "look and feel" as your own Website. When making a purchase, users may not even be aware that they have left your site.

PayPal also offers a recurring payment option. For example, perhaps you have created an investing tips Website and want to charge subscribers five dollars a month to read your pearls of wisdom. PayPal lets you set up a way for users to make automatic monthly payments for their subscription.

**Figure 10.1.** A PayPal Buy Now button lets users pay for a specific product using the PayPal service.

One thing I like about the PayPal service is that you create your own Website to display and describe your products and the customer goes to a PayPal site only for the purchase part of the process. Fees are reasonable, too—you pay only a percentage of each sale with no setup or software fees.

## eBay Stores

Almost everyone has heard of eBay, the online auction site (www.ebay.com). In addition to its auction services, it offers something called eBay Stores, a way for a merchant to have their own shop on the eBay site. Your store will consist of one or more pages (depending on the number of items you have for sale) containing pictures and descriptions of the items and a Buy It Now button for each one.

There are several downsides to eBay stores. You have essentially no control over the appearance of the listings—they are displayed in eBay's format, shown in Figure

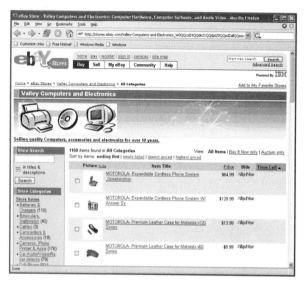

**Figure 10.2.** Listings in an eBay Store are in the standard eBay listing format.

10.2. There's never any doubt that the customer is on an eBay site, and there's really no way for you to make your store and listings stand out from other ones (except with a lower price perhaps!). There's a monthly listing fee for each item that you must pay regardless of whether it sells and then a percentage commission on each sale.

There are advantages as well. Your store's inventory will be included in eBay's powerful search tool, letting potential customers find items in your store even if they have never heard of you and your store. Also, there's no doubt that eBay attracts millions of potential customers, but that has to be weighed against the competition from the many other eBay merchants.

## Yahoo! Store

Yahoo! Store is one of the oldest online storefronts out there. Shown in Figure 10.3, Yahoo! Store is not by any means the lowest-priced product on the market, but

it is probably the most popular one. Unlike eBay and PayPal, Yahoo! Store is not targeted at one particular type of online merchants. Instead it has the flexibility built in to allow inexperienced users to quickly build good stores while giving more advanced users the capability to build a store to their exact specifications, which means they are very customizable. They offer comprehensive reporting and statistics packages that make Yahoo! Store one of the best e-commerce solutions available.

The major downside for many merchants is that Yahoo! still does not allow non-U.S. merchants to sign up for its Store product. If you are willing to pay the premium price, this may be a good solution for you.

**Figure 10.2.** Listings in an eBay Store are in the standard eBay listing format.

I do want to make this extremely clear: using your own merchant account and shopping cart software is always the best way to go. Using an online store is not a very high selling point to a potential customer.

## Shopping Carts

A shopping card provides the most flexible Web shopping experience. If you have done any online ordering, you have probably used a shopping cart. Users can browse all of your merchandise and, for each item, click an "add to cart" button. Users can also view the contents of their cart, deleting items or changing the quantity. When they are finished shopping, they check out by entering their payment and shipping information.

Shopping carts differ greatly in their features, ease of use, cost, and number of customizable features. Some shopping carts provide a merchant account as part of the service, while others must be used with your existing merchant account. If your business has grown to the point where it needs a full-fledged shopping cart, it is wise to shop around to find the combination of features and costs that you need. Here is a list of some providers of shopping carts:

www.paypal.com
www.2checkout.com
www.monstercommerce.com
www.mycart.net
www.litecommerce.com

Some Web hosting providers offer shopping carts as well. For example, Yahoo! Merchant Services (smallbusiness.yahoo.com) offers several packages that combine Web hosting with shopping carts and other services for the online business.

# Website Security

Standard Web traffic—HTTP requests and responses—travel over the Internet in unencrypted form. Anyone who intercepts such traffic can read it with no effort whatsoever. Obviously this is not good for requests that include personal information and credit card information! To meet this need, Netscape developed a protocol called Hypertext Transfer Protocol Over Secure Sockets Layer, usually abbreviated HTTP over SSL or simply HTTPS. This protocol is supported by essentially all Web browsers and servers.

## How Does Encryption Work?

Almost all encryption used on the internet is public key encryption. This technique is based on creating two long numbers that are related to one another. One number, called the public key, is used to encrypt messages. The other number, called the private key, is required to decrypt messages. As the name implies, you make your public key public so anyone can send you an encrypted message. Because only you have the private key, only you can decrypt the message. When HTTPS is used, the keys are handled automatically by the server and browser.

Here's how it works. When you are submitting sensitive information from a Web page to the server, the URL will start with https:// rather than http:// — a signal to use encryption. The information is encrypted by the browser so that anyone intercepting it cannot read it. When the server receives the information, it is decrypted and processed. Information coming back to the user is encrypted by the server and decrypted by the browser. The HTTPS protocol supports the use of digital certificates to permit identity verification. Your browser will display a symbol, usually a small padlock, when you are using a secure connection. This is shown for Internet Explorer in Figure 10.4.

**Figure 10.4.** Internet Explorer displays a small padlock in the status bar when using a secure connection.

## Security beyond the Website

When you are accepting credit card payments, your security arrangements need to include more than your Website. Specifically, what records are kept of credit card information? If you keep paper or electronic records of customers' credit card numbers, you must secure these against theft or unauthorized access. The best approach, in my opinion, is to destroy this information after the transaction is complete — there's no valid reason to keep it, after all. At most you might retain the last four digits of the card number in case the customer inquires about the order.

There's nothing special about creating a secure page — it's the server configuration that provides the security, and there are various ways in which this can be accomplished. You cannot establish a secure connection simply by accessing a page on a regular server using HTTPS — it will not work. Not all Web service providers offer HTTPS, so you'll have to check. Then follow the instructions from your service provider for setting up the site.

Note that if you decide to use one of the commercial solutions, such as PayPal or a shopping cart, all the security will be — or at least should be — taken care of.

## Summary

Online shopping is becoming more and more popular. If you want to get in on this growing method of doing business, you have numerous options. The one common feature is the ability to accept credit card payments. Depending on the number of items you have to sell and the complexity of your business, you should be able to find an online merchant solution that's right for you.

# Part 3

. . . . . . . . . . . . . . . . . . . . . . .

# Deconstructing Web Pages – Some Real Life Dos and Don'ts

Many artists have become better by learning from the techniques of other artists. By seeing how the experts do things, you have a good start on expressing your own creativity. In these three chapters you will see how the Web Design gurus behind nine popular Websites worked their magic.

. . . . . . . . . . . . . . . . . . . . . . .

# CHAPTER 11

# Deconstructing Web Pages, Part I

One of the best ways to fine-tune your Web design skills is to look at the work of other Webmasters. There are millions of Web pages out there, ranging from the horrid to the excellent, and each one has the potential to teach you a lesson, even if it's a lesson on what not to do! This is the first of three chapters on deconstructing Web pages—that is, looking at specific Websites and then examining the code behind their pages to see how it was done. For the most part I will emphasize the positive, but where appropriate I may point out a few places where things could have been done better—at least in my opinion! I will not be deconstructing every aspect of each page's design, just those things that are most important.

Is it legitimate to examine and copy other people's pages? Of course you will not really be copying them, otherwise your page would be identical! But it's perfectly okay to examine the HTML of other pages and adapt the same coding techniques to your own pages. The Web is, after all, an open medium by definition, and anyone who posts a Web page knows it isn't secret.

## Deconstructing — How To

Before we get started, let's look at the techniques used to deconstruct a Web page. The most important is, of course, to get the page's HTML source code. In Internet Explorer this is done with the View|Source command, and other browsers have equivalent commands. This opens the page's HTML source in Notepad, from where you can view, print, or save the source.

You'll soon find that the HTML for many pages is a mess, with no attention paid to formatting. Tags are run together on the same line or split over lines, and it can be very difficult to read. Of course the browser does not care—remember, white space is irrelevant in HTML—

> ## Quick Tip:
>
> If you are serious about Web design, I highly recommend that you download and install Mozilla Firefox. Why? Several reasons. First, it is fully standards compliant. This means that your page will be displayed correctly according to the HTML specification. Second, there is a nifty extension written by Chris Pederick called Web Developer. This extension adds to the browser's interface a toolbar that has all sorts of tools to make your job as a Webmaster easier. You can download Firefox from www.getfirefox.com nd then get the Web Developer plug-in from http://downloads.mozdev.org/Web developer/Webdeveloper.xpi.

but we humans certainly do care! Fortunately, there are several free or inexpensive programs called HTML formatters available that will automatically turn messy HTML into nicely formatted HTML that is easy to dissect. Search Google for "HTML formatter" to see what's available.

The next step that I take is to see if the page uses Cascading Style Sheets (CSS). If so, much of the page formatting will be defined in the style sheet and not in the HTML, and it can be very confusing to figure out why a page displays a certain way if you are not aware of its style sheet! Look for a tag like this in the document's **<head>** section:

```
<link rel="stylesheet" href="/index.css" type="text/css" />
```

You can download and view the style sheet by combining the page's URL with the href attribute from the **<link>** tag. For example, suppose the **<link>** tag in the preceding line of code was in a page with the URL www.somewhere.com. Putting them together gives you www.somewhere.com/index.css. Navigate to that URL with your browser and the style sheet will be displayed.

The final tool for deconstructing a Web page is sorting out the images. In some pages it may not be clear which **<img>** tag in the HTML corresponds with which image on the page. You can identify most images by right-clicking them in the browser and selecting Save Picture As from the pop-up menu (this is Internet Explorer's command, but other browsers have something similar). The name suggested is the image file name, and you can then easily locate the corresponding **<img>** tag in the HTML source (you do not have to actually save the image).

This does not work, however, if the image is a link because the pop-up menu will have link-related rather than image-related commands. Then you will have to work backwards, starting with the **<img>** tag to identify the image. Here's how:

1. Locate the **<img>** tag of interest in the HTML source.

2. Make note of its **src** attribute.

## Watch for Absolute Style Sheet and Image URLs.

For the techniques described in the preceding section for getting a page's images and style sheet, it is assumed that the links are *relative*—in other words, they give the location of the image or style sheet relative to the location of the page itself. This is the way most pages are done, but not all. A few give the absolute URLs of style sheets and/or images and in some cases keep these items on a totally different server from the page itself (eBay is one example of this). You'll have to look out for this and use the style sheet or image URL by itself, not combined with the page's URL.

3. Combine the src attribute with the URL of the page. You would end up with something like www.somewhere.com/images/banner.gif.

4. Navigate to that URL in your browser. The corresponding image will display by itself.

With these techniques at your disposal, you are ready to get started. In the following sections I will concentrate on deconstructing the more interesting elements of a page design. To explain every detail of the page would not be very interesting, but with the information you have learned in the other chapters of this book, you will be able to figure it out. I'll start by deconstructing my own company's Website.

## Remember, Things Change!

Few major Websites remain unchanged for long periods of time. The pages I am deconstructing in this chapter are as they were as this book was being written. If you go there now, things may be different. Use the screen shots that I have provided in this chapter as your guide and not the page's current appearance.

# Deconstructing CoffeeCup.com

My company started as a small outfit offering only a single software product and has grown into a successful operation offering Web hosting as well as a wide range of Web design and other software. The home page, shown in Figure 11.1, is the portal for thousands of existing and potential customers to evaluate and purchase CoffeeCup's products. It has to be attractive and easy to navigate. Let's see how we accomplished this.

**Figure 11.1.** The CoffeeCup.com home page.

## The Head Section

First, look at the page's **<head>** section. While this is not visible to the user, it is, as you have learned, important for the search engines. Here are the important parts of this section of the HTML:

```
<head>
<title>CoffeeCup - HTML Editor, Web Hosting, FTP &amp; Web
Design Software</title>
<meta name="description" content="An Internet Pioneering
Software and Web Hosting Company. Download HTML Editor, FTP,
&amp; Web Design Software" />
<meta name="keywords" content="html, editor, html editor,
Web, hosting, Web design, host, ftp, flash, java, download,
free, software, shareware, site, page, Website, Webpage,
internet, templates, search engine submission" />
<link rel="stylesheet" href="/index.css" type="text/css" />
</head>
```

You can see that in this part of the page we followed good authoring practices and provided a descriptive title, a description, and a list of keywords. In addition, there is a link to a style sheet, which, as you will soon see, is an important part of this page's design.

Now let's get to the visual parts of the page, starting from the top

## The Navigation Tabs

At the top of the CoffeeCup home page is a series of navigation tabs. The CoffeeCup tab is active and the other tabs are links that take you other pages on the site. Tabs are a popular and effective way to design a page, and there are various ways they can be created. We accomplished this with a combination of HTML and style sheet rules. The HTML for these tabs is shown here:

```
<div id="navTab">
    <h1 class="cc"><a
href="http://www.coffeecup.com/"><span>HTML
    Editor - FTP - Web Design - Software</span></a></h1>

    <h1 class="bd"><a href="http://bluedomino.coffeecup.com">
<span>Web Hosting</span></a></h1>

    <b class="sf"><a href="http://submitfire.coffeecup.com/">
<span>Search Engine Submission</span></a></b>

    <b class="ic"><a href="http://instant.coffeecup.com/">
<span>Website Templates</span></a></b>
```

```
<b class="cs"><a href="http://copysite.coffeecup.com/">
<span>Copyright Registration</span></a></b>
</div>
```

Examining this code, you can see the following:

- The HTML for the entire set of tabs is enclosed in a **<div>** tag with the **id** attribute of "**navTab**".

- Each tab is in its own tag, either an **<h1>** or a **<b>** tag, and each tag is assigned a different **class** attribute.

- Each tab tag includes a hyperlink to the destination URL and some text that is within a **<span>** tag.

Looking at this HTML, you may wonder where the tab display, which is clearly images and not text, comes from. Enter the style sheet, stage left. We did this with a style sheet, and the relevant part of the style sheet is shown here:

```
#navTab              { margin:auto;
padding:0px; width:770px; display:block; }

#navTab span     { display:none; }

#navTab h1.cc a { width:181px;
height:35px; background:
url(/images/tab_lg_coffeecup.gif) no-
repeat; cursor:pointer; display:block;
float:left; }

#navTab h1.bd a { width:118px;
height:35px; background:
url(/images/tab_sm_bluedomino.gif) no-
repeat; cursor:pointer; display:block;
float:left; }

#navTab b.sf a  { width:118px; height:35px; background:
url(/images/tab_sm_submitfire.gif) no-repeat; cursor:pointer;
display:block; float:left; }

#navTab b.ic a  { width:118px; height:35px; background:
url(/images/tab_sm_instant.gif) no-repeat; cursor:pointer;
display:block; float:left; }

#navTab b.cs a  { width:118px; height:35px; background:
url(/images/tab_sm_copysite.gif) no-repeat; cursor:pointer;
display:block; float:left; }
```

## Class vs. id

The main difference between these two attributes is that you can assign a given **id** value to only one tag in the document, whereas the same **class** value can be given to as many tags as needed. That's true in theory, at least. Most browsers do not enforce the unique id rule, so if you use the same id value more than once you won't get an error message. Don't do it, however! The value of an id attribute often lies in the fact that it is unique, and having multiple id attributes with the same value may give unpredictable results in some situations.

Now you can see how the tabs are created. Let's examine these style rules one at a time.

- The first rule defines some basic formatting for the **<div>** tag that has an **id** attribute of "**navTab**".

- The second rule specifies that anything within a **<span>** tag is not displayed. Thus, the text in the HTML will not be displayed.

- The selector for the third style rule, **h1.cc a**, is rather complex. In plain English it says, "Apply this rule to **<a>** tags that are within **<h1>** tags that have the **class** attribute set to 'cc'." The rule says to display in the background the image /images/tab_lg_coffeecup.gif at a size of 181 x 35 pixels. Since this rule applies only to the first **<h1>** tag in the HTML, the end result is that the specified image is displayed as the hyperlink for that tab.

- The remaining style rules define selectors and rules for the other four tabs and work in much the same way.

You may be wondering why we created two of the tabs with **<h1>** tags and the others with **<b>** tags. This has nothing to do with visual appearance because the final display of these elements is controlled completely by the style sheet rules. Rather it is for the search engines. Information in heading tags such as **<h1>** is often given more weight than other content, and we wanted to emphasize the information in these two tabs.

## The Navigation Bar and Banner

Immediately below the tabs you'll see a navigation bar that displays three important links on the left and the current date on the right. Note that this bar is the same color as the active tab, which makes it look as if the active tab is part of the page—a nice visual touch if I do say so myself! The HTML for the navigation bar is this:

```
<div id="navBar">

<a href="http://www.coffeecup.com/sales/" title="Order
CoffeeCup Software">Order Software</a>

<a href="http://www.coffeecup.com/software/" title="Download
Trial Versions of CoffeeCup Software">Trial Software
Downloads</a>

<a href="http://www.coffeecup.com/help/" title="Get Sales and
Software Support">Customer Care</a>

</div>

<div id="navDate">12-13-2004</div>
```

Note how we used **<div>** tags and **id** attributes to associate these page elements with the style sheet rules. The appearance of these elements is totally controlled by the style sheet, and the relevant rules are shown here:

```
#navBar          { width:772px; height:20px; clear:both;
text-indent:1em; padding-top:4px; background-color:#606;
font:bold .9em arial,sans-serif; color:#fff; }

#navBar a        { padding:0px 6px; font:bold 1em
tahoma,arial,sans-serif; color:#fff; text-decoration:none; }

#navBar a:hover { text-decoration:underline; color:#ffffcc; }

#navDate         { position:absolute; top:42px; left:auto;
right:8px; font:bold .8em tahoma,arial,sans-serif;
color:#fff; }
```

There are four rules here, as follows:

- The first rule applies to anything in the **<div>** tag with the id attribute equal to "**navBar**"—in other words, the three hyperlinks. Among other things, this rule sets the display width, the font color and size, and the background color.

- The second rule applies to hyperlinks within the same **<div>** tag and specifies details of their display such as font and color.

- The third rule applies to hyperlinks over which the mouse is hovering and specifies an underline effect.

- The last rule applies to anything in the **<div>** tag with the **id** attribute equal to "**navDate**"—in other words, the date.

The page banner—with the photo of the person holding the puzzle pieces—is done with the following **<img>** tag:

```
<img src="/images/html-software.gif" height="120" width="770"
alt="CoffeeCup - HTML Editor, Web Hosting, FTP, &amp; Web
Design Software" />
```

Note how we used the **alt** attribute to include some keywords for the search engines.

## The Main Page Content

The main content of the page is contained in the two columns below the banner. The left column contains three lists of links to software downloads, and the right column contains three independent sections with information about and links to other services and products. I will not analyze every detail of these parts of the page but rather pull out the design techniques that are most interesting. There are two basic ways to create the kind of block layout that is used in this section of the page: tables and style sheets. As you'll see, both are used in this page.

The entire left column is contained within the following tags:

```
<div id="leftCol>
...
</div>
```

You can probably already guess that this tag is used to associate the column with style sheet rules—and here is the rule:

```
#leftCol          { margin:6px 0px 0px; padding-left:6px;
width:375px; float:left; }
```

The important parts of this rule are **width** and **float**. By specifying that the content within this **<div>** tag be 375 pixels wide and float on the left, this simple rule has defined it as a column. There's a similar rule for the right column that differs only in having **float** set to **right**, defining the right column. Yes, you could do essentially the same thing with tables, but we think this is simpler and more elegant. Plus, when we want to change the layout of the page, we only need to edit the CSS and can leave the HTML code unchanged!

Within the **<div id="leftCol">** tag are nested several more **<div>** tags, each with its own **id** or **class** attribute. Each of these has its own style rules that specify the precise placement and appearance. Within some of these **<div>** tabs are HTML tables to arrange the software titles and download links. Style sheet rules are also used for the table. For example, here's the code for a single table row:

```
<tr>
<td class="ttlName">&raquo;   <a href="/free-ftp/"
title="Free FTP">Free FTP</a></td>
<td class="ttlLink"><a href="/freestuff/" title="Download
Free FTP"><span>Download Free FTP</span></a></td>
</tr>
```

You can see that the cell for the first column, which contains the software description, has a different **class** attribute than the cell for the second column, which contains the link. The associated style rules, shown here, control the display of these two cells (the **#buildit** selector references the **<div>** tag that the table is within). These rules specify the appearance and placement of the elements in the table as well as the link formatting:

```
#buildIt .ttlName { width:235px; font: bold 1em arial,sans-
serif; color:#F80; text-indent:10px; text-align:left; }
```

```
#buildIt .ttlName a, #buildIt .ttlName  a:visited { font:
bold 1em arial,sans-serif; color:#000; text-decoration:none;
}

#buildIt .ttlName a:hover, #buildIt .ttlName a:active { text-
decoration:underline; }

#buildIt .ttlLink span { width:135px; }

#buildIt .ttlLink span { display:none; }

#buildIt .ttlLink a { width:94px; height:16px; background:
url(/images/fpdlnow.gif) no-repeat; cursor:pointer;
display:block; }
```

We created the right column of the CoffeeCup.com home page in the same manner, using **<div>** tags and style sheet rules to control placement and formatting.

## Summary

If there's one lesson I'd like you to take home from the CoffeeCup.com home page, it's that you can do your entire page formatting with style sheets. Not only that, using style sheets is often easier than using embedded HTML formatting tags. Some people hesitate to use style sheets because the HTML tags they already know seem easier in some way. In the long run, however, you will certainly save time and hassles by getting a good grounding in CSS and using it for your page design.

# Deconstructing eBay.com

eBay is one of the best known and most visited sites on the Web. It sells, mostly by auction, pretty much everything and anything under the sun. The home page, shown in Figure 11.2, provides links to different parts of the eBay site and ways to search for items or browse by category. Let's look at some of the more interesting parts of the page.

**Figure 11.2.** eBay's home page is the entry point into its auction services.

## The Head Section

Starting with the **<head>** section, let's look at the various elements it contains. First are three important tags for search engines, the meta tags for keywords and descriptions and the **<title>** tag:

```
<meta name="description" content="Buy and sell electronics,
cars, clothing, apparel, collectibles, sporting goods, digi-
tal cameras, and everything else on eBay, the world's online
marketplace. Sign up and begin to buy and sell - auction or
buy it now - almost anything on eBay.com.">
<meta name="keywords" content="ebay, electronics, cars,
clothing, apparel, collectibles, sporting goods, ebay, digi-
tal cameras, antiques, tickets, jewelry, online shopping,
auction, online auction">
<title>eBay - New & used electronics, cars, apparel, col-
lectibles, sporting goods & more at low prices</title>
```

Next we find a script include that imports the script from the specified file into the page:

```
<SCRIPT
SRC="http://include.ebaystatic.com/js/v/us/homepage.js">
</SCRIPT>
```

You can view included script files such as this one by navigating to the URL in your browser. You will be given the option of opening or saving the file; you should select Save. Then open the file in a text editor to view the code. You can look at this file if you wish, but I am not going to go into details about what it does.

Next there's a link to an external style sheet:

```
<link rel="stylesheet" type="text/css"
href="http://include.ebaystatic.com/aw/pics/us/css/homepage.c
ss" />
```

You can view the contents of the CSS file as described earlier in this chapter. You'll see, however, that the eBay page does not make use of styles as heavily as some pages do, such as the CoffeeCup.com page that was deconstructed earlier in the chapter.

Finally we see some embedded style rules. Why did the page author include an external style sheet as well as embedded rules? This is actually a useful technique. Because the embedded rules override any conflicting rules in the external style sheet, you can make minor modifications to the page appearance without having to edit the main style sheet.

```
<style type="text/css">
.buttonsm {font-size: 11px; cursor: hand;}
</style>
```

```
<style type="text/css">
.buttonsm {font-size: 11px; cursor: hand;}
</style>
```

## The Navigation Tabs

Near the top of eBay's home page is a set of five navigation tabs—Buy, Sell, My eBay, and so on. These tabs are created very simply. The structure of the top portion of the page is accomplished with an HTML table, and the five tabs are hyperlink images within one of the table cells. Here's the code:

```
<td height="24" nowrap valign="bottom" width="100%">

<a href="http://hub.ebay.com/buy?ssPageName=h:h:cat:US">
<img border="0" alt="Shop for items" title="Shop for items"
src="http://pics.ebaystatic.com/aw/pics/navbar/buy.gif">
</a>

<a href="http://sell.ebay.com/sell?ssPageName=h:h:syi:US">
<img border="0" alt="Sell your item" title="Sell your item"
src="http://pics.ebaystatic.com/aw/pics/navbar/sell.gif">
</a>

<a
href="http://my.ebay.com/ws/eBayISAPI.dll?MyeBay&amp;ssPageNa
me=H:H:MYEBAY:US">
<img border="0" alt="Track your eBay activities" title="Track
your eBay activities"
src="http://pics.ebaystatic.com/aw/pics/navbar/myebay.gif">
</a>

<a
href="http://pages.ebay.com/community/index.html?ssPageName=h
:h:over:US">
<img border="0" alt="Chat, news and events" title="Chat, news
and events"
src="http://pics.ebaystatic.com/aw/pics/navbar/comm.gif">
</a>

<a
href="http://pages.ebay.com/help/index.html?ssPageName=h:h:he
lp:US"><img border="0" alt="Get help, find answers & contact
Customer Support" title="Get help, find answers & contact
Customer Support"
src="http://pics.ebaystatic.com/aw/pics/navbar/help.gif">
</a>

</td>
```

This is a very straightforward way to create a tabbed interface.

## Search Capabilities

You can't buy something if you can't find it, so searching is an important part of eBay's tools. eBay's page has three fields where the user can enter information to search or browse. They work in pretty much the same way—let's take a look at the one in the middle of the page where it says, "What are you looking for?" As you would expect, this uses an HTML form element for user input and submitting data to the server. Here's the first tag:

```
<form name="searchform"
ACTION="http://search.ebay.com/search/search.dll"
METHOD="GET" onsubmit="setPopOutSwitch(false); return
handleSubmit(this, 'http://search.ebay.com/');">
```

This tag marks the start of the form and specifies that the form data be submitted to http://search.ebay.com/search/search.dll. When the search is submitted, code in search.dll will perform the search and display the results to the user. The JavaScript in the **onsubmit** section is executed when the form is submitted. The next elements in the form are for three **<input>** elements:

```
<input type="hidden" name="cgiurl"
value="http://cgi.ebay.com/ws/">
<input type="hidden" name="sokeywordredirect" value="1">
<input type="hidden" name="from" value="R8">
```

You can see that all these elements are hidden—the user does not see them and cannot change them. They are still submitted as part of the search and provide information needed by the searching engine.

The next section of code displays some visual elements, primarily the image at the top of the form that has the numeral 1 and the word *Find*. The HTML is as follows:

```
<tr bgcolor="#FFFFCC">
<td colspan="5"><IMG
SRC="http://pics.ebaystatic.com/aw/pics/hp/holiday04/imgOne_2
46x63.gif" WIDTH="247" HEIGHT="61" alt="Find: Search or
Browse for an item" /></td>
</tr>
```

The next part of the form may be puzzling:

```
<tr bgcolor="#DDFDC2">
<td colspan="2"><IMG
SRC="http://pics.ebaystatic.com/aw/pics/x.gif" WIDTH="1"
HEIGHT="1" /></td>
```

You can see that this is a table cell that spans two columns. It contains an image that is only 1 x 1 pixel. What gives with this—the image is not visible, certainly, so what purpose does it serve? It is a placeholder, nothing more. HTML does not like empty table cells, and by inserting a tiny image in the cell you can make it essentially vanish.

Next and finally is the HTML code for the field where the user enters the search term and for the submit button.

```
<td><font face="arial, helvetica, sans-serif"
size="2"><B><BR>
What are you looking for?<BR><FONT FACE="arial narrow"
size="2">
<input name="satitle" type="text" size="25" maxlength=300
/></font> 
<input type="submit" value="Search" class="buttonsm">
```

You can see that the input field is specified to have a size (width) of 25 characters and that the maximum length of the search term is 300 characters—more than enough for any search!

## Summary

There's lots more to the eBay home page, but these are the most interesting features from a page author's perspective. Compared with some other pages, the eBay home page makes a lot more use of HTML formatting codes and tables and less use of style sheet rules. Clearly you can use either approach to get a great Web page!

# Deconstructing Ford.com

Everyone knows the Ford Motor Company, and you would expect it to have a slick and completely professional Web presence. Its home page, shown in Figure 11.3, does not disappoint. It's clean and elegant, and not apparent in the figure, the main graphic near the top of the page is animated, changing to show different automobiles as the user is watching.

Now we can look at some of the more interesting parts of this page.

**Figure 11.3.** The Ford Motor Company's home page.

## The Head Section

The **\<head>** section of the Ford home page contains the usual tags for title, key-words, and description as well as a link to a style sheet:

```
<TITLE>Ford Motor Company Home Page</TITLE>

<META name="keywords" CONTENT="ford motor company Ford Motor
Company FORD MOTOR COMPANY blue oval lincoln mercury mazda
volvo jaguar aston martin land rover ford credit quality
care motorcraft hertz vehicle ford cars automobiles trucks
suv explorer sport utility">
<META name="description" CONTENT="The corporate Website "
for Ford Motor Company and its vehicle (car and truck) and
service brands, featuring investor, career, news and media
information.">
<LINK REL="stylesheet" href="/NR/fordcom/css/global_ie.css"
type="text/css">
```

There are also some embedded styles, shown here:

```
<STYLE>
          /* home page styles */
          body, input, select {
                  margin:0;
                  padding:0;
          }
          select {
                  width:135px;
          }
          body, div, td, a, input, select {
                  font-family:arial, helvetica, sans-serif;
                  font-size:11px;
          }
          #header {
              width:760px;
              margin: 13px 0px 0px 0px;
          }
          #header table {
              margin: 0px 0px 9px 0px;
          }
          #main {
                  margin:10px 0px 10px 10px;
          }
          #homeTable a {
                  text-decoration:none;
          }
          .contentRow {
                  background-color:#DDE9F7;
          }
```

```
.inliner, .inliner form {
        display: inline;
}
.dropdownHome {
        width: 210px;
}
.newsHeadline {
        font-weight:bold;
        color:#CC6602;
}
.newsDesc {
        color:#1F5C9D;
}
</STYLE>
```

As the comment near the start of the styles indicates, these are styles that are specific for the home page (this page) and will override any competing styles in the external style sheet.

The **<head>** section also contains some script code. This is related to the use of Flash to create the page's animation, something I'll discuss more later. To play the animation, the user must have the Flash player installed. In case the user does not, the page author did not want a blank space displayed on the page but rather wanted-ed to display alternate content. This script (which is executed when the page loads) checks to see if the Flash player is installed. But wait, things are even more complicated. Different browsers use different script code to check for plug-ins like the Flash player; specifically, Internet Explorer is different from other browsers. The author wanted to be sure the page would work properly in all browsers, so two sections of script were included. The first is for non-IE browsers:

```
<SCRIPT language="javascript">
    var showFlash;
    var plugin = (navigator.mimeTypes &&
      navigator.mimeTypes["application/x-shockwave-flash"]) ?
      navigator.mimeTypes["application/x-shockwave-
      flash"].enabledPlugin : 0;

    showFlash = false;

    // Non-IE Test for Flash
    if (plugin)
    {
        whichPlugin =
parseInt(plugin.description.substring(plugin.description.inde
xOf(".")-1));
        if (whichPlugin >= 6)
        {
```

```
            showFlash = true;
        } else {
            showFlash = false;
        }
    }
</SCRIPT>
```

And the second works in IE only, using the VBScript language rather than JavaScript:

```
<SCRIPT language="VBScript">
    'IE Test for Flash
    On Error Resume Next

    showFlash =

IsObject(CreateObject("ShockwaveFlash.ShockwaveFlash.6"))
</SCRIPT>
```

You may not understand the details of how these scripts work, but the bottom line is that the variable named **showFlash** is set to the value 'TRUE' if the Flash player is installed and to 'FALSE' if it is not. You'll see how this value is used later in the page.

## The Flash Animation

Flash animations are created with a program called Macromedia Flash. In addition to images, animations, and sound, they can contain links, as with the Ford.com Flash presentation. The details of creating Flash animations are beyond the scope of this book, but the end result is a file with the .swf extension that is placed on your Web server along with the Web page that uses it. Code in the Web page indicates where the animation is to be displayed and other details of its appearance. When a user views the page, the SWF file is automatically downloaded and played. To take into account people who do not have the Flash player installed, the page author wrote the following script code and placed it in the **<body>** section of the page at the location where the animation should be displayed:

```
<SCRIPT language="JavaScript">
if (showFlash)
    {
    var skipIntro = getCookie("skipIntro");
    var flashVars = 'xmlsrc=/en/channels.xml&skipIntro=' +
        skipIntro;
    writeFlashEmbed('/NR/fordcom/images/en/home/flash/
    channels.swf',
    760, 330, 'FFFFFF','6,0,0,0',flashVars);
        }
```

```
else {
document.write('<TABLE cellpadding="0" cellspacing="0"
border="0"><TR><TD rowspan="3" width="10"></TD><TD><IMG
src="/NR/fordcom/images/en/home/flash/noflash_top.jpg"
width="750" height="254" border="0"
alt=""></TD></TR><TR><TD><A href="/en/links/General/
www_fordvehicles_com/default.htm?referrer=home"><IMG
src="/NR/fordcom/images/en/home/flash/noflash_nav_ford.gif"
width="79" height="46" border="0" alt="Ford"></A><A
href="/en/links/General/www_lincoln_com/default.htm?referrer=h
ome"><IMG
src="/NR/fordcom/images/en/home/flash/noflash_nav_lincoln.gif"
width="81" height="46" border="0" alt="Lincoln"></A><A
href="/en/links/General/www_mercuryvehicles_com/default.htm?
referrer=home"><IMG
src="/NR/fordcom/images/en/home/flash/noflash_nav_mecury.gif"
width="81" height="46" border="0" alt="Mercury"></A><A
href="/en/links/General/www_mazdausa_com/default.htm?
referrer=home"><IMG
src="/NR/fordcom/images/en/home/flash/noflash_nav_mazda.gif"
width="81" height="46" border="0" alt="Mazda"></A><A
href="/en/links/General/www_volvocars_us/default.htm?
referrer=home"><IMG
src="/NR/fordcom/images/en/home/flash/noflash_nav_volvo.gif"
width="81" height="46" border="0" alt="Volvo"></A><A
href="/en/links/General/www_jaguarusa_com/default.htm?refer-
rer=home"><IMG
src="/NR/fordcom/images/en/home/flash/noflash_nav_jaguar.gif"
width="81" height="46" border="0" alt="Jaguar"></A><A
href="/en/links/General/www_landroverusa_com/default.htm?
referrer=home"><IMG
src="/NR/fordcom/images/en/home/flash/noflash_nav_landrover.
gif" width="82" height="46" border="0" alt="Land Rover"></A><A
href="/en/links/General/www_astonmartin_com/default.htm?
referrer=home"><IMG
src="/NR/fordcom/images/en/home/flash/noflash_nav_aston.gif"
width="80" height="46" border="0" alt="Aston Martin"></A><A
href="/en/company/about/countrySites/default.htm?referrer=
home&source=botnav"><IMG
src="/NR/fordcom/images/en/home/flash/noflash_nav_global.gif"
width="104" height="46" border="0" alt="Global
Sites"></A></TD></TR><TR><TD><IMG
src="/NR/fordcom/images/en/home/flash/noflash_bottom.jpg"
width="750" height="23" border="0"
alt=""></TD></TR></TABLE>');
}
</SCRIPT>
```

This code tests the value of the variable **showFlash**, which was set to **TRUE** or **FALSE** by the script in the document's **<head>** section, as explained earlier. Then the following rules apply:

- If **showFlash** is **TRUE**, the script code displays the Flash animation in the file /NR/fordcom/images/en/home/flash/channels.swf.

- If **showFlash** is **FALSE**, the code uses the **document.write** method to write a block of HTML to the document. This HTML comprises a table containing text and images that provide similar information as the Flash animation but without requiring the player.

This may seem unnecessarily complicated—after all, almost everyone has the Flash player, don't they? But it's good programming practice. Successful Web pages get that way by catering not to most visitors but to all visitors!

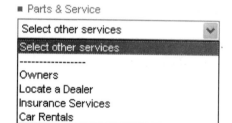

**Figure 11.4.** Hyperlinks in a drop-down list.

## Drop-Down Links

The Ford page makes use of a technique that presents links in a drop-down list, as shown in Figure 11.4. The user clicks the box and the list drops down; by selecting an entry in the list, the user navigates to the corresponding page. Let's see how this is done.

The technique is to use an HTML form element, specifically a Select element. In this case it is not being used as part of a form, and its data is not submitted anywhere, just used for links:

```
<SELECT class=dropdownHome
onchange=if(this.options[this.selectedIndex].value.length!=0)
{window.location.href=this.options[this.selectedIndex].value;
}>
<OPTION selected>Select other services</OPTION>
<OPTION>-----------------</OPTION>
<OPTION
value=http://www.ford.com/en/vehicles/owners/default.htm?refe
rrer=home>Owners</OPTION>
<OPTION
value=http://www.ford.com/en/vehicles/vehicleShowroom/deal-
ers.htm?referrer=home>Locate a Dealer</OPTION>
<OPTION value=http://www.ford.com/en/links/General/www_ford-
vip_com/default.htm?referrer=home>Insurance Services</OPTION>
<OPTION
value=http://www.ford.com/en/vehicles/vehicleShowroom/carRent
als/default.htm?referrer=home>Car Rentals</OPTION>
</SELECT>
```

First, look at the several individual **<option>** tags and note the following:

- Each one contains text between the **<option>** and **</option>** tags—this is the text that is displayed in the drop-down list.
- The first one specifies **selected** in the tag, indicating that this is the list item that will be selected when the page is displayed.
- The second one is simply a row of hyphens, serving as a separator in the list.
- The third through sixth **<option>** tags each have a **value** attribute, and each one consists of a URL. The first and second **<option>** tags do not have a **value** attribute.

Next, look at the opening **<select>** tag. It has an **onchange** event handler, code that is executed whenever the selected item in the list is changed. The code makes use of the **value** attribute of whatever list item is selected. Translating this into English, the code says, "If the value of the selected list item has a length that is not zero, then navigate to the URL contained in the value." Since the first two list items do not have a value, selecting them has no effect.

Using a drop-down list to present links is useful when you have a lot of links and do not want them cluttering up the page. The downside is that the links are not visible unless the user clicks the list.

## The Navigation Bar

Near the top of the Ford.com home page is a navigation bar with five buttons. Each button is an image, and the navigation bar is constructed simply by displaying those five images, as hyperlinks, across the page. For this sort of approach to be effective, you need to design nice buttons, but the HTML code is quite simple:

```
<A href="/en/vehicles/default.htm?referrer=home"><IMG
src="/NR/fordcom/images/en/vehicles/1nav_vehicles.gif"
width="175" height="27" border="0" alt="Vehicles and
Services"></A>
<A href="/en/heritage/default.htm?referrer=home"><IMG
src="/NR/fordcom/images/en/heritage/1nav_heritage.gif"
width="145" height="27" border="0" alt="Heritage"></A>
<A href="/en/innovation/default.htm?referrer=home"><IMG
src="/NR/fordcom/images/en/innovation/1nav_innovation.gif"
width="146" height="27" border="0" alt="Innovation"></A>
<A href="/en/goodWorks/default.htm?referrer=home"><IMG
src="/NR/fordcom/images/en/goodWorks/1nav_goodWorks.gif"
width="147" height="27" border="0" alt="Good Works"></A>
<A href="/en/company/default.htm?referrer=home"><IMG
src="/NR/fordcom/images/en/company/1nav_company.gif"
width="147" height="27" border="0" alt="Company"></A>
```

If you look closely at the navigation bar you'll notice that it has a shadow under it—a subtle touch but one that I think adds to the visual attractiveness of the page. The shadow is a separate image and is displayed below the row of buttons as a result of including a **\<br>** tag to move to a new line before displaying the image at the same width as the five buttons:

```
<BR><IMG src="/NR/fordcom/images/en/global/header_bar.gif"
width="760" height="16" border="0" alt="">
```

## Summary

The Ford.com page presents a clean and easy-to-use interface, and the sophistication of the Flash animation is a terrific way to present Ford's products. You may want to consider exploring Flash on your own. It's not the easiest thing to learn, but the results can be well worth the effort.

# CHAPTER 12

# Deconstructing Web Pages, Part II

This is the second of three chapters in which I deconstruct Web pages, showing how the page authors created specific features for the sites. Please refer back to Chapter 11 for introductory material on this process.

## Deconstructing Amazon.com

Amazon.com is one of the best-known names in online sales. It started with books but has branched out to offer merchandise in a wide array of areas, including electronics, apparel, pet supplies, and jewelry. Its home page, shown in Figure 12.1, has to provide visitors with access to all of Amazon.com's stores and departments without being confusing and cluttered. There are several nice features on this page that I will cover.

### The Head Section

The Amazon.com home page includes a <title> tag in its <head> section but, interestingly enough, no tags for keywords or a description. My guess is that the page authors simply are not concerned with the search engines—after all, Amazon.com is one of the best-known URLs on the Web and a few more search engine listings one way or another will not affect its traffic.

The <head> section also includes an embedded style sheet but no link to an external style sheet. I will not reproduce the entire style sheet here—it is quite long—but let's look at some of its more interesting rules.

The style sheet defines a large number rules with class selectors. Here are a few of them:

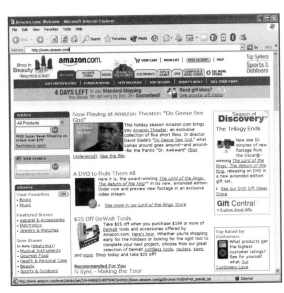

**Figure 12.1.** The Amazon.com home page.

```
.serif { font-family: times,serif; font-size: small; }
.sans { font-family: verdana,arial,helvetica,sans-serif;
font-size: small; }
.small { font-family: verdana,arial,helvetica,sans-serif;
font-size: x-small; }
.h1 { font-family: verdana,arial,helvetica,sans-serif; color:
#CC6600; font-size: small; }
.h3color { font-family: verdana,arial,helvetica,sans-serif;
color: #CC6600; font-size: x-small; }
.tiny { font-family: verdana,arial,helvetica,sans-serif;
font-size: xx-small; }
.Websearch-string {font-family: verdana,arial,helvetica,sans-
serif; font-size: xx-small; }
.listprice { font-family: arial,verdana,sans-serif; text-dec-
oration: line-through; font-size: x-small; }
.price { font-family: verdana,arial,helvetica,sans-serif;
color: #990000; font-size: x-small; }
```

It may seem like a lot of work to create all these rules, but it saves time in the long run when you want to apply different text formatting to different elements in your Web page.

Here's a rule that, if you believe its selector name, is used for page elements that the user's attention should be called to. It does nothing more then set the background color to a light yellow:

```
.attention { background-color: #FFFFD5; }
```

Here's a more complex rule that is used to format text sans serif, 10 pixels high, boldface, white, and all uppercase:

```
.eyebrow {font-family: verdana,arial,helvetica,sans-serif;
font-size: 10px; font-weight: bold; text-transform: upper-
case; text-decoration: none; color: #FFFFFF;}
```

This next rule applies underlining to hyperlinks with the "horizontal-advanced-Websearch" class when the mouse is hovering over them:

```
A.horizontal-advanced-Websearch:hover {text-decoration:
underline}
```

Looking at the rules in various Websites' style sheets can be a great way to get ideas for your own pages.

## The Top Navigation Bar

At the top of the page toward the right is a small navigation bar containing four links: View Cart, Wish List, Your Account, and Help. This bar is created using an image map. In other words, the bar itself is a single image and is divided into four functional regions, each with its own destination URL, by an image map. The map code is shown here:

```
<map name="right_top_nav_map">

<area shape="rect"
href=http://www.amazon.com/gp/cart/view.html/ref=top_nav_sb_g
ateway/104-9482653-8979946 coords="0,0,80,21">

 <area shape="rect"
href=http://www.amazon.com/gp/registry/registry.html/ref=cm_w
l_topnav_gateway/104-9482653-8979946?type=wishlist
coords="85,0,151,21" id="topnav_wishlist">

 <area shape="rect" href=/exec/obidos/account-access-
login/ref=top_nav_ya_gateway/104-9482653-8979946
coords="155,0,256,21">

 <area shape="rect" href=/exec/obidos/tg/browse/-
/508510/ref=top_nav_hp_gateway/104-9482653-8979946
coords="260,0,299,21">

 </map>
```

You can see, for example, the following details about the first area in the map:

- It's a rectangle.
- It extends from coordinates 0,0 (the top-left corner of the image) to coordinates 80,21.
- It links to http://www.amazon.com/gp/registry/registry.html.

The other three areas are defined in a similar manner. The image itself is inserted in the page with the usual **<img>** tag, being sure to use the **usemap** attribute to identify the name of the map to use:

```
<img src="http://g-images.amazon.com/images /G/01/nav/person-
alized/cartwish/right-topnav-default-2.gif" width=300
height=22 alt="" USEMAP=#right_top_nav_map border=0>
```

The Amazon.com home page uses several image maps. This is one of several ways to get navigation bar functionality in your page.

## The Navigation Tabs

The main navigation feature on this page is the set of tabs across the page near the top. Each tab is a separate image, and they are arranged, along with other elements in this part of the page, in table cells. Please note two things about these tabs. First, the active tab—the one for the page the user is currently on—is a different color than the inactive tabs. For example, here's the image for the active Welcome tab:

And here's the image for the inactive Electronics tab:

When the user moves from one page to another, tab images of the appropriate colors are used to maintain the active tab distinction.

Second, note that one tab is not just a plain tab but an image of a shirt—appropriate for the Apparel tab! Because this tab image is taller than the others, special steps were needed to get the desired appearance. The shirt tab image is actually two images, the top and bottom parts, shown here:

The HTML that displays the top part is as follows:

```
<td valign=bottom><a href="/exec/obidos/tg/browse/-
/1036592/ref=tab_xs_ap_4/104-9482653-8979946"><img
src="http://g-images.amazon.com/images/G/01/apparel/apparel-
coat-tab_top.gif" width=70 height=34 border=0></a></td>
```

Then, the following HTML code displays the other tabs, including the bottom of the shirt image:

```
<a
href=/exec/obidos/subst/home/home.html/ref%3Dtab%5Fgw%5Fgw%5F
1/104-9482653-8979946><img src="http://g-images.amazon.com
/images/G/01/marketing/holiday-2001/welcome_red.gif" width=60
height=26 border=0 id=tb_gateway></a>

<a href=/exec/obidos/tg/stores/your/store-home/-/0/
ref%3Dpd%5Fysl%5Fgw%5Ffr%5F2/104-9482653-8979946><img
src="http://g-images.amazon.com/images/G/01/nav/personalized/
tabs/yourstore-off-sliced._ZCPETER%27S,0,2,0,0,verdenab,7,
90,90,80_.gif" width=81 height=26 border=0></a>

<a href=/exec/obidos/tg/browse/-/283155/
ref%3Dtab%5Fgw%5Fb%5F3/104-9482653-8979946><img
src="http://g-images.amazon.com/images/G/01/nav/
personalized/tabs/books-off-sliced.gif" width=39 height=26
border=0 id=tb_books></a></td>
```

```
<td colspan=2><nobr><a href=/exec/obidos/tg/browse/-
/1036592/ref%3Dtab%5Fgw%5Fap%5F4/104-9482653-8979946><img
src="http://g-images.amazon.com/images/G/01/apparel/apparel-
coat-tab_btm.gif" width=70 height=26 border=0></a>

<a href=/exec/obidos/tg/browse/-
/172282/ref%3Dtab%5Fgw%5Fe%5F5/104-9482653-8979946><img
src="http://g-images.amazon.com/images/G/01/nav/personal-
ized/tabs/electronics-off-sliced.gif" width=74 height=26 bor-
der=0 id=tb_electronics></a>

<a href=/exec/obidos/tg/browse/-
/171280/ref%3Dtab%5Fgw%5Ft%5F6/104-9482653-8979946><img
src="http://g-images.amazon.com/images/G/01/nav/personal-
ized/tabs/toys-off-sliced.gif" width=47 height=26 border=0
id=tb_toys></a>

<a href=/exec/obidos/tg/browse/-
/130/ref%3Dtab%5Fgw%5Fd%5F7/104-9482653-8979946><img
src="http://g-images.amazon.com/images/G/01/nav/personal-
ized/tabs/dvd-off-sliced.gif" width=35 height=26 border=0
id=tb_dvd></a>

<a href=/exec/obidos/tg/browse/-
/468642/ref%3Dtab%5Fgw%5Fvg%5F8/104-9482653-8979946><img
src="http://g-images.amazon.com/images/G/01/nav/personal-
ized/tabs/videogames-off-sliced.gif" width=73 height=26 bor-
der=0 id=tb_videogames></a>

<a href=http://www.amazon.com/exec/obidos/subst/home/all-
stores.html/ref%3Dtab_gw_storesdirectory/104-9482653-
8979946><img src="http://g-
images.amazon.com/images/G/01/nav/personalized/tabs/see-more-
off-sliced.gif" width=70 height=26 border=0></a></td>
```
By carefully aligning the two images, the page designers
made them appear as one, and the desired visual effect is
achieved.

## The Animation

Take a look on the Amazon.com home page at the heading "Season of
Discovery." You cannot by looking at Figure 12.1, of course, but this heading is animated. Every few seconds it vanishes only to reappear from left to right. It's a very
effective way to draw people's attention to that part of the page.

The animation itself is a Macromedia Flash file. Even though the Flash player
is free, not everyone has it or wants to be bothered downloading it just to view a

specific page. The Amazon.com page programmers wisely took this into account. As you might expect, this is accomplished with JavaScript. But wait, there's more. The programmers knew that not all browsers support JavaScript, and some people have script support turned off for security reasons, and while it's a tiny percentage, they want everyone to have a good experience at their site. Therefore, they also took into account people who, for whatever reasons, do not run scripts in their browser.

Look at the script here. It checks the variable **MM_FlashCanPlay** and, if it is true (more on this in a moment), uses the **Document.write** method to write the HTML to the document that loads the Flash file into the Flash player. If **MM_FlashCanPlay** is False, HTML is written that displays a static image:

```
<SCRIPT LANGUAGE=JavaScript1.1>
<!--
if ( MM_FlashCanPlay ) {
document.write('<OBJECT classid="clsid:D27CDB6E-AE6D-11cf-
96B8-444553540000"');
document.write('
codebase="http://download.macromedia.com/pub/shockwave/cabs/f
lash/swflash.cab#version=6,0,0,0" ');
document.write(' ID="flashPlayer"');
document.write(' WIDTH="169" HEIGHT="40" ALIGN="right">');
document.write(' <PARAM NAME=movie VALUE="http://images.ama-
zon.com/media/i3d/01/season-discovery_hol-blue.swf"> <PARAM
NAME=loop VALUE=true> <PARAM NAME=quality VALUE=high> ');
document.write(' <EMBED
src="http://images.amazon.com/media/i3d/01/season-
discovery_hol-blue.swf" loop=true quality=high ');
document.write(' ID="flashPlayerEmbed"');
document.write(' swLiveConnect=FALSE WIDTH="169" HEIGHT="40"
NAME="amazonFlash" ALIGN="right"');
document.write(' TYPE="application/x-shockwave-flash" PLUG-
INSPAGE="http://www.macromedia.com/go/getflashplayer">');
document.write(' </EMBED>');
document.write(' </OBJECT>');
} else {
document.write('<img src="http://g-
images.amazon.com/images/G/01/marketing/holiday-04/heads/sea-
son-red-bl2.gif" width=169 height=40 align=right border=0>');
}
//-->
</SCRIPT>
```

To take into account people whose browsers are not running scripts, this HTML is included:

```
<NOSCRIPT><img src="http://g-
images.amazon.com/images/G/01/marketing/holiday-04/heads/
season-red-bl2.gif" width=169 height=40 align=right bor-
der=0></NOSCRIPT>
```

The **<NOSCRIPT>** tag tells browsers to pay attention to this HTML only if scripts are not running. The result is that the static image is displayed in the page.

What about the **MM_FlashCanPlay** variable? Earlier in the page, the following script sets its value to True orFalse depending on whether the Flash player is available:

```
<SCRIPT LANGUAGE=JavaScript1.1>
<!--
var MM_contentVersion = 6;
var plugin = (navigator.mimeTypes &&
navigator.mimeTypes["application/x-shockwave-flash"]) ? navi-
gator.mimeTypes["application/x-shockwave-
flash"].enabledPlugin : 0;
if ( plugin ) {
var words = navigator.plugins["Shockwave Flash"].descrip-
tion.split(" ");
for (var i = 0; i < words.length; ++i){
if (isNaN(parseInt(words[i])))
continue;
var MM_PluginVersion = words[i]; }
var MM_FlashCanPlay = MM_PluginVersion >= MM_contentVersion;
}
else if (navigator.userAgent &&
navigator.userAgent.indexOf("MSIE")>=0 &&
(navigator.appVersion.indexOf("Win") != -1)) {
document.write('<SCR' + 'IPT LANGUAGE=VBScript\> \n'); //FS
hide this from IE4.5 Mac by splitting the tag
document.write('on error resume next \n');
document.write('MM_FlashCanPlay = (
IsObject(CreateObject("ShockwaveFlash.ShockwaveFlash." &
MM_contentVersion)))\n');
document.write('</SCR' + 'IPT\> \n');
}
//-->
</SCRIPT>
```

## Summary

The Amazon.com home page is one of the most visited anywhere. Big bucks are riding on how well it attracts customers, and you can be sure that a lot of attention was lavished on its coding. We have looked at some of the techniques used on this page, techniques that you may want to adapt for your own Web pages.

**Figure 12.2.** The CNN.com home page.

# Deconstructing CNN.com

CNN.com is the Website of the Cable News Network, and as you might expect, it displays a variety of breaking news stories. The home page, shown in Figure 12.2, displays the top story along with links to other stories and to other areas of the Website that are devoted to particular topics, such as business, technology, and sports.

## The Head Section

The **<head>** section of the CNN.com home page includes a **<title>** tag but no keywords or description. As with some other well-known sites, the authors do not seem to believe that the search engines are important in generating traffic and so do not bother to include these elements. In this section you'll also find links to an external style sheet and an external JavaScript file:

```
<link rel="stylesheet" href="http://i.a.cnn.net/cnn/.ele-
ment/ssi/css/1.1/main.css" type="text/css">
<script language="JavaScript1.2"
src="http://i.a.cnn.net/cnn/.element/ssi/js/1.1/main.js"
type="text/javascript"></script>
```

You can use the techniques that were explained in Chapter 11 to view the contents of these files. You'll also see some more styles and JavaScript in the HTML document itself. The CNN.com home page makes extensive use of JavaScript.

## The Main Navigation Bar

On the left side of the page you'll see a couple of vertical navigation bars with links to other pages on the CNN Website—World, U.S., Weather, and so on. You will note two things about these navigation bars:

- The button corresponding to the current page is in a different color than the other buttons (Home Page in the figure).

- As you move the mouse cursor over the buttons, the one under the cursor changes color. This is called a hover effect and is useful to make it perfectly clear which button will be selected by clicking.

There are several ways to implement a hover effect in a Web page. Let's see how it is done here. I'll deal with the upper of the two navigation bars, the one that ends with the Special Reports link.

The entire navigation bar is created in an HTML table. Let's look at the code for the table and then deconstruct it piece by piece. I have included code for only the top two buttons to avoid repetition since the other buttons are created the same way.

```
<table id="cnnNavBar" width="126" bgcolor="#EEEEEE"
border="0" cellpadding="0" cellspacing="0" summary="CNN.com
Navigation">
<col width="8" align="left" valign="top">
<col width="118" align="left" valign="top">

<tr bgcolor="#CCCCCC" class="cnnNavHiliteRow"><td width="8"
class="swath"> </td>
<td class="cnnNavHilite" onClick="CNN_goTo('/')"><div
class="cnnNavText"><a href="/">Home Page</a></div></td></tr>

<tr class="cnnNavRow"><td class="swath"> </td>
<td class="cnnNav" onMouseOver="CNN_navBar(this,1,1)"
onMouseOut="CNN_navBar(this,0,1)"
onClick="CNN_navBarClick(this,1,'/WORLD/')"><div
class="cnnNavText"><a
href="/WORLD/">World</a></div></td></tr>

</table>
```

The first tag is the **\<table\>** tag that starts the table:

```
<table id="cnnNavBar" width="126" bgcolor="#EEEEEE"
border="0" cellpadding="0" cellspacing="0" summary="CNN.com
Navigation">
```

You can see that this tag defines a table that is exactly 126 pixels wide with a light gray background, no border, and no cell spacing or padding. Note also that the tag is assigned an **id** attribute of **cnnNavBar**. This would normally be used to connect the table with a style sheet rule, but a search of both the external and internal style sheets does not turn up a selector for this attribute value. One can only assume the attribute was used in the past or is included for possible use in the future.

The next tags in the table are two **\<column\>** tags:

```
<col width="8" align="left" valign="top">
<col width="118" align="left" valign="top">
```

These define the table as having two columns that are respectively 8 and 118 pixels wide—which add up to the total table width of 126 as it should. Content in each column will be top and left aligned.

The next tag starts a table row:

```
<tr bgcolor="#CCCCCC" class="cnnNavHiliteRow">
```

The background color is defined as a medium gray, and the tag is assigned the **class** attribute of **cnnNavHiliteRow**. Looking through the external style sheet we find two rules that will select this class when assigned to a **<TR>** tag:

```
TR.cnnNavHiliteRow TD {
    vertical-align: middle;
    border: 1px solid;
    border-color: #f66 #600 #600;
    border-left: none;
}

TR.cnnNavHiliteRow TD.swath {
    background-color: #f66;
    border-right: none;
}
```

The selectors are slightly different for these two rules:

- The first selector applies to and any all **<TD>** tags that are inside a **<TR>** tag that has the **class** attribute set to cnnNavHiliteRow.

- The second selector applies to only those **<TD>** tags that have their **class** attribute set to **swath** and are inside a **<TR>** tag that has the **class** attribute set to **cnnNavHiliteRow**.

This is a good example of using the cascading feature of Cascading Style Sheets—the second rule needs only to define those style details that are different from the first rule.

The next tag defines a table cell, the first one in the row:

```
<td width="8" class="swath"> </td>
```

The **width** attribute is redundant because the earlier **<col>** tag already defined the first column as 8 pixels wide—however, this does no harm. The **class** attribute set to **swath** connects the cell with the second style sheet rule that was shown earlier. Thus, this cell will have a background color of #f66 (a grayish blue) and no right border in addition to the other formatting assigned by style rules higher in the cascade. This cell contains only a space and in effect serves only as a spacer that separates the actual navigation buttons from the left edge of the page.

The next tag defines another table cell, the cell that contains the button for the current page. Because it is the current page, the button does not have a hover effect:

```
<td class="cnnNavHilite" onClick="CNN_goTo('/')"><div
class="cnnNavText"><a href="/">Home Page</a></div></td>
```

The **class** attribute connects the cell to the following style sheet rules:

```
.cnnNavHilite {
    background-color: #c00;
    color: #fff;
    cursor: pointer;
}

.cnnNavHilite A:link, .cnnNavHilite A:visited {
    color: #fff;

TR TD.cnnNavHilite A:link, TR TD.cnnNavHilite A:visited {
    text-decoration: none;
}
```

The first rule specifies the background and text colors and the mouse pointer appearance. The other two rules control how links are displayed.

The **onClick** attribute specifies a JavaScript function that will be called when the cell is clicked. The argument "/" will be passed to the function. We'll see how this function works in a bit.

The next tag is a **<div>** tag with the **class** attribute set to **cnnNavText**:

```
<div class="cnnNavText">
```

This attribute connects the tag to the following style sheet rule:

```
.cnnNavText {
    font-family: verdana, arial, sans-serif;
    font-size: 10px;
    font-weight: bold;
    line-height: 14px;
    padding-left: 4px;
}
```

The result is that any text within the **<div>** tag will be displayed with the specified font, line height, and left padding.

Inside the **<div>** tag is the innermost tag that represents the actual hyperlink:

```
<a href="/">Home Page</a>
```

This is simply the text displayed on the button (which is not really a button *per se*, just a table cell that looks and acts like a button) with the associated URL.

Now let's look at the code for the second button in the navigation bar. This one is similar to the first one in many ways but differs because it is not for the current page but for another page. First of all, the **<tr>** tag has a different **class** attribute:

```
<tr class="cnnNavRow">
```

This attribute connects it to the following style rules:

```
TR.cnnNavRow TD {
    vertical-align: middle;
    border: 1px solid;
    border-color: #369 #003 #003;
    border-left: none;
}

TR.cnnNavRow TD.swath {
    background-color: #369;
    border-right: none;
}
```

The result is that buttons for other pages are displayed differently from the button for the current page.

The first cell in the row is the same as before, providing a narrow left spacing for the navigation button:

```
<td class="swath"> </td>
```

The tag that starts the second cell, the actual button, is where most of the differences lie:

```
<td class="cnnNav" onMouseOver="CNN_navBar(this,1,1)"
onMouseOut="CNN_navBar(this,0,1)"
onClick="CNN_navBarClick(this,1,'/WORLD/')">
```

The **class** attribute **cnnNav** connects the tag to these style sheet rules, which give to these buttons a totally different appearance than that of the "current page" button:

```
.cnnNav {
    background-color: #036;
    color: #fff;
    cursor: pointer;
}
.cnnNav A:link, .cnnNav A:visited {
    color: #fff;
}
TR TD.cnnNav A:link, TR TD.cnnNav A:visited {
    text-decoration: none;
}
```

You'll also note references to three JavaScript functions in this tag. Here's where the hover effect is achieved:

- **onMouseOver** is called when the mouse cursor enters the cell. It changes the cell to its "hover" appearance.

- **onMouseOut** is called when the mouse cursor leaves the cell. It restores it to its normal appearance.

- **onClick** is called when the cell is clicked.

I'll discuss these functions in the next section.

The final part of this table cell is the link tag itself. This is identical to the tag for the current page button, explained earlier, so I will not repeat the details.

Before we get to the JavaScript functions for this part of the page, let's review. This is one of many ways to present a navigation bar to the user. It is a bit more complicated than other techniques you have seen. Part of this added complexity is due to the hover effect, which some of the other navigation bars I have deconstructed did not have. Some of the complexity is due to the fact that the designers used a combination of HTML tags and style sheets for formatting the page. In theory, it is preferable to do all your formatting with style sheet rules, but they are used with relatively few pages.

## The Navigation Bar JavaScript

You have seen three JavaScript functions used in the code for this navigation bar. The first one, **CNN_goTo**, is called when the user clicks the navigation button for the current page. The code for this function is quite simple:

```
function CNN_goTo( url ) {
    window.location.href = url;
}
```

Passed the URL, it simply navigates the current window to that URL. When the current page button is clicked, the URL "/" is passed, causing the browser to reload the current page. Why navigate at all? After all, the current page is by definition already displayed. My belief is that, because it is a news page that changes frequently, they wanted to always load the most current version.

## Cascading Confusion

Cascading Style Sheets are great for the page developer but can sometimes be confusing when you are trying to deconstruct a page. It's the cascading that can cause problems. When you see a particular page element formatted in a certain way, it may be difficult to locate the source of that formatting. Is it is a style sheet rule that applies specifically to that element? Does it cascade down from a higher-level rule? Or is it the result of an HTML formatting tag in the document? It can sometimes take a bit of sleuthing to figure things out!

The function **CNN_navBarClick** is called when the user clicks a navigation button for another page. Its code is shown here:

```
function CNN_navBarClick( tableCellRef, navStyle, url ) {
    CNN_navBar( tableCellRef, 0, navStyle );
    CNN_goTo( url );
}
```

This function is passed three arguments:

- A reference to the current table cell (passed as the **this** keyword)
- A numerical argument **navStyle** that can be 0 or 1
- The target URL

The code in this function does nothing more than call two other functions. The first one it calls, **CNN_navBar**, deals with changing the cell's appearance and will be explained in a moment. The second, **CNN_goTo**, was explained earlier and simply navigates the browser to the supplied URL.

The third function used by this navigation bar is **CNN_navBar**. The code is shown here:

```
function CNN_navBar( tableCellRef, hoverFlag, navStyle ) {
    if ( hoverFlag ) {
        switch ( navStyle ) {
            case 1:
                tableCellRef.style.backgroundColor = '#69c';
                break;
            default:
                if ( document.getElementsByTagName ) {
                    tableCellRef.getElementsByTagName( 'a' )[0].
                        style.color = '#c00';
                }
        }
    } else {
        switch ( navStyle ) {
            case 1:
                tableCellRef.style.backgroundColor = '#036';
                break;
            default:
                if ( document.getElementsByTagName ) {
                tableCellRef.getElementsByTagName( 'a' )[0].
                        style.color = '#000';
                }
            }
        }
    }
}
```

This function is called under three situations: when the **onMouseOver** event occurs, when the **onMouseOut** event occurs, and from the **CNN_navBarClick** function when the user clicks the button. These three situations all require that the button's appearance changes, and the page programmer has cleverly put the required code in a single function. Here's how it works:

- The first argument, **tableCellRef**, is always a reference to the current cell, allowing code in the function to modify the current cell's appearance.
- The second argument, **hoverFlag**, is 0 for the **mouseOut** and **onClick** events and 1 for the **onMouseOver** event.
- The third argument, **navStyle**, is always 1.

Why include the third argument if it is always 1? This function is probably called from elsewhere on the page with a different argument, but that's beyond the scope of the present discussion.

When the function is called from the **onMouseOver** event, **hoverFlag** is 1 and the first part of the **if** is executed. Since **navStyle** is always 1, the result is to set the current cell's background color to #69c. When the function is called from the **mouseOut** and **onClick** events, **hoverFlag** is 0 and the **else** section is executed. Again, **navStyle** is always 1 so the result is to set the current cell's background color to #36. The result—a button that changes color when hovered over and clicked.

## Summary

We have looked at only a small part of the CNN.com home page, but it's an important part. Navigation is an essential part of Web pages, particularly so when a page needs to present links to many destination URLs. The HTML, style sheet, and JavaScript approach used on this page may seem a bit complex, but it is very effective and flexible.

# Deconstructing Webpagesthatsuck.com

The URL of this site says it all—it's a compendium of bad Website design ideas taken from real life. It dates back some eight years and has become very popular. Aside from deconstructing it, the site is a useful place for novice Web designers to visit to learn about what is and is not considered bad design. Of course this site is only one person's opinions and should not be taken as gospel, but in my opinion he hits the mark most of the time. Vincent mentioned our software in his first book, so I'm returning the favor by adding his Website to my first book. Did we find anything wrong?

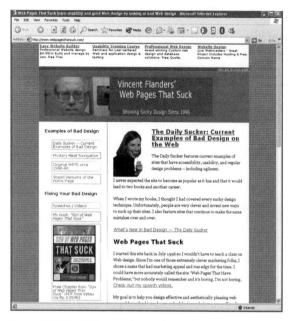

**Figure 12.3.** The Webpagesthatsuck.com home page.

The site's home page is shown in Figure 12.3.

## The Head Section

The **<head>** section of this page contains an excellent **<title>** tag that describes the site very well:

```
<title>Web Pages That Suck
learn usability and good Web
design by looking at bad Web
design</title>
```

And guess what—the **description** meta tag is almost exactly the same! Nothing like reinforcing your message:

```
<meta name="description"
content="Web Pages That Suck--
learn good Web design by
looking at bad design" />
```

Other meta tags include information for the author, keywords, and copyright:

```
<meta name="Author" content="Vincent Flanders" />
<meta name="keywords" content="Web pages, accessibility,
section 508, user interface design, Web page design, intranet
design, intranet, Vincent Flanders, design techniques, sucky
pages, Web design, Web books, Web designer, usability, page
design, page layout, page design and layout" />
<meta name="Copyright" content="Copyright (c) 1996-2004
Vincent Flanders" />
```

The next tag tells search engine robots that they can index all content on the page. This is probably unnecessary, as indexing all content is usually the default, but it does no harm:

```
<meta name="ROBOTS" content="ALL" />
```

The final tag tells the Google robot that older versions of this page should not be archived:

```
<meta name="GOOGLEBOT" content="NOARCHIVE" />
```

## The Advertisements

At the top of the Webpagesthatsuck.com home page you see what look like....yep, they are ads. The giveaway is the Adds by Goooooogle link in the lower-right corner. This is program run by the Google search people that lets Website owners earn income by placing ads on their sites. What makes the program appealing to many people is that Google targets the ads specifically so they are relevant to the site content. For Webpagesthatsuck.com, the ads are all for products and services related to Web design. The JavaScript code for these ads is inserted near the top of the page:

```
<script type="text/javascript"><!--
google_ad_client = "pub-2027241362013109";
google_ad_width = 728;
google_ad_height = 90;
google_ad_format = "728x90_as";
google_ad_channel ="9215558010";
google_color_border = "0474A4";
google_color_bg = "FFFFFF";
google_color_link = "0000FF";
google_color_url = "008000";
google_color_text = "000000";
//--></script>
<script type="text/javascript"

src="http://pagead2.googlesyndication.com/pagead/show_ads.js"
>
</script>
```

Most of the script sets variables with values that identify the Web page it is on and specify various aspects of how the ads will be displayed. The script show_ads.js does the real work of displaying the ads. This script is provided by Google, so it's very easy to put the ads on your page. I am not advocating for or against this ad program, but it's something you should know about.

## The Main Table

The entire remainder of the page consists of a single HTML table in two columns. The opening **<table>** tag is as follows:

```
<table border="0" align="center" cellpadding="20"
cellspacing="0" id="mainTable">
```

The id attribute connects the table to this style sheet rule:

```
#mainTable {
    border: 1px solid #9999cd;
    background:url('images/white.gif');
    /*/*/line-height: 1.5em
  }
```

You may notice two things here. For one, the **border** specification in the **<table>** tag contradicts the **border** specification in the style sheet rule. The former takes precedence, of course, so the table has no border. Also, the table background is specified in the style sheet rule as an image that is solid white, something that is hardly necessary since the default background for tables is white. The end result is fine, but these two design factors point out that even a well-designed Web page created by an experienced designer does not always do things in the most straightforward and efficient manner.

## The Banner

The main banner, just below the ads, is displayed in a single table cell that spans the table's two columns. The code is as follows:

```
<tr>
<td colspan="2" id="header"><img src="images/Web-pages-that-
suck.jpg" alt="Vincent Flanders' Web Pages That Suck"
width="580" height="130" border="0" class="imgfloatleft"
/><br /></td>
</tr>
```

The cell itself is linked by the **id** attribute to this style sheet rule that specifies the background and foreground colors for the cell. Since there is no text in the cell, the color rule is not relevant, but it would be if the page author adds text to the cell in the future:

```
#header {
    background-color: #787fad;
    color: #787fad;
```

The **<img>** tag itself is assigned a **class** attribute that links it to this style sheet rule:

```
.imgfloatleft { float : left;  padding-right : 5px; }
```

The result is that the image floats on the left with 5 pixels of padding.

The remainder of the table is divided into narrower left and wider right columns. Each column is in fact a single cell.

## The Left Column

The left column is a single cell that is opened by this HTML tag:

```
<td id="sidebar">
```

The **id** attribute links this cell to the following style sheet rule:

```
#sidebar {
    width: 190px;
    font-size: 12px;
    vertical-align: top;
    background:url('images/white.gif') repeat-y;
    /*/*/font-size: 85%
}
```

Most important here is that the cell width is specified as a fixed 190 pixels. You can see how this affects the page display by changing the width of the browser window—the left column remains at a fixed width while the right column expands and contracts.

## The Right Column

Here's the opening tag for the right column:

```
<td id="maincontent">
```

The id attribute of this tag links it to this style rule:

```
#maincontent {
    border-left: 2px dotted #9999cd;
    background-color: #ffffff;
    vertical-align: top;
    /*/*/font-size: 100%; /* */
}
```

Note that this rule does not specify a width, hence the column will expand and contract as the browser window size changes. Note also how it specifies the dotted border between the columns.

## The Column Content

The content of the two columns in this table is mostly standard HTML that uses some style sheet rules for formatting. You will not have any trouble figuring out how these are done. One technique I do want to point is the use of HTML list elements in this column. On the page, under Examples of Bad Design, you see four links that are surrounded by dotted borders. Each of these links is its own image, but they are formatted as an unordered list:

```
<ul>
<li><a
href="http://www.Webpagesthatsuck.com/dailysucker/">Daily
Sucker -- Current Examples of Bad Design</a></li>
<li><a href="http://www.Webpagesthatsuck.com/
mysterymeatnavigation.html">Mystery Meat Navigation</a></li>
<li><a
href="http://www.Webpagesthatsuck.com/begin.htm">Original
WPTS circa 1996-98</a></li>
<li><a href="http://www.Webpagesthatsuck.com/stupid-versions-
of-the-home-page.html">Stupid Versions of the Home
Page</a></li>
</ul>
```

Normally an unordered list displays with bullets, but the page author changed the display with the following style sheet rules for the <ul> and <li> tags (the **#sidebar** specifier refers to the **id** of the table cell element):

```
#sidebar ul {
    /*/*/padding-left: 1em;
    list-style-type: none;
    margin-left: 1em; /* */
}
#sidebar li {
    /*/*/margin: 0px 0px 6px 0px; /* */
}
```

# Summary

The Webpagesthatsuck.com home page combines the use of tables, HTML formatting, and style sheet rules to create a clean, attractive, and easy-to-use interface. While there are a few inconsistencies in the details, the end result is fine—and that, after all, is what counts!

# Deconstructing Web Pages, Part III

This is the last of the three chapters n this book devoted to deconstructing Websites. By looking at the code behind top-quality, successful Websites and seeing how they did things, you can learn a lot of techniques for your own Website. Please refer back to Chapter 11 for some introductory material on this topic.

## Deconstructing useit.com

The www.useit.com Website is a lot different from some of the other Web pages we have been deconstructing. Shown in Figure 13.1, it is a "plain vanilla" site in terms of its design—no animations, images, fancy fonts, or clever layout. Does it look boring? If you think so, then you are valuing style over content. This site is loaded with useful information for Website developers and the philosophy behind the home page is simplicity. The name, by the ways, stands for "usable information technology." Jakob Nielsen is a recognized usability expert and one of the pioneers of successful Web design through careful planning and forethought.

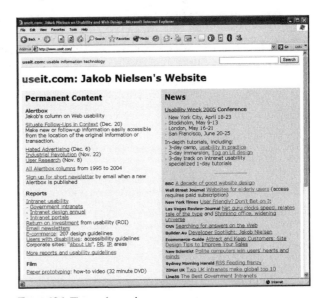

**Figure 13.1.** The useit.com home page.

### The Head Section

The <head> section of useit.com is just the essentials:

```
<head>
<title>useit.com: Jakob
Nielsen on Usability and Web
Design</title>
<meta name="keywords" con-
tent="Jakob Nielsen, Jacob
Nielsen, Jakob Nielson,
Neilsen, Neilson, Web
usability, user interface
design, discount usability
engineering, user testing,
```

```
heuristic evaluation, hypertext, Website design, UI, GUI,
HCI, CHI, UCD, user-centered design, human-computer interac-
tion">
<meta name="description" content="Alertbox column, Web
usability, usability engineering, and Jakob's minimalist
approach to Web quality; Jakob's biography. Conferences and
training events.">
<link title="Useit House Style" rel="stylesheet"
href="./useit_style.css" type="text/css">
<link rel="shortcut icon" href="/favicon.ico">
</head>
```

It's interesting to note how the author, Jakob Nielsen, has included several common misspellings of his name, such as Jacob Nielsen, in the keywords. There's no reason to loose visitors just because they misspell your name when using a search engine! There's a link to a style sheet and also a link to a "favorites" icon. By specifying this icon in a **<link>** tag like this and placing the icon file in the Website's root folder, you can have most browsers use the specified icon if the user adds the site to their favorites list (instead of the default icon).

## The Search Bar

At the top of the page is a horizontal bar with a search field and button. This lets the user search the site for information or keywords they are interested in. The code that creates this bar is shown here:

```
<form action="http://useit.mondosearch.com/cgi-
bin/MsmFind.exe" name="MONDOSEARCHFORM" method="GET">
<table bgcolor="#ffff66" width="100%" class="navbar">
<tr>
<td>
<small>
<strong>useit.com:</strong> usable information technology
</small>
</td>
<td align="right">
<input type="TEXT" name="QUERY" size="30" value=""
style="font-size: 80%">
<input type="submit" value="Search" style="font-size:
80%"></td>
</tr>
</table>
</form>
```

The search bar is created with a table that has two cells. The table is inside an HTML form, permitting the search query to be submitted. The form elements are a text field and a Submit button. You can see that the search information is directed to a program at mondosearch.com. This is the site of a company that provides searching for Websites in a more sophisticated manner than most Web authors could provide themselves. You can find more information at www.mondosearch.com.

## The Page Content

The remainder of the page content is done is the simplest possible manner. A table is used to define the two columns, and the content is formatted very simply using HTML tags. While there is an external style sheet associated with the page, it is used minimally. You can look at this HTML yourself, but I will not discuss it because there is nothing unusual to see.

## Summary

By its very simplicity, useit.com stands out from the other Web pages that have been covered here. No animations, no fancy graphics—heck, no graphics at all! The page author has simply put the information he has to offer on the Web, assuming that visitors to his page will be able to find what they need without extra decoration. While you may not want to make your own site quite so utilitarian, there is a valuable lesson to be learned from this site. Are you putting up a Website to win design awards or so people can find information? If the latter, a simpler approach may be a good idea.

# Deconstructing Download.com

Download.com is a Website that provides you with a wide variety of downloadable material ranging from software to music and games. Many downloads are free. The home page, shown in Figure 13.2, provides a clean and uncluttered interface to the site's many offerings. We know all of the people at Download.com, so if I didn't mention them, they might get mad and make all of our software listings "disappear."

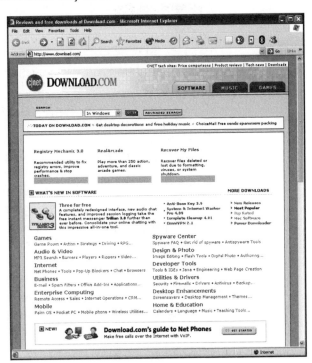

**Figure 13.2.** The Download.com home page.

## The Head Section

The Download.com home page's **<head>** section contains the usual title, keyword, and description tags as well as author and copyright tags. Looking at these tags in this and other Web pages can help you to see how experienced Web authors use these tags to optimize their sites for search engines.

```
<title>Reviews and free downloads at Download.com</title>
```

```
<meta name="description" content="Find the software you're
looking for at  Download.com, the most comprehensive source
for free-to-try software downloads  on the Web. Includes
audio programs, utilities, Internet and desktop software,
applications for developers, downloads for small business
users, and more.">
```

```
<meta name="keywords" content="download, utilities, windows,
mac, internet,  macintosh, software, application, applica-
tions, app, downloadable, dl,  shareware, freeware, demo,
osx, linux, xp, windows, 95, 98, 2000, win,  winfiles, file,
files, downloads, zip, downloader, exe">
```

```
<meta name="author" content="download.com">
```

```
<meta name="copyright" content="Copyright (c) 1995-2004 by
CNET Networks, Inc.">
```

The **<head>** section also contains a couple of tags that you may not have seen before:

```
<meta name="distribution" content="world">
<meta name="revisit-after" content="1">
```

The **distribution** meta tag indicates the intended distribution of the page content. By setting the value to "**global**" or "**world**", you specify your intent to distribute globally without restriction, but including this tag is a waste of time because that's the default for Web pages anyway. Setting the value to "**local**" or "IU" (internal use) specifies your intent for more limited distribution. Of course, this tag does not actually limit distribution; it just indicates the page author's intent.

The **revisit-after** meta tag is very rare for the very good reason that it is not supported by any of the major search engines and probably never will be. It is specific to the VancouverBC search engine, located in Vancouver, Canada, and tells the engine how often it should revisit the page to update its index.

As regards style sheets, this page goes wild! There are links to four external style sheets, as shown here:

```
<link rel="stylesheet" type="text/css"
```

```
href="http://i.i.com.com/cnwk.1d/css/all.css" />
<link rel="stylesheet" type="text/css"
href="/css/browser_specific.css" />
<link rel="stylesheet" type="text/css"
href="http://i.i.com.com/cnwk.1d/css/dl/dl_common.css" />
<link rel="stylesheet" type="text/css"
href="/css/dl/dl_fd_sponsored.css" />
```

In addition there are two separate **<style>** sections:

```
<style type="text/css">
.toppad {padding: 0 10px 0 10px;}
.mainpad {padding: 0 10px 0 15px;}
.bottompad {padding: 0 10px 0 10px;}
</style>

<style>
h2.ont {
color: #336699;
font-family: verdana;
font-size: 14px;
margin: 0px;
line-height: 5mm
}

h3.ont {
color: #336699;
font-family: verdana;
font-size: 11px;
margin: 0px;
font-weight: normal;
margin-bottom: 1mm;
}
</style>
```

It's rare to see a page that spreads its style rules out so much. In general, this sort of arrangement can be confusing because when you want to change a style detail, it can be very difficult to figure out where exactly it is defined! Also, the effects of the cascade can be difficult to determine—is this style rule superseded by another rule farther down the cascade? Unless you have a very good reason for spreading your styles out over multiple external files and internal styles, it's probably better to limit yourself to one external file and one internal <style> section.

## The Small Navigation Bar

At the very top of the page, above the tabs, is small navigation bar that starts with "CNET tech sites." While you might think that such links should be more visible, making them small saves screen real estate. This is useful too when you want to include the same links in more than one location on the page. The HTML for these links is as follows:

```
<div style="background-color:#ffffff">
<div id="cnetSites">
<a href="http://www.cnet.com/2001-1_1-0.html?tag=hd.ts">CNET
</a> tech sites:

<a href="http://shopper.cnet.com/2001-1_9-
0.html?tag=hd.ts">Price comparisons </a> |

<a href="http://reviews.cnet.com/2001-1_7-
0.html?tag=hd.ts">Product reviews</a> |

<a href="http://news.com.com/2001-1_3-0.html?tag=hd.ts">Tech
news</a> |

<a href="/2001-20_4-0.html?tag=hd.ts">Downloads</a>
</div></div>
```

You can see that the inner **<div>** tag has its **id** attribute set to "**cnetSites**". This connects it to the following style sheet rule:

```
#cnetSites {
margin: 0;
padding: 2px 5px 0;
text-align: right;
font-family: verdana, geneva;
font-size: 9px;
color: #000;
}
```

This rule displays the links at the right margin and in a small font size.

## The Main Header

The Download.com home page's main header contains the site's logo as well as three navigation tabs for software, music, and games. The logo itself is a link—two links, actually—as are the tabs. Let's see how this section of the page was created.

To start with, the entire header is enclosed in a **<div>** tag:

```
<div id="header">
```

The **id** attribute of "**header**" connects this section to the following style sheet rule:

```
#header {
position: relative;
```

```
height: 71px;
margin: 0;
border-bottom: 1px solid #000;
background: #FFF
url('http://i.i.com.com/cnwk.1d/i/dl/hdr/dl_pixelfade_bg.jpg'
) no-repeat top right;
text-align:left;
font-size:0px
}
```

Note that this rule specifies not only a bottom border and an overall size but also a background image (as well as other formatting characteristics). Why does it specify a background color if there is also a background image? My guess is that it's in case the image cannot be found; if that happens, the color will be displayed.

The logo itself is displayed using a regular **<img>** tag:

```
<img src="/i/dl/hdr/dl_logo_hed.gif" width="290" height="65"
border="0" usemap="#redball" alt="CNET Download.com" />
```

You can see that this tag specifies an image map for the two links that the logo represents. The image map, which actually comes before the **<img>** tag in the HTML, is shown here. It divides the images into two areas, one circle and one rectangle, for the two links:

```
<map name="redball">
<area shape="circle" coords="47,37,25"
href="http://www.cnet.com/2001-1_1-0.html?tag=hd.ts" />
<area shape="rectangle" coords="80,20,284,50" href="/
2001-20_4-0.html?tag=hd.ts" />
</map>
```

The three tabs are within their own **<div>** tag, which is nested within the outer **<div>** tag:

```
<div id="headerButtons">
```

The **id** attribute connects this division to this style sheet rule. The rule specifies not only the size of the area but also its precise position:

```
#headerButtons {
    position: absolute;
    width:335px;
    height:32px;
    top: 38px;
    right: 0px;
    font-size: 10px;
}
```

Then finally, the three images for the tabs are displayed:

```
<a href="/2001-20_4-0.html?tag=tab"><img
src="http://i.i.com.com/cnwk.1d/i/dl/hdr/sw_tab_on.gif"
width="111" height="32" border="0" id="dlSoftTab"
alt="Software" class="on" /></a>

<a href="http://music.download.com/2001-1_32-
0.html?tag=tab"><img
src="http://i.i.com.com/cnwk.1d/i/dl/hdr/mdl_tab_off.gif"
width="104" height="29" border="0" id="dlMusicTab"
alt="Music" class="off" /></a>

<a href="/2001-2012_4-0.html?tag=tab"><img
src="http://i.i.com.com/cnwk.1d/i/dl/hdr/games_tab_off.gif"
width="104" height="29" border="0" id="dlGamesTab"
alt="Games" class="off" /></a>
Colorful Links
```

On the right side of the page about halfway down there is a heading "More Downloads" with a list of five links under it. You cannot see this in the figure, but each of these links is a different color—a rather attractive effect. Also, each link is preceded by a small arrow. Let's see how this was done. The links are in a table, as you might expect, and here's the full HTML code for that table. This code is contained within a cell of another, outer table that determines its position on the page. I do not show the code for the outer table, however:

```
<table width="140" cellpadding="1" cellspacing="0"
border="0">
<tr valign="middle"><td ><img alt="" src="/b.gif" width="15"
height="1" /></td>
<td><img src="/i/dl/glb/arrow_gr.gif"></td>
<td valign="middle"><b class="v1">
<a href="/3140-2001_4-0-1-2.html?tag=dir"
style="color:#009933">New Releases</a>
</td></tr>
<tr valign="middle"><td ><img alt="" src="/b.gif" width="1"
height="1" /></td>
<td><img src="/i/dl/glb/arrow_gr.gif"></td>
<td valign="middle"><b class="v1">
<a href="/3101-2001_4-0-1.html?tag=dir"
style="color:#000000">Most Popular</a>
</td></tr>
<tr valign="middle"><td ><img alt="" src="/b.gif" width="1"
height="1" /></td>
<td><img src="/i/dl/glb/arrow_gr.gif"></td>
<td valign="middle"><b class="v1">
```

```
<a href="/3130-2001_4-0-1-2.html?tag=dir"
style="color:#CC9933">Top Rated</a>
</td></tr>
<tr valign="middle"><td ><img alt="" src="/b.gif" width="1"
height="1" /></td>
<td style="color:#336699"><img
src="/i/dl/glb/arrow_gr.gif"></td>
<td valign="middle"><b class="v1">
<a href="/2001-2003_4-0.html?tag=dir" style="color:
#FF0000">Mac Software</a>
</td></tr>
<tr valign="middle"><td ><img alt="" src="/b.gif" width="1"
height="1" /></td>
<td style="color:#336699"><img
src="/i/dl/glb/arrow_gr.gif"></td>
<td valign="middle"><b class="v1">
<a href="/2001-2645_4-0.html?tag=dir">Power Downloader</a>
</td></tr>
</table>
```

The first tag is the **<table>** tag that sets the basic parameters of the table:

```
<table width="140" cellpadding="1" cellspacing="0"
border="0">
```

Then, for each of the five links there is a row that specifies only the vertical alignment of the row contents:

```
<tr valign="middle">
```

Each row contains three cells. The first cell contains only an image displayed at 1 x 1 pixels, serving as a spacer:

```
<td><img alt="" src="/b.gif" width="1" height="1" /></td>
```

The second cell contains the image of the arrow:

```
<td><img src="/i/dl/glb/arrow_gr.gif"></td>
```

The third cell contains the link itself:

```
<td valign="middle">
<a href="/2001-2003_4-0.html?tag=dir" style="color:
#FF0000">Mac Software</a>
</td>
```

The **valign="middle"** attribute is not really necessary because this alignment was already specified in the **<tr>** tag, but including it again does no harm. You can see that the **<a>** tag includes a **style** attribute that sets the link's color—red in this case. The other four links in this table have different color values.

## Summary

The Download.com Website provides some useful lessons in Web design. It manages to include a lot of information and links while maintaining a clean and uncluttered design. Not only that, it has some great downloads you may find useful, including Web page design tools.

# Deconstructing google.com

By far, the most successful search engine is Google. It's become so widely used that it has even spawned a new word—to "google" something means to look it up on Google. With all this success and attention you might think that the Google home page is really impressive. Think again—it is amazingly simple, as shown in Figure 13.3.

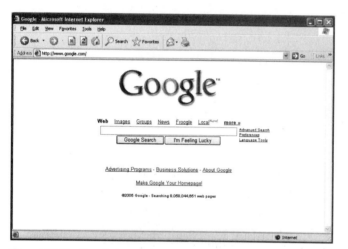

**Figure 13.3.** The Google home page.

The fact is that Google's success lies in the breadth and accuracy of its searches and not in the appearance of its home page. Let's take a look at the inner working of this page.

### The Head Section

The **<head>** section is quite simple. There's a **<title>** tag of course:

```
<title>Google</title>
```

What about meta tags for keywords and description? Not a trace of them—and this makes sense when you think about it because Google is hardly worried about being listed in the search engines!

While there is no external style sheet, there is one internal style rule:

```
<style><!--
body,td,a,p,.h{font-family:arial,sans-serif;}
.h{font-size: 20px;}
.q{color:#0000cc;}
//-->
</style>
```

## The Body Tag

The **<body>** tag of the Google home page is as follows:

```
<body bgcolor=#ffffff text=#000000 link=#0000cc vlink=#551a8b
alink=#ff0000 onLoad=sf()>
```

You can see that it defines text as black and the background as white and also specifies colors for links, active links, and visited links. It also uses the **onLoad** attribute to specify that the JavaScript function **sf()** be executed when the page loads. That function is short and sweet:

```
function sf(){document.f.q.focus();}
```

This might not make sense at first, but will once you know the following points:

- The page's **<form>** element has its name attribute set to **f**.
- On the form, the **<input>** element (where the user enters their search term) has its **name** attribute set to **q**.

Now you can see that when the page loads, this function sets the focus to the input element so the user can start typing right away—a nice design touch!

## How the Search Works

There's no way we can look inside the internal workings of Google, but we can figure out how the home page submits the information to the search engine. For pages that submit form information, you can often gain some insight into how they work by examining the URL they submit. Assuming they are using the default **GET** method of form submission, the information they are sending is encoded in the URL. For example, if I enter "Iceland" into the search field and click the Google Search button, here's the URL that is used:

```
http://www.google.com/search?hl=en&q=Iceland&btnG=Google+Sear
ch
```

There are three parts to this:

- http://www.google.com is the base URL.
- /search is the action specified in the **<form>** tag.
- Everything after the question mark is the submitted data.

Submitted data is organized in variable name=value pairs. If there is more than one item being submitted, they are separated by the ampersand symbol (&). Spaces are replaced by plus signs. Now you can see that this submission includes:

- A variable named **hl** with the value **en**.

- A variable named **q** with the value **Iceland**.
- A variable named **btnG** with the value **Google Search**.

We know that each value in a form submission comes from an element on the form. Obviously the element **q** is the field where you enter the search term. To finish deconstructing the form, we must look for elements with the names **hl** and **btnG**. And indeed we find them. **hl** is the name of a hidden element:

```
<input type=hidden name=hl value=en>
```

Hidden elements let you submit data as part of the form without letting the user see or edit it. My guess is that this element is used to signal the search engine that the English language is in use.

The **btnG** element turns out to be a button, or more specifically a submit element:

```
<input type=submit value="Google Search" name=btnG>
```

When this value is included in the form submission, the search engine knows that the Search Google button was clicked and not the I'm Feeling Lucky button.

## Summary

The Google home page derives its power and popularity not from the page content itself, but from what's behind the page—namely Google's powerful search capabilities. The page is very simple and leaves no doubt in the user's mind as to how to proceed. The page emphasizes function over style, and that's a great lesson for a Web designer to learn.

# Part 4

• • • • • • • • • • • • • • • • • • • • • •

# Advice From a
# Professional Webmaster

You've accomplished a lot by now, and are well on your way to

becoming a great Webmaster. In these final five chapters I will cover

a variety of topics that any Web Designer should know about,

including search engine optimization, blogging, and images.

• • • • • • • • • • • • • • • • • • • • • •

# Website Usability Concerns

Webmasters often pay too much attention to the appearance of their pages at the expense of something equally if not more important—usability. A Website is a tool that serves specific purposes. A personal site may be just to let the world know about your family, pets, and hobbies. A business site will be designed to let potential customers locate information about your company and products. A university site should make it easy for guests to locate information on admissions, courses, expenses, and campus life. No matter how gorgeous a Website is, if it does not fulfill its intended task it is a failure—sort of like a beautiful, sleek sports car with a 40-horsepower engine, bad brakes, and a leaky roof! In this chapter, I cover a range of usability concerns that you should be aware of.

## Navigational Structure

If you have a one-page Website, then there's no navigational structure to worry about. As soon as you go beyond a few pages, however, it's a good idea to give the matter some thought. I am using the term to mean two related things:

- The way information is divided between the pages
- The way the links between pages are organized

Let's look at these in turn.

### Planning Your Pages

Completely separate from the question of page appearance and design is deciding what material goes on a page. The general rule is, of course, that related material should be kept together. On a personal Website, for example, one page might be devoted to baby pictures, another page to family history, and so on. This is only logical, and site visitors expect this kind of organization.

But what if a topic includes only a little bit of information, enough to fill, let's say, one third of a typical browser window? That wouldn't look good, so it's okay to combine skimpy topics on the same page as long as they are clearly identified.

You can also face the opposite problem—a topic with too much information to fit on one page. Visitors can always scroll down in the browser window to view it, but you may prefer to have everything visible at once. In that case, you can divide the material over two or more pages and use Next and Previous links to let people move between them. If you do want to have the entire page visible, you have to take screen size into consideration, as discussed later in this chapter.

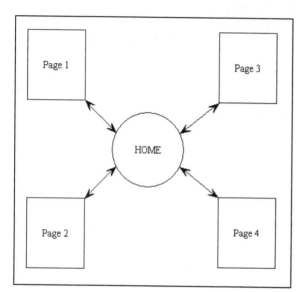

**Figure 14.1.** A simple hub-and-spoke link structure.

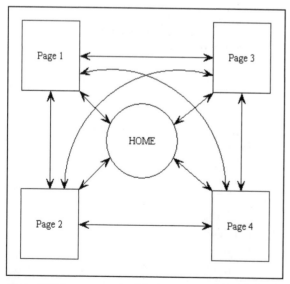

**Figure 14.2.** A more complex link structure in which each page links to every other page.

## Planning Your Links

You've probably had the experience of getting bogged down in a Website and not being able to find what you want or even get back to where you started. Few things are more frustrating, and you certainly do not want this happening to your visitors! It's only a problem on more complex sites—that is, sites with a lot of pages—but even with simpler sites you should give some thought to your navigational structure.

Many simpler sites use a traditional hub-and-spoke design. The hub is the home page, of course, and each spoke is a link to a topic page. Then, each topic page includes a link back to the home page. This is diagrammed in Figure 14.1.

To provide your users with more flexibility, you may want each page on the site to contain a link to every other page. Figure 14.2 shows a diagram of this kind of link structure. When you use this approach, it is a good idea to display the links similarly in each page—in other words, with the same formatting and in the same location, so users will be able to find them easily.

Problems are rare with either of the link structures presented so far. This is because no page is more than one or two jumps away from any other. Problems are much more likely to arise when your site's link structure gets deeper than two levels with a large number of pages. Look, for instance, at the link structure in Figure 14.3. Here we have two "branches" of related pages, each starting at the home page. I think you can see why a user who has found themselves on Page 3 might have trouble finding Page C! And, just think how these problems can be multiplied on a site with dozens of pages and five or six levels of links! There's no way you could link every page to every other page. It's all too easy for a visitor to get lost on such a site, and that's a guarantee for frustration!

What's to be done for large, complex Websites? There's no easy answer, but here are some tips:

- Include a link to the home page on every page.

- Be consistent in the way you format, display, and use links in all parts of the site.

- Use "breadcrumbs," or link trails, that show the visitor where they are in the site.

- Include a site map, covered next.

## Site Maps

A site map is a Web page that displays the names of all the site's pages with links to each one. For example, Figure 14.4 shows the site map for the CoffeeCup Website. You can see how the page titles are organized in related groups and each one is a link. You can get to any page on the site from the site map in a single click.

Of course, for a site map to be useful, the page titles must be accurate and descriptive. Some Web design software offers automatic site map generation, but it's not very difficult to do it yourself. Be sure to keep it up-to-date when you make changes to the site! Generally you should have a link to the site map on every page in the site.

## Browser Compatibility Issues

While Microsoft has done a pretty good job of taking over the browser world with

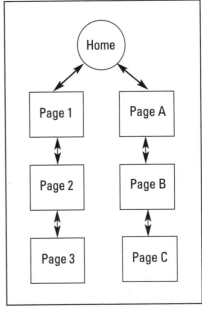

**Figure 14.3.** A link structure with four levels.

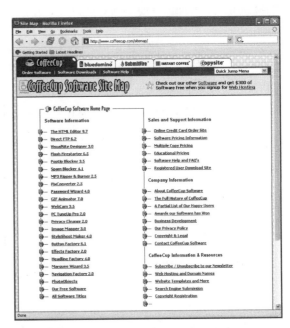

**Figure 14.4.** The site map for the CoffeeCup Website.

Internet Explorer, it hasn't quite vanquished all other browser platforms. My information has Internet Explorer being used by somewhere between 70 and 75 percent of users. Of the remainder, the vast majority uses Netscape Navigator and other Mozilla-based browsers, primarily Firefox. What does this mean to the Webmaster?

## What Kind of Incompatibilities Exist?

What sort of problems do the incompatibilities between the browsers cause? They range from the trivial to the serious. On the less-serious side, you may see table borders not display quite as intended or style sheet rules interpreted in slightly different ways. On the serious side, whole sections of a page may not display at all (although this kind of thing is rare). Testing is the only sure way to tell.

In an ideal world, it would not mean anything—all browsers would follow the same standards and would work the same when it come to rendering HTML, interpreting style sheets, and executing JavaScript. As you may have noticed, however, this is not an ideal world! While the various browsers have excellent compatibility with one another, it is not 100 percent.

The bottom line is that you have two choices, as I see it. You can do your testing in just Internet Explorer, know that 80 to 85 percent of users will see your pages fine, and hope that whatever incompatibilities exist will not prevent Netscape and Firefox users from enjoying your pages. Or you can test in all three browsers to be sure. My opinion is that the best way to create and test your pages is to create them in the most current, standards-compliant browser you can (this would be Firefox) and then tweak your pages for Internet Explorer. This will save you lots of time when you do find a little bug that needs to be squashed in IE.

Fortunately the browsers are all free, and in my experience there is no problem having them all installed on the same system. Here's where to get them:

Firefox: http://www.getfirefox.com

Internet Explorer: http://www.microsoft.com/windows/ie/default.mspx

Netscape: http://channels.netscape.com/ns/browsers/default.jsp

Opera: http://www.opera.com

## Screen Size Concerns

People who visit your page will have a variety of monitor types and sizes, ranging from a small 800x600 laptop screen to a giant 1600x1200 21 inch monitor. It's only natural for a page designer to create pages that look good on his or her own monitor, but you should be concerned about all your viewers. Most important, you should consider the possibility that many site visitors will have a monitor that has lower resolution than yours. The result can be that a beautiful Web page that displays nicely on your monitor is too big and will display only partially, requiring the user to scroll vertically and horizontally to view all the content.

There's no universal solution to potential screen size problems, but there are steps you can take to minimize them. For maximum usability I suggest testing your pages at the 800x600 or 1024x768 screen resolution because these are the lowest screen resolutions in common use. Of course you need do this only if your own screen resolution is higher. Here's how:

1. Right-click an empty spot on your Windows Desktop.

2. Select Properties from the popup menu to display the Display Properties dialog box.

3. Click the Settings tab.

4. Change the Screen Resolution setting to either 800x600 or 1024x768.

5. Click OK.

Your screen will resize to the new resolution and you can evaluate your pages to see how they will look and work. When you are finished, repeat the above steps to return the display to your normal resolution.

## Download Times

While broadband Internet access, mainly cable and DSL, is getting more and more common, there are still millions of people who use a dial-up (modem) connection. If your pages are slow to download for these users, they may give up in frustration! You may want to estimate the download times for your pages and decide if they are too long.

To estimate download time, use Windows Explorer to determine the file size for each HTML file and for all the images that the file displays. Add these values together to get the total download size. Then use Table 14.1 to estimate the download time. Note that 56k is the speed of the fastest modems under ideal conditions, and 28.8k is the speed of some older modems.

**Table 14.1.** Estimating dial-up download times.

| FILE SIZE | MODEM SPEED | |
|---|---|---|
| | 28.8k | 56k |
| 250 KB | 2 min | 1 min |
| 500 KB | 4 min | 2 min |
| 1 MB | 7 min | 4 min |
| 5 MB | 37 min | 22 min |

What can you do if you feel that the download time for one of your pages is excessive? At times there will be nothing you can do except warn users, but in other situations there are corrective actions to take:

• Split the large page into two or more smaller pages that link to each other. The total download time will not change, but user frustration will be decreased because each page loads faster.

- Decrease image size. This includes both decreasing the pixel size when possible and, for JPEG files, increasing the compression level to get smaller files.

## Creating Accessible Web Pages

Much of the power of the Web derives from its universality, and this means that access to information on the Web should be available to everyone regardless of disability. For Web pages, this applies mostly to people with visual impairments, which can range from total blindness to an inability to read small type or distinguish certain colors. Following are some general guidelines for creating accessible Web pages:

- Use standard HTML. Many visually impaired people use special browsers that assist them by doing things such as converting text to speech or displaying text in extra-large letters. Such browsers may not be able to interpret nonstandard HTML, special plug-ins, and other proprietary page elements.

- Maintain a consistent page layout. Having your links in the same location, with the same formatting, on every page makes them easier to locate.

- Maintain readability. This means keeping backgrounds simple and ensuring good contrast between the text and the background. Text against a busy background, or dark text against a black background, can be difficult for anyone to read!

- Make links descriptive. Instead of just "Click Here," a link should be a description of what it points to. Thus, instead of

  ```
  <A HREF="about.htm">Click here</A> for company information.
  ```

  you would create the link as follows:

  ```
  <A HREF="about.htm">View company information</a>
  ```

- Use **alt** attributes to describe images. Text-to-speech browsers typically read the **alt** attribute of each **<img>** tag to provide a description of the image for the user.

Web page accessibility is an evolving topic. You can keep abreast of developments at the World Wide Web Consortium's page here: http://www.w3.org/WAI/

## Summary

Websites are like people in one way—looks are not everything! In addition to being visually attractive, your site should be usable. In my experience, it is usability more than anything else (except content, of course) that keeps people coming back to your Website.

# Optimizing Your Site for the Search Engines

It goes almost without saying that if you have created a Website, you want people to visit it. Perhaps the best way to attract new visitors is with a listing on one or more of the search engines such as Google, Yahoo!, and AltaVista. This chapter shows you some strategies that will help you get listed—and listed at a good position—on the search engines. This is called *search engine optimization*, or *SEO*.

## Search Engine Basics

All of the search engines work in basically the same way, at least from the user's perspective. You go to the engine's Website and type in the term of interest, say *digital photography* or *Chinese cooking*, and hit the Search button. A few seconds later you'll see a list of related Websites. Unless you are searching for a very obscure topic you are likely to get a huge number of hits. Table 15.1 shows some examples from Google.

These results may give you some idea of how big the Web is and how much information is available on it. They should also bring home the point that being included in a search engine's listings is not in itself enough—you want a decent placement so people will actually find you! Let's face it, if your site is at the 450th position, very few people will find you through the search engine because they will almost surely find what they are looking for before they get to your listing.

Table 15.1. Number of Google hits for various search terms.

| SEARCH TERM | NUMBER OF HITS |
| --- | --- |
| Chinese cooking | 2,180,000 |
| Boxing | 6,870,000 |
| Digital photography | 6,080,000 |
| Rock and roll | 6,100,000 |
| Marilyn Monroe | 1,430,000 |
| History of Norway | 2,650,000 |

## How Search Engines Work

Most search engines—about 95 percent by latest estimates—use automated software programs to perform their indexing. These programs are called *spider robots* because they "crawl" the World Wide Web in much the same way a real spider moves around its Web. These programs move from page to page using the hyperlinks that are the heart of the Web. The content of each page is analyzed and that information is used to determine if the page will be included n the listings and, if so, where. The "where" part includes both the topic the site will be listed under and its position within each topic listing.

How exactly does a spider robot analyze a page? That's the $64,000 question and I cannot answer it for you. As you might well expect, each search engine keeps its listing and ranking algorithms secret. After all, if this information were made public, Web page authors would be able to tailor their pages specifically to do well in the listings, something the search engine people do not want. Of course, while we cannot know exactly how a specific search engine rates and ranks Web pages, we can certainly make some educated guesses. Along with my experience in the SEO field, this provides the basis for the information presented in this chapter.

## Submitting Your Site

Spiders find most of their targets by following links on the Web. Of course, this means they will revisit pages on a regular basis, but that's part of the plan. On second and subsequent visits the spider can, first of all, verify that the page still exists so that, if it doesn't, dead links can be removed from the search engine database. It will also examine the information in the page to see if anything has changed and, if appropriate, change the site's listing topic and/or position.

But what about the brand-new site that you just created? Being new, there will not be any links to it, so how will the search engine spiders find it? The answer lies in submitting your site to the search engines. Once you have submitted your site, the search engine will know about your URL and will put it in the list of URLs to be visited by the spider.

CoffeeCup also has a service called SubmitFire that submits your site to over 3,000 of the most popular search engines and directories, considerably increasing the chances of someone finding your Website. SubmitFire will save you valuable time, effort, and money. The automatic monthly submissions are essential in preventing newly submitted competitors from taking your place in the search results.

Table 15.2 lists the major search engines and information about how to submit a site to each one. Be aware that some search engines share databases, so submitting to one gets you submitted to the others too. For example, as this book is being written, the database used by the Microsoft Network is also used by America Online, Excite, and Overture. Likewise, the Open Directory Project database is used by Ask Jeeves, Lycos, and Netscape.

Keep in mind that submission is not an instant process. You cannot expect to submit your site to a search engine and be listed the next day—it may take weeks for the process to complete. Also, submission is no guarantee that you'll be listed at all. The search engines have various listing criteria, and if your site does not meet them, you will not be listed, no notice or explanation given. But don't be discouraged—if you follow the advice in this chapter, it is very unlikely this will happen to you.

**Table 15.2.** Information for submitting sites to the major search engines.

| SEARCH ENGINE | URL | COMMENTS |
| --- | --- | --- |
| Google | http://www.google.com/addurl.html | Enter your site's URL and some brief comments to help the spider categorize the site. |
| Yahoo! | http://www.yahoo.com | Start by displaying the category that is most appropriate for your site. Then click the Suggest a Site link in the upper-right portion of the category page. |
| AltaVista | http://www.altavista.com | Click the Submit a Site link on the home page. |
| Open Directory | http://dmoz.org/add.html | Read the guidelines and then go to dmoz.org. Find the category that is most appropriate for your site and click the Suggest URL link. |
| Microsoft Network | http://submitit.bcentral.com/msnsubmit.htm | Enter your URL and email address and then click Submit Site. |

# Outside Links

It's very important to have some outside links pointing to your page. Some search engines consider this an important parameter in ranking pages. The more outside sites that link to a page, in theory, the more valuable and interesting that page must be. There's some validity to this, but the fact that search engines use outside links as a ranking factor has led to a lot of abuse. People would go to a lot of effort to exchange links with others even if the links made no sense. Joe would link his fishing page to Nancy's knitting page and vice versa just to increase link count. The search engines have caught on and are no longer using raw link count as they used to. Again, the details are kept secret, but other factors such as link relevancy are being considered, so you can no longer count on boosting your ranking just by getting a lot of irrelevant links to your page.

But how does a new Web page get outside links? There's no getting around that it just takes some effort on your part, particularly at the beginning when your site is new and unknown. Your strategy will depend to some extent on the type of page.

Commercial pages are trying to sell something, whether a product or service. You can't expect to get links from your competitor's pages, but you can try the following:

- If you belong to any professional associations or trade groups, see if they have member listings on their Website. It might even be worth joining a group just to be included in their listings.

- Try for links from the pages of related businesses (reciprocating of course with a link from your page to theirs). For example, a flooring contractor might trade links with a professional house painter, or a graphics designer might trade links with a printing shop.

- Look for private or governmental agencies whose job it is to promote trade and business. Your town or county might have a Web page promoting local businesses, for example.

For personal pages—pages that are first and foremost about the author—the process is a bit different. Your best bet is to try to get reciprocal links with other people's personal pages. Friends and family are the first place to try; then you can keep your eyes out for interesting personal pages of people you do not know and inquire about a reciprocal link.

Topic pages are pages that are about a specific topic, such as fly-fishing, car racing, sewing, or what have you. When trying to develop some external links to your topic page, your best bet is to find other people who are interested in the same topic. Most Web authors are more than happy to swap links with other pages on the same topic as theirs. You can also look for "links" pages that provide a comprehensive set of links to pages on a specific topic and submit your page there.

## Keep Your Topics Separate

A lot of people get a great deal of satisfaction from creating Web pages dealing with topics they find interesting. It can be a lot of fun to do research, seek out images, and put together a useful reference site on some topic. No matter how strange you think your interest is, trust me—there are plenty of other people with the same interest, and a well-designed Web page is a great way to meet them. But be sure to keep your topics separate, one to a page. Combining two or more topics on a single page will confuse the search engines and lead to lower and/or improper search engine listings. You can have a single home page with links to all the other pages on your site.

# Page Optimization Techniques

The following sections describe the technique you will use to optimize your page content for the search engines. Page layout and design considerations will be covered later in the chapter.

## Your Keyword Strategy

The key to site optimization lies in your selections of keywords. A keyword is a word or short phrase that describes your site's content accurately and concisely. Site optimization is largely a matter of selecting and using keywords carefully. When a search engine examines your site, it looks for keywords. Where does it look?

Everywhere! While you can designate specific words as "official keywords" using a meta tag (discussed soon), the search engines don't really care about this—they look at the entire content of the document when deciding the page's keywords. More than anything else, the frequency with which a word or phrase occurs on a page determines the weight it is given.

Needless to say, common words such as *the* and *and* are ignored by the search engines. For this reason, it is advisable to avoid common words in key phrases. For example, aviation history is a better key phrase than *history of aviation*.

For each page, you should decide on a single key word or phrase and use it consistently throughout the page. Because of the way keywords work, each page can have only one primary keyword. A search engine may well pick up on other keywords for the page, but they will unavoidably be secondary. This is one reason why it is a good idea to place individual topics each on its own page, as I mentioned earlier. For example, rather than having a single "programming tips" page that covers both Visual Basic and Delphi, it would be better to have a separate page for each language.

## Page Title

Many people believe that the title tag is the most important part of your optimization strategy. There are two reasons for this.

First, the title of a page provides—or at least should provide—a concise description of the page and its contents. Because the title is displayed in the browser title bar, Web page authors are hesitant to load it up with extra irrelevant keywords or other junk.

## Don't Fake It

Upon learning that the search engines pay attention to the frequency of keywords, some Web designers have tried various sneaky techniques to fool them. One example is including HTML comments in the page with the keyword repeated dozens of times. Another is to include an invisible paragraph (white text on a white background) with the keyword repeated over and over. Guess what? The search engines have caught on to these tactics, and if anything, you will end up with a lower ranking. Yes, you want to repeat your keyword frequently, but you need to do so in a valid manner that is not detected as an attempt to trick the search engine ranking process.

Second, the page title is the first thing displayed in a search engine listing. Take a look at Google, for example. Each listing in a search result consists of the page title first, serving as the link to the page, followed by a brief excerpt and the URL. It's the title that users see first, and it is the title that will tempt them to click through to your page—or will make them pass you by for some other page.

Your page title should tie in with your keyword strategy. Ideally the title will contain your primary keyword or phrase. But a good title by itself is rarely enough. If your page has a really odd and unusual topic, a good title by itself may get you a high ranking on the search engines, but for most of us the title is just part, albeit a very important part, of your overall SEO strategy.

## Your Text

Perhaps the most important part of the page is the text. After all, this (along with images) is the content of the page and is what visitors will see, and the search engines take this into account when ranking a page. You want to write what is called *keyword-rich* text without having it come across as stilted or artificial. There's no perfect formula for doing this, and it can be a challenge, but it's an important part of your SEO strategy. Let's look at an example. Here's a hypothetical first paragraph for a page that deals with *Visual Basic* programming (the key phrase of course is Visual Basic).

I have always loved programming in Visual Basic since it was first released. It is a powerful and intuitive programming tool that lets you create sophisticated Windows applications quickly. VB is pretty easy to learn also because it has a simple syntax and no complex rules. I highly recommend it for people just getting started in programming.

The preceding paragraph is an example of poor text writing, at least from the SEO standpoint. Let's see how it would look after an SEO expert got through editing it.

Visual Basic has been my favorite programming language ever since it was first released. Visual Basic is a powerful and intuitive programming tool that lets you create sophisticated Windows applications quickly. You'll find that Visual Basic is pretty easy to learn because it has a simple syntax and no complex rules. I highly recommend Visual Basic for people just getting started in programming.

Why is this second paragraph better? There are two reasons. First, the key phrase is the very first thing in the paragraph, and since this is the first paragraph on the page, it is also the first thing on the page. Search engines pay attention to things like this! Second, the key phrase occurs four times rather than just once. This was easily accomplished by not using the abbreviation VB or pronouns such as it in places where the full phrase could be spelled out.

## Using alt Attributes

The **<img>** tag used to display images can include an optional **alt** attribute that specifies text to be displayed if the image file cannot be found. Many people omit the **alt** attribute from image tags because they are confident that the image file will be available, particularly if it is on the same Website. However, **alt** attributes can be part of your optimization scheme. Spiders may not be able to look at your images and determine the content, but they can read **alt** attributes. Each **alt** attribute can provide the spider with a bit more information with which to judge and rank your page. By simply using your keywords or key phrase in all your alt attributes, you can increase the impact of the page on the search engines.

But is blind repetition of the same keywords a good idea? Maybe not. Many search engines have caught on to the fact that some Web page authors repeat the same keywords dozens if not hundreds of times simply hoping to improve their ranking. By varying things to some degree, you are more likely to make an impression. One way to do this is to repeat your primary keyword while including a different secondary keyword in each attribute. For example, a fishing Web page could use "fishing trout" as the first **alt** attribute, "fishing bass" as the second, "fishing perch" as the third, and so on. Another approach is to include sequential numbers in the **alt** attributes so no two are the same: "fishing 1," "fishing 2," and so on.

## Using Meta Tags

You learned in Chapter 2 how meta tags can be used to include various kinds of information n the head section of an HTML document. There are two meta tags that have a role in SEO: description and keywords.

The description tag, as you might well expect, provides a brief description of the page. Descriptions tend to be used by search engines when someone searches for your page not by keyword but by your company name or URL. It's a good idea to include a brief—as in a short paragraph at most—description for each page. Here's an example:

> ## Accessibility and the alt Attribute
>
> Unfortunately, using the **<img>** tag's **alt** attribute as an SEO strategy will conflict with efforts to create a Website that is accessible to visually impaired people. Such people often use specialized browsers that convert the text on a Web page to speech, including the **alt** attribute of images. To be effective in this context, the **alt** attribute must contain a good description of the image that will let those who cannot see the image understand the Web page. Such descriptions may work with your SEO strategy, but if they don't, you will have to choose.

Acme Sportswear provides a wide selection of men's, women's, and children's sportswear at hard-to-beat prices. Whether it is for skiing, surfing, hiking, or scuba diving, Acme has just the sportswear you need. Our convenient online catalog and ordering system makes it easy for you to find and purchase your sportswear needs without leaving the comfort of your home.

Note that the keyword—*sportswear*—was featured prominently in the description, always a good idea. As a reminder, to create a description meta tag you would put the following in the head section of the document:

```
<meta name="description" content="Description goes here" />
```

The second meta tag you need to know about is the keyword tag. Meta keywords are thought by many people to be the most important part of SEO. Unfortunately, they are wrong. It's true that search engines used to give a lot of weight to meta keywords, but it soon became apparent that meta keywords were being heavily abused. The problem is that a Web page author can include any meta keywords they like even if they have nothing to do with the actual content of your page. Authors were including popular meta keywords just to attract traffic. A page that sold vitamins might include *Elvis Presley*, *sex*, and *free money* in the meta keywords just in the hopes of attracting a few people who would stick around to buy something. As a result, search engines stopped paying much attention to meta keywords and started concentrating on the page's actual content.

There's no harm in including meta keywords in your page. After all, a few search engines still give them some weight, and they do no harm with engines that ignore them. The syntax is as follows:

```
<meta name="keywords" content="keyword1, keyword2, ..." />
```

# Page Design Considerations

The first part of this chapter showed you some techniques for creating Website content that will maximize your chances of getting an appropriate listing and good position on the major search engines. But content is not all there is to SEO—the way your pages are designed and laid out is important too. Design and layout considerations are mostly a matter of knowing what to avoid. Why is this? Certain design techniques may create visually stunning pages, but they hide content from the search engines. You may have the best page anywhere on a certain topic, but if the content is hidden from the search engines, you won't get many visitors.

## Frames

I explained in an earlier chapter why I think frames are best avoided altogether. If you need another reason to avoid frames, here it is: frames can seriously hinder or prevent altogether the proper indexing of a page by the search engines.

Remember, frames are a way to present two or more independent windows on a single page. The main page—the one that you want listed n the search engines—usually does not contain any content but just the frame definitions. Each frame then displays a separate HTML document where the real content is located. But—and this is crucial—the search engines do not see this because these separate documents are loaded by the user's browser and the search engines see only your content-free frames page. This is not good!

## Flash Animations

Flash is a popular program that can create truly stunning animations, complete with sound, navigation buttons, and dynamic content, for display on your Web page. The problem with Flash is that, as you may have guessed, it too hides content from the search engines. Anything in a Flash animation might as well not exist as far as the search engines are concerned—including the hyperlinks, which means that the search engine cannot follow the links to locate other pages on your site to index.

Used within reason, Flash is fine. There's no reason not to have an attractive Flash banner at the top of your page. But the program is powerful enough to create complete pages, and that's not a good idea from the SEO standpoint. Google will find a link to your Flash file off your Website, but it will not able to index the contents of it. You want your page content available where the search engines can find it.

## PDF Files

PDF stands for *Portable Document Format*, a file format developed by Adobe specifically for distribution and printing of complex formatted documents. Many Websites use PDF files to allow the user to download and view or print documents such as product manuals, catalogs, and instruction sheets. When used properly, PDF files are a great tool, but search engines cannot index their content.

## Image Maps

An image map is an image that has been divided up into several sections, each section serving as a hyperlink to another page. You have probably seen them used for geographical maps where you click the state or country of interest to go to the relevant Web page. All very nice, but links in an image map are not readable by a spider robot, thus preventing further indexing of your site. If you must use an image map, you should also include a more traditional set of links using HTML for the search engines to use.

## JavaScript Navigation

Links that are within JavaScript code cannot be followed by search engines. If you want to use JavaScript for navigation within your site, it's a good idea to also include traditional HTML links for the spiders to follow.

# Standards Compliance and Valid HTML

It only makes sense that the search engines spiders are designed to read HTML so that they can figure out what your page is about. I feel another solid argument for creating standards-compliant, valid HTML pages is that these spiders can read your content easier with fewer errors. That makes them even more search engine friendly, and I've seen cases in which it can have a very positive impact on your search rankings.

## Summary

Search engines are an essential part of the World Wide Web. There's a huge amount of information on the Web, and I cannot imagine how anyone would find anything without using a search engine. To drive traffic to your site—something every Webmaster wants—you need a search engine listing. Following the techniques in this chapter for Web page design and submission is your best bet to get an accurate listing and good ranking.

# Images for Your Website

A Website without any images will be pretty boring. Even if most or all of the information on your site is text, it's a good idea to include a few images simply for decoration and to break up solid blocks of text. Many Websites, of course, are mostly images. HTML provides you with tags for placing images on your pages, controlling their size, and adding features such as borders. However, Web pages are limited to displaying only a few of a many dozens of different image file formats that are available. Don't worry. These few formats are more than adequate for your page design needs, but you need to understand how they differ, which one to use for a given situation, and how to optimize images for use on the Web. This chapter starts out with a brief primer on image basics and then gets into the specifics of using images on your Web pages.

To work with images, you will need a graphics program. There are many on the market, and most of them will do everything that the typical Webmaster needs. The industry standard (whatever that means!) is Adobe Photoshop, and that's what I use for the examples in this chapter (version 7 to be specific). Any other program, such as Paint Shop Pro or Photoshop Elements, will have most of the same capabilities although the menu commands and dialog boxes may be different.

## Image Basics

You may already know all about digital images, in which case you can skip this section. If not, or if you want to review, please read on. You need to know these fundamentals to make the most of the remainder of the chapter.

All images that can be used on the Web are *bitmap* images, sometimes also called raster images. A bitmap image comprises a grid of dots, or pixels, and the file where the image is stored contains a series of numbers for each pixel, specifying the color. Most of the images that are used on computers are this type.

Another type of image is the vector image. Rather than pixel information strung together, vector images are stored as a series of instructions required to create the image. For example, a circle might be stored as numbers that specify the position of the circle, its radius, the thickness of the line used to draw it, and the color. Vector images are converted to pixels for display, but internally they are stored as I just described. You cannot use vector images on the Web without first converting them to a bitmap images. The remainder of this chapter is devoted to bitmap images.

## Resolution and Size

Every bitmap image has a size—that is, the number of pixels it has both horizontally and vertically. This is usually expressed as width x height, so an image that is 200 pixels wide and 150 pixels would be described as being 200 x 150.

An image's pixel size is sometimes referred to as its resolution—but this is incorrect. The term resolution actually means how many pixels an image has per inch, or pixels per inch (ppi). Thus, an image might have a resolution of 72 ppi, 150 ppi, and so on. With rare exception, an image's resolution will be the same both vertically and horizontally.

But wait just a minute—a digital image exists in a disk file and in computer memory, so how can you assign pixels to physical units such as inches? The truth is you cannot really do so, and this is an important point: digital images do not have an inherent physical size. You can print a digital image at any size you like, and you can also display it on screen at different sizes. So, where do the "inches" come from?

The fact is that most graphics programs assign a resolution to every image for purely practical reasons. When an image has a resolution assigned to it, then it also has a physical size associated with it (as I'll explain soon). This will be the size that the image is printed at by default.

You may have already realized that an image's pixel size, its resolution, and its physical size are all related. The relationship is expressed by this formula:

physical width = (pixel width) / (horizontal resolution)

physical height = (pixel height) / (vertical resolution)

## When Resolution Matters

There is one situation in which an image's resolution and physical size are meaningful. This is when you are scanning images and there is an original image with an actual physical size. Scanning software will—or at least should—create a digital image that has the correct measurements for size and resolution.

You can see that in order to change one of these items, you must change at least one of the others. But here's what makes the Webmaster's life easier—all you need to be concerned with is the pixel size. That's right; for the Web, an image's physical size is meaningless, so you can forget about it. The process of changing an image's pixel size is called *resampling*, and essentially any graphics program will have this capability.

## Color Depth

Digital images do not all contain the same amount of color information. There are four levels of color information that you will encounter most often:

- Two color: Every pixel in the image is either black or white. This mode is appropriate for line drawings and text.

- Gray scale: The image is made up of 256 shades of gray ranging from pure white to pure black. This mode is most commonly used for black-and-white photos.

- 256 color: The image contains a maximum of 256 different colors. This mode is appropriate for nonphotographic color images such as charts and logos.

- True color: The image contains up to 16 million+ colors. This is called true color because it can accurately represent any color image including photographs.

Color depth is important because the Web image file formats support different color depths. Knowing the depth most appropriate for a given image can help you to select the best file format to use.

## Compression

Computer scientists realized long ago that many kinds of data can be compressed. The result is a file that contains all or most of the data but is smaller. Smaller files not only save disk space but can be transmitted over a network more quickly. If you have ever used a ZIP utility, you know what compression is. The image file formats that are used on the Web are all compressed formats. There are two types of compression:

- **Lossless compression:** When the compressed data is extracted, you get back an exact byte-for-byte copy of the original.

- **Lossy compression:** When the compressed data is extracted, you get back a close but not exact copy of the original. Lossy compression results in smaller files than does lossless compression.

For most kinds of data, such as text documents, lossless compression is obviously needed. For images, however, it was noted that some of the information could be lost and when displayed the image would still look fine. One of the Web file formats makes use of this fact to create image files that are as small as possible.

### 256 Color Mode – Not as Bad as It Seems

Limiting an image to 256 colors may seem very restrictive, but it's a lot more flexible than you might think. This is because the 256 colors are not fixed but are selected for each image based on the image itself. For example, if you saved a photograph of a tree in 256 color mode, the selection of colors—the image's *palette*—would consist mostly of various shades of green. Likewise, the palette of an image of someone's face would consist mostly of skin tones. As a result, this mode can provide a lot more color realism that you might expect. Even so, it is rarely appropriate for color photographs.

# The Web Image File Formats

Now that you understand the fundamentals of digital images, let's take a look at the image file formats that are used on the Web. You may be surprised to learn that there are only three.

## Be Careful with JPEG Images

JPEG is a terrific image file format but there's one drawback that you need to be aware of so you can avoid it. Each time a JPEG file is opened—in your graphics editor for example—it is decompressed so it can be displayed and manipulated. When you again save the image, it is recompressed with the attendant loss of data (remember, JPEG uses lossy compression). Repeated opening/saving cycles can eventually degrade an image. To avoid this potential problem, you should always save images you are editing in another format, preferably your graphics program's native format. Then you can open and save them as many times as needed without loss. Only when the image is ready should you save it in JPEG format.

## PNG Transparency— Maybe Not!

While the PNG format was designed to support transparency, it has been quirky at best, at least in early implementations of the format. If you want to use PNG files with transparency, you should test first to ensure that it comes out the way you want. If not, you will be limited to using GIF format for images with transparent backgrounds.

Perhaps the most commonly used Web image file format is JPEG. This is an acronym for Joint Photographic Experts Group, and the files are saved with the .jpg (or, less commonly, .jpeg) extension. When you see a photograph on the Web, it is almost always in JPEG format, and other kinds of images are often in JPEG too. JPEG is a true color format with lossy compression. Perhaps most important is that this format lets you specify the compression level to suit your needs. More compression results in a smaller file size but lower image quality, while less compression has the opposite effect. JPEG does not offer transparency.

The other common Web image file format is GIF, for Graphics Interchange Format. GIF format is limited to 256 color mode, so it is most appropriate for drawings and charts rather than photographs. GIF files are compressed (using lossless compression) and also support transparency.

The third Web file format is PNG, which stands for Portable Network Graphics. PNG is relatively new and was developed in response to the shortcomings of JPEG and GIF. Another way to put it is that PNG was designed to combine the advantages of JPEG and GIF, specifically these:

- Like JPEG, it supports true color and therefore is suitable for photographs.

- Like GIF, it has lossless compression and supports transparency.

PNG has been slow to gain widespread acceptance because the other formats, JPEG and GIF, fill essentially every need. But still, it's nice to know that PNG is available for special situations, such as when you need to have both true color and transparency.

PNG files are often smaller than the same quality image in JPG or GIF format, and for this reason, they are now more widespread than ever before.

To summarize, JPEG is the preferred format for photographs and for drawings that use a lot of colors. Try out the different compression levels and see which one provides the combination of image quality and file size that suits your needs. Use GIF for drawings, icons, charts, and other images that have relatively few colors and when you need transparency.

## Image Display in Browsers

You learned in Chapter 2 that you use the **<img>** tag to display images on a Web page. The size at which the image is displayed is determined in one of two ways:

- You can include the height and width attributes in the **<img>** tag to display the image at a specific size.

- You can omit the height and width attributes to display the image at its native size.

What does "native size" mean? This means that the image is displayed so that each pixel in the image corresponds to one pixel on the screen. The final display size therefore depends on the monitor in use—specifically, its resolution or pixels per inch (ppi). Monitors are not the same, of course, but as a general rule you can expect monitors to have a resolution of 72 to 96 ppi, with the lower value common on older monitors. From this information, you can estimate how large an image will display on the screen when it is part of a Web page. Here are the required steps:

1. Open the image in Photoshop.

2. Select Image|Image Size to display the Image Size dialog box (Figure 16.1).

3. Read the pixel size from the Width and Height boxes in the Pixel Dimensions section of the dialog box.

4. Divide the pixel size by 72, 96, or some intermediate value to get the approximate image display size in inches.

Of course, you can also simply add the image to the Web page you are editing and see its size directly. If necessary, you can then optimize the image size, covered next.

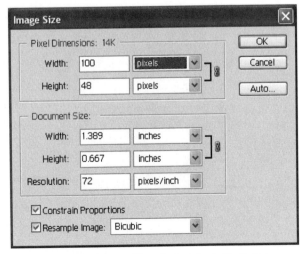

**Figure 16.1.** Determining an image's pixel size in Photoshop.

# Optimizing Image Size

For Web design, an optimized image is one that is just large enough and no larger. This gives you the smallest image size while maintaining a high-quality visual appearance. The other options are as follows:

- If the image is too large, the file will be larger than needed, slowing the page load time without increasing the visual quality.

- If the image is too small, it will be stretched by the browser to fit the size you specify and the visual quality will suffer.

It's advisable to optimize an image's size first, before inserting it into a Web page and uploading it to your site. If your image is larger than needed, this works quite well. If it is smaller than needed, the results will be less than ideal simply because increasing an image's size always results in loss of detail and visual quality. However, it is always better to increase the size in your graphics program rather than let the browser do it for you. Here are the steps required to change an image's size in Photoshop:

1. Determine the desired image size. This can be either as a specific pixel dimension or as a percent of the original.

2. Open the image in Photoshop.

3. Select Image|Image Size to display the Image Size dialog box (shown earlier in Figure 16.1).

4. Make sure that the Constrain Proportions and Resample Image options are selected.

## Transparency

Some image file formats, specifically the GIF and PNG formats, support transparency. This option lets you make the background of the image transparent so that whatever is behind the image shows through. Figure 16.2 shows an example. For this example, I used my graphics program to create a rectangular button that has a white background. I saved the button image two ways: with transparency and without transparency. I then inserted both images on a Web page that has a gray background.

5. For a specific pixel size, be sure Pixels is selected in the pull-down list next to the Width and Height boxes, and then enter the new value for either Width or Height. If you enter a Width value, the Height value will change accordingly and vice versa (this is what the Constrain Proportion option does, keeping the width-to-height ratio the same).

6. For a percent change, select percent in the drop-down list next to Width and Height, and then enter the desired percentage in the Width or Height box.

7. Click OK.

8. Select File|Save As and save the file under a new name.

You can see that the button image without transparency is displayed along with its white background—not too attractive! With transparency in place, however, the white image background is not shown and the gray page background shows through—much nicer! In this case, you could have cropped the original image to remove the white background, but with more complex images this would not be an option.

Here's how to create and save an image with a transparent background using Photoshop:

**Figure 16.2.** Demonstrating images with (bottom) and without (top) transparency.

1. Create the image on a solid white background. You can also use a solid background of any other color, but white is most common. It is best to use a background color that is not used in the image itself. Figure 16.3 shows such an image, in this case a logo for use on a Web page.

2. Use the Magic Wand tool to select the entire background.

3. Use the Magic Erase tool to erase the background, in effect making it transparent. The background will now display as a checkered pattern, as shown in Figure 16.4.

4. To save the file, select File|Save As to display the Save As dialog box.

5. Open the Format list and select CompuServe GIF.

6. Enter a name for the file in the File Name box.

7. Click Save to display the Indexed Color dialog box (Figure 16.5).

8. Select the Transparency option.

9. Click OK.

The GIF file is now ready to be inserted on your Web page.

## Saving PNG Files with Transparency

As mentioned earlier in the chapter, transparency in PNG files does not always work the way it should, so you must test before publishing your Web pages. To save an image as PNG, follow the steps outlined except in step 5, select PNG from the Format list. There is no Transparency option to select because PNG files always contain any transparency that is present in the original image.

**Figure 16.3.** An image to be saved with a transparent background.

**Figure 16.4.** After making the background transparent, it displays as a checkered pattern.

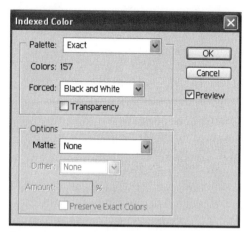

**Figure 16.5.** You must select the Transparency option when saving a GIF file with a transparent background.

Another option in Photoshop is to use the Save for Web tool. This will open another dialog where you can choose the transparency, color depth, and file format. This is also handy because you can see the effects of using different file formats and compression levels and work with optimization tools, all with a snazzy live preview.

# Making the Most of the <img> Tag

There are a couple of tips for using the **<img>** tag to include images in a Web page. The first one involves the use of the **height** and **width** attributes to specify the size at which the image will be displayed. Here's an example:

```
<img src="images/logo.gif" height="150" width="95" />
```

Ideally you will optimize your images to the desired display size. This means that you can omit the **Height** and **Width** attributes, right? Technically this is true, but it's a bad idea, and here's why.

When a user navigates to a Web page, the first thing that happen is the page—in other words the HTML file—is downloaded. As the page is being loaded into the browser, whenever an **<img>** tag is encountered, the actual image file has to be downloaded separately. If the **<img>** tag includes **Height** and **Width** attributes, the browser knows how big the image will be, so it can set aside space on the screen for the image and continue rendering other parts of the page while the image is being downloaded. Without the **Height** and **Width** attributes, the browser must wait for the entire image file to be downloaded before it knows how large it will be, and this slows things down. It is wise, therefore, to always include the **Height** and **Width** attributes in your **<img>** tags even when the image will be displayed at its native size.

The second tip involves the **alt** attribute. You learned in Chapter 2 that this attribute is used to specify "alternate" text that is displayed if the image file cannot be found. When you are displaying images on your own Website, this should never be a problem because you can make sure the image files are located where they should be. Instead you can use the **Alt** attribute to include information for the search engines. Please refer to Chapter 15 for more information on this strategy.

# Creating Simple Animations

You have probably seen Websites that display small, simple animated drawings. These can be an effective way to call attention to specific areas of a Web page. They can be overdone, it is true, but used in moderation they are an effective tool for the Web designer.

Animated drawings are created as animated GIF files. This is a variant of the standard GIF file, which contains only a single image, to contain multiple images. When the animated GIF is displayed, it automatically "flips" from one image to another, creating an illusion of movement. There are numerous GIF animation creation programs on the market, but the one I like best is from CoffeeCup Software, and it's called the CoffeeCup GIF Animator. Let's take a look at how it works.

Before you start, you must create the frames in your animation using a graphics program such as Photoshop. The GIF Animator is used to stitch the frames together into an animation. You can create the frames in a variety of graphics file formats, including GIF, JPG, BMP, ICO, WMF, and EMF. The result, of course, is always a GIF animation. As may be obvious, all the frames should be the same size. There's no size limit to animations, but generally they are relatively small.

For this demonstration my goal was to create a simple animation of a moving clock hand. The four images that will make up the animation each consist of a circle with a line in it, with the line at a different angle in each image. These four images are shown in Figure 16.6.

**Figure 16.6.** The four images that will be used to make the GIF animation.

Once the images are ready, creating the animation is easy. Here are the steps to follow:

1. Start the CoffeeCup GIF Animator. It will open with a blank animation ready to work on.

2. Press Ctrl+I or click the Insert Frame button on the toolbar to add the first frame. In the dialog box that is displayed, select the image file that contains the first frame.

3. Repeat step 2 for the second and subsequent frames. For the demonstration, the screen will look like Figure 16.7.

4. Set the animation options (described in detail shortly).

5. Select File|Save to save the GIF animation.

Note that you insert a GIF animation in a Web page as you would any other GIF image—the animation is taken care of automatically.

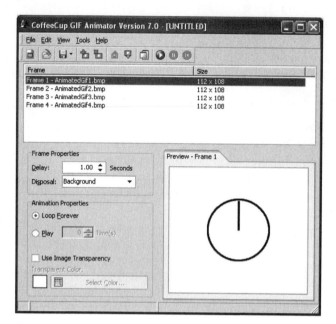

**Figure 16.7.** After adding the four frames to the animation.

The program options you'll use most often are as follows:

- Delay: The time that the selected frame is displayed.

- Loop Forever: Animation plays repeatedly without end.

- Plax X Times: The animation plays a specified number of times and then stops.

You can experiment with the other Animator options as needed. All in all, it is so easy to make GIF animations that you may want to use one or more on your Web pages.

# Creating Image Maps

Image maps provide a clever way of using graphical images as hyperlinks. You have already seen how to use an entire image as a hyperlink, but with an image map you can have different parts of the image link to different URLs. Most image maps in use today are so-called client-side maps because they run in the browser.

Conceptually, an image map is quite simple. It is based on information that you include in the HTML of the page. This information specifies the coordinates of one or more regions of the image, each of which is an independent hyperlink. Here's an example:

```
<map NAME="mymapareas">
<area SHAPE=RECT COORDS="90,30 126,90"
HREF="http://www.ford.com"
    ALT="Ford">
<area SHAPE=CIRCLE COORDS="20,75 35,87"
    HREF="http://www.chevy.com" ALT="Chevy">
<area SHAPE=POLY COORDS="9,125 82,78 99,126 59,122 85,175
48,206"
    HREF="http://www.bmw.com" ALT="BMW">
</map>
```

Let's analyze this code.

- The first tag defines a map definition named "**mymapareas**".

- The second tag defines a rectangular hyperlink area in the image with the specified coordinates. It links to http://www.ford.com and has the **alt** attribute "**Ford**".

- The third tag specifies a circular hyperlink area with the specified coordinate, URL, and **alt** attribute.

- The fourth tag specifies a polygonal hyperlink area with the specified coordinate, URL, and **alt** attribute.

- The final tag is the closing element of the **<map>** tag.

Then, at the document location where you want the image displayed, you would place HTML like the following:

```
<A HREF="mymap.map">
<IMG SRC="mymap.gif" HEIGHT="255" WIDTH="300" ISMAP
    USEMAP="#mymapareas" />
</A>
```

The first tag is the start of a hyperlink. The **HREF** attribute in this case is simply a unique name for the map—it has no other purpose as the actual URLs are included in the map information. The second tag, the **<IMG>** tag, is where the action is. It has these attributes:

- **SRC**: The name of the image to display.

- **HEIGHT**, **WIDTH**: The size to display the image.

- **ISMAP**: Tells the browser that the image is an image map.

- **USEMAP**: Tells the browser which image map information to use. In other words, this is the **name** attribute of the **<map>** tag that contains the coordinate and URL information for the map.

Here's how to create an image map using the Map Wizard utility:

1. Select File|Map Wizard to start the Map Wizard utility.

2. On the first wizard screen, select the Create a New Map option; then click Next.

3. On the next wizard screen, which is shown in Figure 16.8, enter the following information, and then click Next:

  - Select the image...: Click the Browse button to locate the image that will be used for the map.

  - Choose a name...: Enter a unique name for the map.

  - If someone misclicks...: Enter the URL that users will go to if they click a part of the image that is not defined as a link. This is optional, and if omitted, misclicking will have no effect.

- In which frame...: If your page uses frames, specify the frame to go to in the misclick URL.

4. On the final wizard page, click Finish.

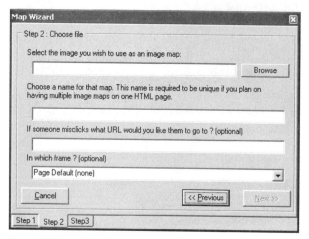

**Figure 16.8.** Starting a new image map.

**Figure 16.9.** An image displayed in the Image Mapper, ready for defining link areas.

At this point the Image Mapper will display the selected image, as shown in Figure 16.9. You can zoom in and out on the image by clicking the magnifier buttons on the toolbar. To define a link area, click one of the shape buttons on the toolbar depending on whether you want to create a rectangle, a circle, or a polygon.

The next part of the process is as follows:

- To create a rectangular link area, click the upper-left corner of the area and then click the lower-right corner.

- To create a circular link area, click the center of the circle and then click on the circle's edge.

- To create a polygonal link area, click the first, second, and subsequent points in order and then double-click the last point.

Whichever shape you are creating, the program displays a dialog box for entering the URL and other information for this link area. Each defined area is shown on the image as an outlined, hatched area, as shown in Figure 16.10. The program also displays, in the lower part of its window, the HTML that it has generated for the map.

To modify a map, select the arrow button on the toolbar. Then you can make changes as follows:

- To change the size and/or shape of an area, point at one of the handles (small black boxes) on its outline and drag to the desired size.

- To change the information for an area, right-click it and select Area Attributes from the pop-up menu.

When you have finished creating the map, you have two options for saving the HTML that has been created:

- Select File|Save Map to save the map information in an otherwise empty HTML file.

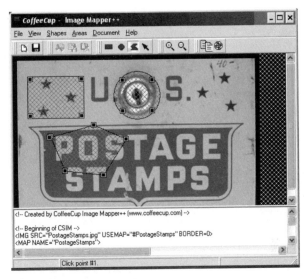

**Figure 16.8.** Starting a new image map.

- Select Document|Copy Map to Clipboard to copy the map HTML to the Windows clipboard. You can then paste it into your HTML document as needed.

Image maps are a nice feature for some Web pages. With a tool like the CoffeeCup Image Mapper, they are easy to create and use.

## Summary

A Web page without images is not very interesting. Images are central to some Websites and merely decorative for others, but in any case, a Web designer needs to know how to create and use images. By choosing your image file formats correctly, and by optimizing the size of your images, you can ensure efficient Web pages that download as quickly as possible. Animations, transparency, and image maps provide additional options for spicing up your pages.

### What about Overlapping Map Areas?

There's nothing to prevent you from defining two or more areas in an image map that overlap. When a user clicks such an overlapping area, what happens? It depends on the order of the region definitions in the map—whichever region comes first in the HTML will be active and that's the URL that the user will navigate to.

# Blogging, RSS, and Flash

As with every other technology, the Web is an ever evolving beast. What was hip even 18 months ago is now commonplace, and there is always something new on the horizon. I'll highlight a few of the newer things that are changing the Web as we know it in this chapter and you can decide what to adopt and what to let pass.

## Blogging

While Web logs, or *blogs* as they are called, are not new by any stretch, they are just now becoming mainstream enough to have an impact on the way we use the Web. What exactly is a blog? Glad you asked.

A blog essentially is a different form of Website generally geared around a chronological organization of *posts*, like an online diary. *Bloggers*, as they are called, are the Webmasters of these sites and are known for posting anything and everything they think of. There are tons of blogs on the Web as I write this, and for the most part, in my opinion, very few of them have any real substance. Don't get me wrong; there are some blog sites rich in good information, tutorials, and insight, but they are often more like some guy in Indiana talking about the daily turmoil of working on his 1982 Honda. Ugh.

Anyone can start a blog quickly and easily. Just go to a popular service like blogger.com or typepad.com and sign up. Within minutes you will have a cookie-cutter Website where you can share anything from random thoughts to well-written articles on the topic of your choice with the world at large. No coding required—just pick a template and go. It's all online with no software to install and practically nothing to learn.

*So this is a great way to create my new Website, right?*

Maybe…but probably not. Blogging is a niche of Web design that fits a very narrow purpose: to have a chronological organization of your thoughts or articles. There is no flexibility without heavy customization for anything beyond that. If you want to have a shopping cart system to sell your products, or if you want to post a company or personal information site, a blog is probably not the route for you. Besides, you will inevitably want to customize the look and feel of your site, and guess what? You can't do it with a blog unless you know some HTML. In fact, the way most blogging systems are set up, you better know a lot about XHTML, CSS, and XML to make even the slightest customizations.

You could also download and install a blogging system on your Website and not use any of the online services that are available. But be prepared to know PHP scripting, and have a MySQL database server handy, because 99 percent of blogging systems require it.

Don't take all this as me being anti-blog because that's not the case. Just understand that blogging requires a specialized type of Website that does an excellent job at what it was designed for, but not much beyond that.

All that said, let me tell you a little more about blogs and how they work.

As I've already told you, blogs are a chronological listing of posts. These posts can include any amount of content that you like, from just a quick thought and a link to some other site to a full-blown article on how to program your TiVo box to do back flips. Usually these posts are created via an online interface, whether that is through blogger.com or a system that you've installed on your Website.

After the post is created, it is automatically added to your *archives*. These archives can be browsed by date, and most systems allow visitors to search the posts as well. Most blogging system also allow for the public to leave comments on the posts. This way, the people that read the blog can add their thoughts as well.

When a blogger links to other bloggers' Websites, this is usually called a *blogroll*. Many bloggers make their blogrolls public by putting them in a sidebar on their Website. This is similar to the Web rings that were so popular a few years ago. Blogrolls are a good way to see who has common interests and who reads what. This can be a great indicator of the popularity of a blog, so when you see the same Website in lots of blogrolls, it's probably a good site.

Now there are a few special ways that bloggers have created to link to each other so that they can stitch related information together across multiple Websites. These are called TrackBack and PingBack.

*TrackBack* and *PingBack* are methods of notification between two Websites.

TrackBack is a way for blogger A to tell blogger B, "Hey, this is something you might be interested in." Blogger A can send a *TrackBack ping* to blogger B. Why would you want to do this? Let's say that you find a blog that has a review of a book you just read. You decide that this person has missed a few key points and so you want to talk about them on your Website. You could send a TrackBack to the other person's blog to notify them (and the other people reading the post) that you have added a similar post on your blog. Everyone who sees that post from then on is aware that you have a similar post.

So what if you want to know when someone links to a post on your blog? That's what a PingBack is for. This is a method to request notification when somebody links to one of your posts. This enables you to keep track of who is linking to, or referring to, your posts. This way, when someone links to you in one of their posts (and they use PingBacks), you will get a notice on your post. Some blogging software supports automatic PingBacks, where all the links in a published article can be pinged when the article is published.

This brings me to one of the greatest tools that is used by the blogging community and is now being embraced by Websites all over, RSS

# Really Simple Syndication (RSS)

RSS is an XML-formatted summary of your Website's content. This can be summaries of articles you've written, the latest news or product updates, or any other information you want to syndicate. Think of it as a news or stock ticker...a stream of short bits of fresh information. You don't need a blog to use RSS (although most blogging systems have it built in), just the ability to create content in this XML format. There are a few versions of RSS available, a competitor called Atom and maybe a few others, but the concept behind them is all the same, so I'll just talk about RSS.

Here is an example of the RSS 2.0 XML format from the Yahoo! News feed:

```
-<rss version="2.0">
-<channel>
   <title>Yahoo! News: Top Stories</title>
   -<copyright>Copyright (c) 2005 Yahoo! Inc. All rights
reserved.</copyright>
   <link>http://news.yahoo.com/news?tmpl=index&cid=716</link>
   <description>Top Stories</description>
   <language>en-us</language>
   <lastBuildDate>Tue, 22 Feb 2005 15:49:24
GMT</lastBuildDate>
   <ttl>5</ttl>
   -<image>
      <title>Yahoo! News</title>
      <width>142</width>
      <height>18</height>
      <link>http://news.yahoo.com/</link>
      -
<url>http://us.i1.yimg.com/us.yimg.com/i/us/nws/th/main_142b.
gif</url>
   </image>
   -<item>
      <title>Iran Earthquake Reportedly Kills 370
(AP)</title>
      -
<link>http://story.news.yahoo.com/news?tmpl=story2&u=/ap/2005
0222/ap_on_re_mi_ea/iran_earthquake</link>
```

```
        <guid isPermaLink="false">
ap/20050222/iran_earthquake</guid>
        <pubDate>Tue, 22 Feb 2005 15:45:33 GMT</pubDate>
        -<description>AP - A powerful earthquake flattened
villages and collapsed mud-brick homes in central Iran on
Tuesday, killing at least 370 people and injuring nearly
1,000, Iranian state-run television said.</description>
        </item>
```

When you provide an RSS summary of content from your Website, it is called a *feed*. Many news Websites and nearly all blogs have RSS feeds. There are a large number of programs that read this special format and display the content for you to read. These are called Feed Readers or sometimes Aggregators. One of the most popular Feed Readers was written by a friend of mine named Nick Bradbury. It is called FeedDemon and is available for trial download at http://www.bradsoft.com. You can use FeedDemon or an online service like bloglines.com, newsgator.com or CNET's NewsBurst.com to go fetch the latest content from RSS feeds you choose and display it all in one spot for you to read at your leisure.

Once you set up one of these programs or services, just look for the RSS feed links on the Websites you visit. Depending on which way you have chosen to read the feeds, you will then add it to your siteor subscribe to the Website's feed. Once you do this, your software will start getting content from that Website. This is a fantastic way to have one place to read all the latest content from your favorite Websites.

So how do you make an RSS feed for your Website? This can be a little tricky, so I recommend you do some research and find the way that is best for you. You could install software on your computer or use an online service. It's really up to you. There are new RSS feeds popping up all the time, and new ways of getting them on your Website are becoming rapidly available. As this book is being written, we are creating RSS-compatible software at CoffeeCup too. You will probably be able to find an RSS tool to suit your needs; it will just take a few searches to do so. Table 17.1 lists some popular RSS feeds.

## Look for the RSS Icon

Most Websites use one of these icons or something similar as a link to their RSS feeds.

**Table 17.1.** Some popular RSS feeds.

| | |
|---|---|
| http://news.yahoo.com/rss/ | About 20 feeds for popular news topics and the ability to create custom feeds of topics that interest you |
| http://www.cnn.com/services/rss/ | The latest news from CNN by category |
| http://biz.yahoo.com/rss.html | Financial news by company name or stock ticker |
| http://cbs.sportsline.com/xml/rss | The latest sports news and updates |
| http://www.feedster.com | A search engine for RSS feeds |

# Flash

Macromedia Flash is a wonderful and powerful tool that may change the face of the Web as we know it. Flash already has a lot of Websites and a truckload of books dedicated to it, so I'll just cover the basics.

Several years ago when Flash was just breaking on to the Web, many people saw it as just another way to add a fancy effect to your Website. Then we went through the phase in which everyone had a snazzy moving and swirling "intro" for their site that you had to watch before seeing the real content. It was soon realized that this was a bad idea and Flash started to fade away. Then Flash started getting more flexible. People used it to create dynamic Web interfaces that allowed the user to actually interact with the Website. We started seeing it used for Website navigation, car manufacturers started using it for live demos and 3D tours of their cars, news Websites are now using it for streaming video, and the list goes on and on.

What is Flash? According to Wikipedia (http://en.wikipedia.org), "Flash is a robust graphics animation program used to create and deliver dynamic content and interactive applications to the web". It's a little hard to describe technically, so think of it as a way to mix cartoons and Websites together. You have the ability to create content—text and images—that you see and read with the power to animate that content and create interaction between the visitor and your Website. You can make certain things happen when the user clicks a button; you can use it to play a slide show of photographs or maybe to create cartoons (the real kind). It is a great tool for Website interaction, navigation, and special effects.

The limits of Flash at this point are rather unknown. It's really up to the creativity and technical ability of the Webmaster. The tools you need to create Flash can be very complex (and quite expensive) with a steep learning curve. If you decide to jump into the world of hardcore Flash development, be prepared to spend a lot of time and money to learn all the software and capabilities of Flash.

Most people just want to use the basic functionality of Flash to make something cool for their Website, so there are a few simple programs like CoffeeCup Firestarter that are good for making quick and easy Flash effects. If this is you, I recommend that you try Firestarter and some other simple Flash tools before looking at Macromedia's software.

Here are some Flash resources where you can learn more about it:

Macromedia Flash:  http://www.macromedia.com/

CoffeeCup Firestarter: http://www.coffeecup.com/

FlashKit: http://www.flashkit.com/

## Summary

Blogs, RSS, and Flash are three of the more specialized tools that are available to Web designers. You may never need any of them, or you might find one or more of them indispensable for your Website.

# Thanks!

Now that you have come to the end of this book,
I just wanted to say I appreciate you reading it and
I hope you got something good out of it. Don't forget
to look over the HTML reference in the next two
sections and please check out our software and other
services at www.coffeecup.com.

Have fun and don't make any ugly Websites!

— Nick

**\<a\>**

Used to anchor one document to another (i.e. hypertext link).
Attributes: id, class, style, title, lang, xml:lang, dir, charset, type, name, href, hreflang, rel, rev, accesskey, shape, coords, tabindex, onfocus, onblur

**\<abbr\>**

Used to indicate an abbreviation.
Attributes: id, class, style, title, lang, xml:lang, dir

**\<acronym\>**

Used to indicate an acronym.
Attributes: id, class, style, title, lang, xml:lang, dir

**\<address\>**

Used to provide contact information about the author of the XHTML document.
Attributes: id, class, style, title, lang, xml:lang, dir

**\<applet\>**

Used to include a Java applet in your web page. (*Transitional DTD*).
Attributes: id, class, style, title, codebase, archive, code, object, alt, name, width, height, align, hspace, vspace

**\<area\>**

Used to define the area of a client-side image map.
Attributes: id, class, style, title, lang, xml:lang, dir, shape, coords, href, nohref, alt (required),tabindex, accesskey, onfocus, onblur

**\<b\>**

Used to provide bold font.
Attributes: id, class, style, title, lang, xml:lang, dir

**\<base\>**

This is the document's base URI. (Part of the \<head\> element.)
Attribute: href

**\<basefont\>**

Used to define the base (i.e. default) font size. (*Transitional DTD*).
Attributes: id, size, color, face

### <bdo>

Used to turn off the bi-directional rendering algorithm.
Attributes: id, class, style, title, lang, xml:lang, dir (required), onclick, ond-blclick, onmousedown, onmouseup, onmousemove, onmouseout, onkeypress, onkeydown, onkeyup

### <big>

Used to provide bigger font.
Attributes: id, class, style, title, lang, xml:lang, dir

### <blockquote>

Used to delaminate a long quotation.
Attributes: id, class, style, title, lang, xml:lang, dir, cite

### <body>

The <body> element contains the document's displayed content.
Attributes: id, class, style, title, lang, xml:lang, dir, onload, onunload

### <br />

Used to provide forced line break — empty element.
Attributes: id, class, style, title

### <button>

Used to provide an XHTML button on your web page.
Attributes: id, class, style, title, lang, xml:lang, dir, name, value, type, disabled, tabindex, accesskey, onfocus, onblur

### <caption>

Used to provide the caption for a table.
Attributes: id, class, style, title, lang, xml:lang, dir

### <center>

Used to centre text on your web page (same as <div align="center">).
(Transitional DTD).
Attributes: id, class, style, title, lang, xml:lang, dir

### <cite>

Used to indicate a citation (reference to other work).
Attributes: id, class, style, title, lang, xml:lang, dir

### <code>

Used to delimit program code.
Attributes: id, class, style, title, lang, xml:lang, dir

**<col>**

Used to denote a table column.
Attributes: id, class, style, title, lang, xml:lang, dir, span, width, char, charoff, align, valign

**<colgroup>**

Used to denote a table column group.
Attributes: id, class, style, title, lang, xml:lang, dir, span, width, char, charoff, align, valign

**<dd>**

Used to provide a definition of the <dd> in a <dl>.
Attributes: id, class, style, title, lang, xml:lang, dir

**<del>**

Used to show the text that has been deleted in order to update a document.
Attributes: id, class, style, title, lang, xml:lang, dir, cite, datetime

**<dfn>**

Used to delimit a definition.
Attributes: id, class, style, title, lang, xml:lang, dir

**<dir>**

Used to define a listing of directories. (*Transitional DTD*).
Attributes: id, class, style, title, lang, xml:lang, dir, compact

**<div>**

A block level language/style container.
Attributes: id, class, style, title, lang, xml:lang, dir

**<dl>**

Used to define a definition list.
Attributes: id, class, style, title, lang, xml:lang, dir

**<dt>**

Used within <dl> to define a definition term.
Attributes: id, class, style, title, lang, xml:lang, dir

**<em>**

Used to proved emphasis.
Attributes: id, class, style, title, lang, xml:lang, dir

**<fieldset>**

Used to group form fields.
Attributes: id, class, style, title, lang, xml:lang, dir

### \<font>

Used to change the font size and colour. (*Transitional DTD*).
Attributes: id, class, style, title, lang, xml:lang, dir, size, color, face

### \<form>

Used to generate an interactive form.
Attributes: id, class, style, title, lang, xml:lang, dir, action (required), method, enctype, onsubmit, onreset, accept-charset

### \<frame>

Used to define a frame (or sub-window). (*Frameset DTD*).
Attributes: id, class, style, title, longdesc, name, src, frameborder, marginwidth, marginheight, noresize, scrolling

### \<frameset>

Used to define a window subdivision. (*Frameset DTD*).
Attributes: id, class, style, title, rows, cols, onload, onunload

### \<h1>

The largest of the six headings.
Attributes: id, class, style, title, lang, xml:lang, dir

### \<h2>

The second largest of the six headings.
Attributes: id, class, style, title, lang, xml:lang, dir

### \<h3>

The third largest of the six headings.
Attributes: id, class, style, title, lang, xml:lang, dir

### \<h4>

The third smallest of the six headings.
Attributes: id, class, style, title, lang, xml:lang, dir

### \<h5>

The second smallest of the six headings.
Attributes: id, class, style, title, lang, xml:lang, dir

### \<h6>

The smallest of the six headings.
Attributes: id, class, style, title, lang, xml:lang, dir

### \<head>

The \<head> element contains a document's non-displayed meta-information.
Attributes: lang, xml:lang, dir, profile

## <hr />

Displays a horizontal rule — empty element.
Attributes: id, class, style, title, lang, xml:lang, dir

## <html>

The root element of each XHTML document (note it has no x).
Attributes: lang, xml:lang, dir, xmlns (fixed, must be
http://www.w3.org/1999/xhtml)

## <I>

Used to provide italic font.
Attributes: id, class, style, title, lang, xml:lang, dir

## <iframe>

Used to create a sub-window within your web page. (*Transitional DTD*).
Attributes: id, class, style, title, longdesc, name, src, frameborder, marginwidth,
marginheight, scrolling, align, height, width

## <img>

Used to include an image within the web page.
Attributes: id, class, style, title, lang, xml:lang, dir, src (required), alt (required),
longdesc, height, width, usemap, ismap

## <input>

Used to specify a form's input control.
Attributes: id, class, style, title, lang, xml:lang, dir, type, name, value, checked,
disabled, readonly, size, maxlength, src, alt, usemap, tabindex, accesskey, onfocus, onblur, onselect, onchange, accept

## <ins>

Used to show the text that has been inserted in order to update a document.
Attributes: id, class, style, title, lang, xml:lang, dir, cite, datetime

## <isindex>

Used to enter a word in a searchable index. (*Transitional DTD*).
Attributes: id, class, style, title, lang, xml:lang, dir, prompt

## <kbd>

Used to indicate material that a user should enter at their keyboard.
Attributes: id, class, style, title, lang, xml:lang, dir

## <label>

Used to label a form field.
Attributes: id, class, style, title, lang, xml:lang, dir, for, accesskey, onfocus, onblur

**<legend>**
Used to label a fieldset grouping.
Attributes: id, class, style, title, lang, xml:lang, dir, accesskey

**<li>**
Used to define each item in your specified list (either <ol> or <ul>).
Attributes: id, class, style, title, lang, xml:lang, dir

**<link>**
A media-independent link. (Part of the <head> element).
Attributes: id, class, style, title, lang, xml:lang, dir, charset, href, hreflang, type, rel, rev, media

**<map>**
Used to specify a client-side image map.
Attributes: lang, xml:lang, dir, id (required), class, style, title, name, onclick, ondblclick, onmousedown, onmouseup, onmousemove, onmouseout, onkeypress, onkeydown, onkeyup

**<menu>**
Used to define a menu list. (*Transitional DTD*).
Attributes: id, class, style, title, lang, xml:lang, dir, compact

**<meta>**
Used to list generic meta-information. (Part of the <head> element).
Attributes: lang, xml:lang, dir, http-equiv, name, content (required), scheme

**<noframes>**
Used to provide alternate content when frames are not available. (*Transitional DTD*).
Attributes: id, class, style, title, lang, xml:lang, dir

**<noscript>**
Used to provide an alternate content when scripting is not available (Part of the <head> element).
Attributes: id, class, style, title, lang, xml:lang, dir

**<object>**
Used to embed an object within your web page.
Attributes: id, class, style, title, lang, xml:lang, dir, declare, classid, codebase, data, type, codetype, archive, standby, height, width, usemap, name, tabindex

**<ol>**
Used to define an ordered (i.e. numbered) list.
Attributes: id, class, style, title, lang, xml:lang, dir

**<optgroup>**

Used to create a list of options.
Attributes: id, class, style, title, lang, xml:lang, dir, disabled, label (required)

**<option>**

Used to define each choice in a <select> list.
Attributes: id, class, style, title, lang, xml:lang, dir, selected, disabled, label, value

**<p>**

Used to begin a new paragraph.
Attributes: id, class, style, title, lang, xml:lang, dir

**<param>**

Used to supply a name property (e.g. within <object>).
Attributes: id, name, value, valuetype, type

**<pre>**

Used to preserve spacing (i.e. preformatted text).
Attributes: id, class, style, title, lang, xml:lang, dir, xml:space

**<q>**

Used to indicate an in-line quote.
Attributes: id, class, style, title, lang, xml:lang, dir, cite

**<s>**

Used to provide strike-through text (same as <strike>). (*Transitional DTD*).
Attributes: id, class, style, title, lang, xml:lang, dir

**<samp>**

Used to delimit program and other sample output.
Attributes: id, class, style, title, lang, xml:lang, dir

**<script>**

Use to include script statements. (Part of the <head> element.)
Attributes: charset, type (required), src, defer, xml:space

**<select>**

Used to provide a menu of options from which a user may select one choice.
Attributes: id, class, style, title, lang, xml:lang, dir, name, size, multiple, disabled, tabindex, onfocus, onblur, onchange

**<small>**

Used to provide smaller font.
Attributes: id, class, style, title, lang, xml:lang, dir

**<span>**

An in line language/style container.
Attributes: id, class, style, title, lang, xml:lang, dir

**<strike>**

Used to provide strike-through text (same as <s>). (*Transitional DTD*).
Attributes: id, class, style, title, lang, xml:lang, dir

**<strong>**

Used to provide strong emphasis.
Attributes: id, class, style, title, lang, xml:lang, dir

**<style>**

Used to include style information. (Part of the <head> element.)
Attributes: lang, xml:lang, dir, type (required), media, title, xml:space

**<sub>**

Used to provide subscripts.
Attributes: id, class, style, title, lang, xml:lang, dir

**<sup>**

Used to provide superscripts.
Attributes: id, class, style, title, lang, xml:lang, dir

**<table>**

Used to define a table.
Attributes: id, class, style, title, lang, xml:lang, dir, summary, width, border, frame, rules, cellspacing, cellpadding

**<tbody>**

Used to delimit the table body.
Attributes: id, class, style, title, lang, xml:lang, dir, char, charoff, align, valign

**<td>**

Used to define a table data cell.
Attributes: id, class, style, title, lang, xml:lang, dir, abbr, axis, headers, scope, rowspan, colspan, char, charoff, align, valign

**<textarea>**

Used to define a multi-line input text field.
Attributes: id, class, style, title, lang, xml:lang, dir, name, rows (required), cols (required), disabled, readonly, tabindex, accesskey, onfocus, onblur, onselect, onchange

**\<tfoot\>**

Used to define the table footer.
Attributes: id, class, style, title, lang, xml:lang, dir, char, charoff, align, valign

**\<th\>**

Used to denote one of the header rows in a table.
Attributes: id, class, style, title, lang, xml:lang, dir, abbr, axis, headers, scope, rowspan, colspan, char, charoff, align, valign

**\<thead\>**

Used to delimit the table head.
Attributes: id, class, style, title, lang, xml:lang, dir, char, charoff, align, valign

**\<title\>**

Used to define the document's title. (Part of the \<head\> element.)
Attributes: lang, xml:lang, dir

**\<tr\>**

Used to define a table row.
Attributes: id, class, style, title, lang, xml:lang, dir, char, charoff, align, valign

**\<tt\>**

Used to provide a fixed width font (teletype).
Attributes: id, class, style, title, lang, xml:lang, dir

**\<u\>**

Used to provide underlined text. (*Transitional DTD*).
Attributes: id, class, style, title, lang, xml:lang, dir

**\<ul\>**

Used to define an unordered list.
Attributes: id, class, style, title, lang, xml:lang, dir

**\<var\>**

Used to indicate a variable.
Attributes: id, class, style, title, lang, xml:lang, dir

| Char | Name of Char | What to Type | Alternate |
|---|---|---|---|
| " | quotation mark | &quot; | &#34; |
| & | ampersand | &amp; | &#38; |
| < | less-than sign | &lt; | &#60; |
| > | greater-than sign | &gt; | &#62; |
|  | non-breaking space |   |   |
| ¡ | inverted exclamation | &iexcl; | &#161; |
| ¢ | cent sign | &cent; | &#162; |
| £ | pound sterling | &pound; | &#163; |
| ¤ | general currency sign | &curren; | &#164; |
| ¥ | yen sign | &yen; | &#165; |
| ¦ | broken vertical bar | &brvbar; | &#166; |
| § | section sign | &sect; | &#167; |
| ¨ | umlaut (dieresis) | &uml; | &#168; |
| © | copyright | &copy; | &#169; |
| ª | feminine ordinal | &ordf; | &#170; |
| « | left angle quote, guillemotleft | &laquo; | &#171; |
| ¬ | not sign | &not; | &#172; |
|  | soft hyphen | &shy; | &#173; |
| ® | registered trademark | &reg; | &#174; |
| ¯ | macron accent | &macr; | &#175; |
| ° | degree sign | &deg; | &#176; |
| ± | plus or minus | &plusmn; | &#177; |
| ² | superscript two | &sup2; | &#178; |
| ³ | superscript three | &sup3; | &#179; |
| ´ | acute accent | &acute; | &#180; |
| µ | micro sign | &micro; | &#181; |
| ¶ | paragraph sign | &para; | &#182; |
| · | middle dot | &middot; | &#183; |
| ¸ | cedilla | &cedil; | &#184; |
| ¹ | superscript one | &sup1; | &#185; |
| º | masculine ordinal | &ordm; | &#186; |
| » | right angle quote, guillemotright | &raquo; | &#187; |
| ¼ | fraction one-fourth | &frac14; | &#188; |

| Char | Name of Char | What to Type | Alternate |
|------|--------------|--------------|-----------|
| ½ | fraction one-half | &frac12; | &#189; |
| ¾ | fraction three-fourths | &frac34; | &#190; |
| ¿ | inverted question mark | &iquest; | &#191; |
| À | capital A, grave accent | &Agrave; | &#192; |
| Á | capital A, acute accent | &Aacute; | &#193; |
| Â | capital A, circumflex accent | &Acirc; | &#194; |
| Ã | capital A, tilde | &Atilde; | &#195; |
| Ä | capital A, dieresis or umlaut mark | &Auml; | &#196; |
| Å | capital A, ring | &Aring; | &#197; |
| Æ | capital AE diphthong (ligature) | &AElig; | &#198; |
| Ç | capital C, cedilla | &Ccedil; | &#199; |
| È | capital E, grave accent | &Egrave; | &#200; |
| É | capital E, acute accent | &Eacute; | &#201; |
| Ê | capital E, circumflex accent | &Ecirc; | &#202; |
| Ë | capital E, dieresis or umlaut mark | &Euml; | &#203; |
| Ì | capital I, grave accent | &Igrave; | &#204; |
| Í | capital I, acute accent | &Iacute; | &#205; |
| Î | capital I, circumflex accent | &Icirc; | &#206; |
| Ï | capital I, dieresis or umlaut mark | &Iuml; | &#207; |
| Ð | capital Eth, Icelandic | &ETH; | &#208; |
| Ñ | capital N, tilde | &Ntilde; | &#209; |
| Ò | capital O, grave accent | &Ograve; | &#210; |
| Ó | capital O, acute accent | &Oacute; | &#211; |
| Ô | capital O, circumflex accent | &Ocirc; | &#212; |
| Õ | capital O, tilde | &Otilde; | &#213; |
| Ö | capital O, dieresis or umlaut mark | &Ouml; | &#214; |
| × | multiply sign | &times; | &#215; |
| Ø | capital O, slash | &Oslash; | &#216; |
| Ù | capital U, grave accent | &Ugrave; | &#217; |
| Ú | capital U, acute accent | &Uacute; | &#218; |
| Û | capital U, circumflex accent | &Ucirc; | &#219; |
| Ü | capital U, dieresis or umlaut mark | &Uuml; | &#220; |
| Ý | capital Y, acute accent | &Yacute; | &#221; |
| Þ | capital THORN, Icelandic | &THORN; | &#222; |
| ß | small sharp s, German (sz ligature) | &szlig; | &#223; |

| Char | Name of Char | What to Type | Alternate |
|------|--------------|--------------|-----------|
| à | small a, grave accent | &agrave; | &#224; |
| á | small a, acute accent | &aacute; | &#225; |
| â | small a, circumflex accent | &acirc; | &#226; |
| ã | small a, tilde | &atilde; | &#227; |
| ä | small a, dieresis or umlaut mark | &auml; | &#228; |
| å | small a, ring | &aring; | &#229; |
| æ | small ae diphthong (ligature) | &aelig; | &#230; |
| ç | small c, cedilla | &ccedil; | &#231; |
| è | small e, grave accent | &egrave; | &#232; |
| é | small e, acute accent | &eacute; | &#233; |
| ê | small e, circumflex accent | &ecirc; | &#234; |
| ë | small e, dieresis or umlaut mark | &euml; | &#235; |
| ì | small i, grave accent | &igrave; | &#236; |
| í | small i, acute accent | &iacute; | &#237; |
| î | small i, circumflex accent | &icirc; | &#238; |
| ï | small i, dieresis or umlaut mark | &iuml; | &#239; |
| ð | small eth, Icelandic | &eth; | &#240; |
| ñ | small n, tilde | &ntilde; | &#241; |
| ò | small o, grave accent | &ograve; | &#242; |
| ó | small o, acute accent | &oacute; | &#243; |
| ô | small o, circumflex accent | &ocirc; | &#244; |
| õ | small o, tilde | &otilde; | &#245; |
| ö | small o, dieresis or umlaut mark | &ouml; | &#246; |
| ÷ | division sign | &divide; | &#247; |
| ø | small o, slash | &oslash; | &#248; |
| ù | small u, grave accent | &ugrave; | &#249; |
| ú | small u, acute accent | &uacute; | &#250; |
| û | small u, circumflex accent | &ucirc; | &#251; |
| ü | small u, dieresis or umlaut mark | &uuml; | &#252; |
| ý | small y, acute accent | &yacute; | &#253; |
| þ | small thorn, Icelandic | &thorn; | &#254; |
| ÿ | small y, dieresis or umlaut mark | &yuml; | &#255; |

# INDEX

## A

<a> (anchor) tag, 30-32
absolute URLs, 25, 150
action attribute, 77
active hyperlinks, 37
Active Server Pages (ASP), 78
adjustable tables, 48-49
advertisements, webpagesthatsuck.com, 185
align attribute
    <h1>...<h6> tags, 42, 44-46
    <hr> tag, 42-43
    <img> tag, 29-30
    <p> tag, 42
    <table> tag, 50
    <td> tag, 52
    <tr> tag, 51
aligning
    horizontal rules, 42-43
    images, 29-30
    paragraphs, 42
    review and practice, 44-46
    tables, 49, 52
    text, 93
    Web page headings, 42, 44-46
alink attribute, 37
alt attribute, 28, 214-215
AltaVista, 211
Amazon.com, deconstructing
animation, 173-175
    <head> section, 169-170
    home page, 169
    navigation bar, 170-171
    navigation tabs, 171-173
    <title> tag, 169-170
&amp (ampersand) character entity, 18
ampersands (&&), AND operator, 119-120
anchor (<a>) tag, 30-32
anchors, creating, 30-32
AND (&&) operator, 119-120
animation
    Amazon.com, 173-175

## C

## D

# I

# J

# M

# N

# P

# Q

&quot (double quote) character entity, 18

# R

radio buttons, 77
radio element, 77
random numbers, 139-140
Really Simple Syndication (RSS), 235-236
registered trademark (®) character entity, 18
relational operators, 118-119
relative URLs, 25
rendering versus source code, 14
Reset button, 76, 124
reset element, 76
resolution, 220
return values, 114-115
RGB color, 35-36
rollovers, 129-131
rows, 51
rowspan attribute, 53-55
RSS (Really Simple Syndication), 235-236

# S

sans-serif fonts, 89-90
scope, 115-116
screen size, 206-207
script codes, identifying, 21
script files, file extensions, 31
<script> (script code) tag, 21
scripting, 101-102
scripts
    *See* also DHTML
    *See* also DOM (Document Object Model)
    *See* also forms
    *See* also JavaScript
    ASP (Active Server Pages), 78
    CGI (Common Gateway Interface), 78
    client-side versus server-side, 79, 101
    installing, 79
    languages, 78  *See* also JavaScript

# U